The Secret Tradition in Freemasonry

And an Analysis of the Inter-Relation Between the Craft and the High Grades

IN RESPECT OF THEIR TERM OF RESEARCH, EXPRESSED BY THE WAY OF SYMBOLISM

BY

ARTHUR EDWARD WAITE

IN TWO VOLUMES

With 28 Full-page Plates, and many other Illustrations

Volume II

British Library Cataloguing-in-Publication Data
A catalogue record for this book is available from
the British Library

Arthur Edward Waite

Arthur Edward Waite was born on the 2nd of October, 1857 in America.

After the death of his father, Waite and his mother returned to her native England, where he was raised in North London, attending St. Charles' College from the age of thirteen. Waite left school to become a clerk, but also wrote verse in his spare time. The death of his sister, Frederika Waite, in 1874 soon attracted him into psychical research. At 21, he began to read regularly in the Library of the British Museum, studying many branches of esotericism.

Waite was a scholarly mystic who wrote extensively on occult and esoteric matters, and was the co-creator of the Rider-Waite Tarot deck. As his biographer, R.A. Gilbert described him, "Waite's name has survived because he was the first to attempt a systematic study of the history of western occultism - viewed as a spiritual tradition rather than as aspects of proto-science or as the pathology of religion."

Waite was a prolific author with many of his works being well received in academic circles. He wrote occult texts on subjects including divination, esotericism, Rosicrucianism, Freemasonry and ceremonial magic, Kabbalism, and alchemy. Waite also translated and reissued several important mystical and alchemical works. His works on the Holy Grail, influenced by his friendship with Arthur Machen, were particularly notable. A number of his volumes remain in print: *The Book of Ceremonial Magic*, *The Holy Kabbalah*, *A New Encyclopedia of Freemasonry*, and his edited translation of Eliphas Levi's *Transcendental Magic, its Doctrine and Ritual*.

Waite is best known as the co-creator of the popular

and widely used Rider-Waite Tarot deck and author of its companion volume, *The Key to the Tarot*, re-published in expanded form the following year, 1911, as *The Pictorial Key to the Tarot, a guide to Tarot reading*. The Rider-Waite-Smith tarot was notable for being one of the first tarot decks to illustrate all 78 cards fully. Golden Dawn member Pamela Colman Smith illustrated the cards for Waite, and the deck was first published in 1909. It remains in publication today.

Other works by Waite are in circulation, many published after his death. They include *Inner and Outer Order Initiations of the Holy Order of the Golden Dawn*, (2005) *The Brotherhood of the Rosy Cross: Being Records of the House of the Holy Spirit in its Inward and Outward History*, (1924), *Israfel: Letters, Visions and* (1886), *A New Encyclopaedia of Freemasonry (Ars Magna Latomorum) and of Cognate Instituted Mysteries: Their Rites, Literature, and History* (1994), *Theories As to the Authorship of the Rosicrucian Manifestoes* (2005), *The Hidden Church of the Holy Grail: Its Legends and Symbolism Considered in Their Affinity with Certain Mysteries of Initiation and Other Traces of a Secret Tradition in Christian Times* (2002).

When Waite was almost 30, he married Ada Lakeman and they had one daughter, Sybil. Some time after Ada's death in 1924, Waite married Mary Broadbent Schofield. He spent most of his life in or near London, connected to various publishing houses, and editing a magazine, The Unknown World.

Waite passed away on the 19th May, 1942.

THE SPIRIT OF FREEMASONRY

TABLE OF CONTENTS

VOLUME II

BOOK V

Of Alchemy in Masonry

Contents

BOOK VI

Of Magical and Kabalistical Degrees

BOOK VII

Of the Mysteries on their Mystical Side, and of this Subject in its Relation to Masonry

Contents

𝕬𝖕𝖕𝖊𝖓𝖉𝖎𝖈𝖊𝖘

vii

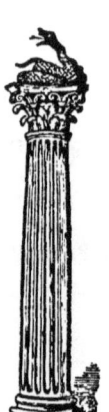

BOOK V

Of Alchemy in Masonry

THE ARGUMENT

I. The Root-Matter of the Alleged Hermetic Connection

The Masonic aspects of Alchemy—Further concerning the gifts of spiritual building—The question of Hermetic interference—That such interference must have been tinctured with Kabalism—That it was not of practical Alchemy—State of the question in the mind of Masonic writers—Slightness of their acquaintance with Hermetic literature—The initiation of Ashmole—Meaning of the term Hermetic in the seventeenth century—High Grades developed in the alchemical sense—The French Rite of Philalethes—Its origin and growth—Nature of its interests—The Grade content—Masonic and philosophical aims—Conventions held at Paris—Dissolution of the Rite—Disappointments in Hermetic Masonry—The term in mystical Alchemy and in Kabalism—Alchemy and the Secret Tradition.

II. The School of Alchemy

History of Alchemy in Europe—The Byzantine alchemists —Some questions for future research—Rise of Latin Alchemy—Of Alchemy in living languages—The Roman de la Rose—The Flamel Legend—Stages in

The Secret Tradition in Freemasonry

III. Masonic Systems of Alchemical Degrees and, Firstly, the Hermetic Rite of Pernety

4

The Argument

IV. Masonic Systems of Alchemic Degrees and, Secondly, the Hermetic Rite of Baron Tschoudy

Publication of L'Étoile Flamboyante—Theory concerning the origin of Masonry—Its connection with chivalry— Hermetic side of the treatise—The Knights of the Morning and Palestine—Their perpetuation from the past—The dream of another Temple in Jerusalem —The first Crusade—Johannite Christians and Essenes—Sons of the Valley—The imputed Masonic connection—Intercourse between the secret chivalry and Crusaders—Rise of the Masonic institution— Relation of this hypothesis to that of Ramsay— Alchemical researches of the Brotherhood—Value of the hypothesis—The hermit Morienus—The Hermetic Tract referred to him—Hermetic Catechism of Baron Tschoudy—The physical work therein—The sense of its Hermetic terminology—Nature of the work delineated — The hypothesis on which it rests— Analogies in Freemasonry—The art of development— The art of emblematic building—Term of research in Alchemy—Term of research in Masonry—Limits of the analogy—Masonry as the spiritual side of the magnum opus—Intimations of the Hermetic Catechism—Something reserved by the writer—The closing formulæ—Baron Tschoudy on Masonic High Grades—His hand in certain Rituals—The Grade of Sublime and Unknown Philosopher—The Statutes of the Unknown Philosophers—Their secret and the mode of its communication—How Postulants are said to have been received—A scheme in embryo— The title of Unknown Philosopher—Testimony of Ragon concerning an Order of the Unknown Judge-Philosophers—The legend of Dionysian Architects—

5

The Secret ·Tradition in Freemasonry

Their alleged connection with Freemasons—The passing of Baron Tschoudy.

V. Masonic Systems of Alchemical Degrees and, Thirdly, the Rite of Mizraïm

The common tolerance of the High Grades—Their system of incorporation—Their borrowings and lendings— Of things set aside—Feeling concerning Grades of the Old Alliance and Grades of Chivalry—Later and encyclopædic Rites—Their derivations and inventions — Of occult science in the Orders of Mizraïm and Memphis—The Grades of Chaos— The Grade of Knight of the Sun—Sovereign Commander of the Stars—Curious alchemical symbolism —Confusions therein—Experience of the Candidate —Grades of Hermetic Mineralogy—The True Mason Adept — Reflections from alchemical literature — Vanity of this Grade—The Perfect Alchemical Master—Conclusion on the Hermetic Masonry of Mizraïm.

VI. Masonic Systems of Alchemical Degrees and, Fourthly, the Hermetic Elements in the Oriental Order of Memphis

The order on its historical side—Varied classification of its Degrees—Reduction into an Antient and Primitive Rite—Hermetic Element in the Order— The Senate of Hermetic Philosophers—The Grade of Knight Hermetic Philosopher—Heads of the instruction on mysteries of nature and science—Presumable grand principles—Follies of the Rite in

6

The Argument

*Summary—Gleanings from the Hermetic Catechism—
Its views on spiritual Alchemy—Conclusion on the
Rite at large.*

VII. LES ARCHIVES MITHO-HERMÉTIQUES

*Of certain forgotten debts to the enemies of Masonry—
Professor Robison on a work of Saint-Martin—
The Loge de Bienfaisance—Statements in respect of
the work here under notice—Its extreme rarity—A
quest after it—Inference concerning its Masonic
connections—Its thesis on the Universal Medicine—
Study of the divine Pymander—Spiritual history
of Man—Man and the Quintessence—Symbolism
of this subject—Whether the Universal Medicine
should be understood mystically or materially—Doubts
as to the intention of the writer—Further analysis
of the text—Generation and destiny of the Spirit—
The Triad above and below—Purpose of this notice.*

BOOK V

Of Alchemy in Masonry

I

THE ROOT-MATTER OF THE ALLEGED HERMETIC CONNECTION

I must not say that one follows devious and hopeless paths more especially in Masonic Rites and literatures than in some other divisions of formulated secret thought, and yet several keen disappointments may await the zealous seeker on side issues of my subject, even if he has brought to it a certain canon of criticism on his own part, to act as a touchstone for possibilities which at a distance may seem alluring. Such ordeals notwithstanding, I believe that if this work should deserve well of its readers, it must not be its least title that I shall have done what lies within me to advise them in which direction it is idle to look for light. The Masonic aspects of Alchemy will prove disillusionary enough when it is a question only of two or three groups of Rituals, but there is another side of the subject on which I must dwell lightly, because a speculation upon origin is involved.

It is impossible to indicate in a printed book the exact lines of consanguinity which subsist between the central thesis of Craft Masonry and Zoharic literature, with its antecedents and derivations. The quest is the same quest, with due respect to the enormous variation of the external side of doctrine and symbolical fable. Craft Masonry is the home of a single legend, but there are many sides to Zoharic allegory. Among the things which they possess in common there is the gift of spiritual building, and there is also the haunting sense of a loss that has not been repaired through the ages ; but this notwithstanding, there is on both sides the certain expectation which causes the quest to continue. Here, and in such phantasmal outline, is sufficient to shew (*a*) that the phase of Hermetic interference which took place in Masonry, if indeed it was Hermetic at all in any rigorous sense of that term, was deeply tinctured with Kabalism, or such interference is a dream ; and (*b*) that its alchemical part was not practised on any plane of physics. Now this conclusion is notable, because, in the first place, it would seem to put out of court once and for all every Hermetic Grade which deals with the material side of the *magnum opus*—that is to say, the transmutation of metals ; and thus, in the second place, we are put in possession beforehand of a casual canon of criticism which will simplify our research into this branch—at once so important antecedently and so involved—of Masonic ceremonial literature.

Some attention has been paid of recent years by Masonic writers of ability, and of large experience along the lines of their proper research, to the possibility of Hermetic intervention in the evolution of Symbolical Masonry. After exhausting all fields, there remains, or there has arisen, a feeling of instability as to the old notion of such an identical connection between the trade and the emblematic mystery that the one could have arisen from the other without an interference of some and indeed of a very specific kind. Because it does not appear with plainness, I do not know exactly what is understood by these writers regarding the horizon and content of the Hermetic schools ; it is in no spirit of adverse criticism if I say that it is perhaps only in a secondary sense that they can be said to have acquaintance therewith, and more especially with the tradition therein. We might have several reserves to establish if I were entering on a serious consideration of the question ; but passing over these, and speaking in a general sense only, I believe that the view has arisen through the coincidence of Elias Ashmole's membership with the period to which the transformation is attributed. Ashmole appears chiefly as an informed amateur of that branch of Hermetic philosophy or science which is connected with the name of Alchemy, and there is evidence of his presence in a London Lodge at the very period when a confessedly speculative branch of Masonry was in session at the same place—that is to say, in 1682.

Whether or not this represents the entire content of the feeling that has actuated the trend of thought, the hand of the Hermetic Schools in Early Symbolical Freemasonry has come to be regarded with sufferance, though it sets aside tacitly the particular importance which Mr. R. F. Gould has attached to the Regius MS. He himself is one of the tolerating parties, and I confess that I do not see how he harmonises the possible Hermetic intervention which could be early only between the limits of the seventeenth century, with the supposed testimony of the fourteenth century manuscript to a speculative art into which the Hermetic motive never entered. Setting this also aside, the first question that arises is, as I have just intimated, the precise significance which would be attached to the term Hermetic in the minds of those who have used it, seeing that they would disclaim any special acquaintance with the schools, their horizon or their term. At the period under notice—I mean in the seventeenth century—it is, I think, exact to say that the word had reference to Alchemy and to nothing else. It is that which it signified for Elias Ash-mole, since it was one of his especial dedications, and he is likely to be remembered by his intro-duction to the *Museum Hermeticum Britannicum* long after the history of the Order of the Garter has passed from the minds of men. Ashmole had certain intimations moving in his mind that the field of Hermetic science was not covered by a simple form of experimental research regarding the transmutation of metals, but the fact had no consequence for himself apparently, and none certainly for his period. If I may assume, there-fore, that the possibility of Hermetic interfer-ence in Masonry signifies—for those who have mentioned it—an interposition on the part of alchemists, then the hypothesis or disposition will seem at first sight to derive a certain colour from the fact that the High Degrees were developed—in one direction—along alchemical lines.

Although in very brief summary, we shall see in the next few sections how curiously the Hermetic preoccupation—so understood—inter-venes in the highways and byways of Masonic history. It is out of all expectation in respect of the broad roads, but it is indubitable, apart from these ; and it took shape in specific Rites which were collections of considerable magnitude. The illustrious RITE OF THE PHILALETHES is an important case in point as a casual centre of the interest.

Amidst the cloud of reveries and false seeming,

this institution came into existence with an express resolution to separate the wheat from the chaff in the matter of historical, philosophical and symbolical Masonry, and during more than a decade of years it sought to perform, within the circle of the Lodge and its connections, what was attempted in 1782 by the memorable Convention of Wilhelmsbad, a kind of œcumenical Council of Masonry. I cannot say that the alchemical predisposition predominated, but it certainly was in evidence, so far as membership was concerned, and that rather conspicuously. The Rite reached no term, and the Revolution, which devoured so much and gave back so little, swallowed it up entirely.

It will serve a more general purpose to dwell, however, for a moment on an experiment which was brilliant during its brief period, and under happier circumstances might have had, as it deserved assuredly, a more permanent lease of life. The question of dates is as usual somewhat doubtful, but a *Loge des Amis Réunis* seems to have been founded at Paris early in 1771 for the express purpose of investigating the basis of Masonry, and the value, comparative and absolute, of its various Rites and systems. In the year 1775 the work had so far matured that it had selected from the vast concourse of Grades a certain number which were regarded as suited to its intention and had added thereto four others, previously unknown, which represented the plenary development of the Masonic subject

14

within the horizon of the Lodge. It was thus in working possession of the LESSER MYSTERIES as follows : . (1) *Apprentice*, (2) *Companion*, (3) *Master*, (4) *Elect*, (5) *Scottish Master*, (6) *Knight of the East* ; and of the GREATER MYSTERIES (7) *Rose Croix*, (8) *Knight of the Temple*, (9) *Unknown Philosopher*, (10) *Sublime Philosopher*, (11) *Initiate*, (12) *Philalethes*, or *Searcher after Truth* and *Master of all Grades*.

In respect of the first seven Degrees, the order and titles are identical with those of the modern French Rite, as professed by the Grand Orient. The eighth Grade is reminiscent of the *Strict Observance*, to which, however, there seems good authority for saying that the system was in some sense opposed in respect of the Templar claim. Herein it was following in part the trend of the time, but more especially the leading of the RITE OF ELECT COHENS. We come therefore to the ninth Grade, which was that of *Unknown Philosopher*, in which we can trace at once the influence of Martines de Pasqually, exercised not by himself, for he was then no longer in Europe or the world, but by the *Loge de Bienfaisance* at Lyons—through its representative in chief, J. B. Willermoz, a member of the RITE OF PHILALETHES practically from the beginning of its activity. Of the last three Grades I can speak by report only. The first is included by name in the modern ORDER OF MIZRAÏM, but the correspondence may be titular only ; the second and third have not been co-opted to other interests. The report is that they were Grades concerned with the perfection of man, his return towards the centre from which he came forth at the beginning ; his regeneration, his reintegration in a state of primitive innocence and the restoration of the rights and privileges which were lost by the averse mystery of the Fall. It is, in a word, a reduction into ritual form of Pasqually's plan of redemption established in his *Traité de la Ré-intégration des Êtres*, as we shall find in a later section.

The system was thus theosophical, as other records have stated, and it was also in some sense alchemical, which, however, is rather a reference to the predispositions of certain members than to the complexion of its acknowledged Grades. The *Archives Mytho-Hermétiques* emanated from this source, as we shall also see. The Roll of the Rite included Court de Gebelin, a celebrated archæologist of his period ; Duchanteau, to whom occultists owe the largest and most erudite of all Calendars of Magic ; the alchemist Clavières, who was also a minister of finance ; the Baron de Gleichen, author of a *Treatise on Metaphysical Heresies ;* Jacques Cazotte, better remembered than any by his story of *Le Diable Amoureux ;* in fine, astrologers, physiognomists, cartomancists, Kabalists and all the choir illuminated of the secret sciences and arts.

The Convention of Lyons, held in 1778, may

A COURT DE GEBELIN.
Auteur du Monde Primitif
De diverses Académies, Président du Musée de Paris
Censeur Royal &c?

COURT DE GEBELIN

have led to the formulation of the four final Degrees, and in this case that Templar chivalry which they included may have approximated to the *Knights Beneficent of the Holy City of Jerusalem*. The RITE OF THE PHILALETHES itself held two Conventions at Paris in 1785 and 1787. As the founder of EGYPTIAN MASONRY, Cagliostro was' summoned to the first, but demanded the destruction of the valuable archives possessed by the Rite as the price of his attendance, and the proposal therefore fell through. The deliberations attained no satisfactory term, and there is hence no reason for the consideration of that which they proposed. Its Hermetic and theosophical tendencies and its reflections from early Martinism are the justification of this brief notice of the Rite. They were part of the hunger and thirst which filled the instructed hearts in all Masonry at the period and led them in a world without religion to seek more wisely than they knew for the religion which is concealed in all.

The comparative byways of Rites and collections will prove more to our purpose than this eclectic experiment, including as they did many Grades and Degrees which were invented or compiled by alchemists to illustrate the Hermetic connections of Masonry for the use of alchemists, who were thus brought into the Fraternity, and for the use of Masons, who might thus be brought into Alchemy.

We shall find, however, much to disappoint even if there is something to encourage us in exploring Hermetic Freemasonry, for in the first place it incorporated a good deal that was extrinsic to its own subject, and gave very little colour to the assumption of real knowledge even in its proper department. I mean to say that—obviously and almost only—it was dedicated to the physical work ; but there is not the least reason to infer that any maker of alchemical Grades in Masonry had attained to the term of his art, while of its higher aspects, or of the mystical side, there was no light in his consciousness. *Ex hypothesi*, mystical Alchemy was the experience of the Divine Union, and it delineated all the processes leading thereto, from that mystery of the black state which corresponds to some part of the Candidate's experience in Craft Masonry. The end in the terminology of the subject was the mystic marriage of the Sun and Moon. On the other hand, and also by the hypothesis, the term of Kabalism was entrance into nuptial joys like those of Rabbi Simeon. The experience of mystical death and resurrection is not less clear in Alchemy than in the Instituted Mysteries like Masonry, but it is anything rather than clear even on the high side of Kabalism ; the great transition therein is from the life of this world, through physical death, to the reward of the just man and the true Sons of the Doctrine in the world to come. I omit what it may perpetuate regarding material resurrection, which is only a burden to the tradition and has no prominent part in the system. That which appears at first sight to be a difficulty, tends, however, to dissolve in the light of one canon of interpretation ; the theosophy of Israel was rooted in things visible, things tangible and material, and on these it worked strange processes of transfiguration, by which they seemed to dissolve and take their part and place in the things that are eternal. After this manner the death which was physical became a mystical death : the resurrection of Rabbi Simeon really took place when he was received into the celestial school. Our triad in this manner is not actually in a state of separation, on the understanding that the traditional schools are for such reason the more distinct as schools and did not derive from one another. But if we suppose for a moment that they did, then the nearest progenitor of Masonry, on the inward side as otherwise on that which I must term in a sense historical, would be Kabalism and not Alchemy. It is not, however, Kabalism on the debased or magical side, and this is one reason why most magical Grades which are in masks under the name of Masonry are little better than abortions. Fortunately they are for the most part so obscure that their very names are almost unknown, and it may well be a matter of surprise that I have unearthed such considerations concerning them as will appear in some later sections.

I am dealing for the moment, however, with

the Hermetic school in Masonry, and as it was in France rather than elsewhere that alchemical Rites rose up, it seems desirable to put on record the mode of regarding the subject which obtained in that country. It is more important for the Secret Tradition than for Masonry as generally understood, but the one reflects on the other, and the question—as it so happens—has some intrinsic interest of its own.

II

THE SCHOOL OF ALCHEMY : AN EXCURSUS

THE history of Alchemy in Europe offers a field of research in which the first steps have as yet been scarcely taken. There is a very fair probability—which does not, however, enter at all into the grade of certitude from any point of view—that what I may call the font of experience in this subject was Byzantium, represented by the extant remains of the Byzantine alchemists. They date from the fourth century and onward to about 700 A.D., and their influence has been traced by the perpetuation of certain characteristic conventions of expression for a considerable period beyond the Middle Ages. These phrases seem to offer a better testimony to the source of knowledge than the instituted technical terminology which Alchemy has used so invariably and which constitutes the chief veil of the art. Having regard to the unknown world in China, and the existence of the same art therein from a period as yet wholly indeterminate, it is very difficult to say that Alchemy was not an importation from that far region, and Byzantium would not have been by necessity the sole port of entrance for the particular class of merchandise. The catch phrases, however, on which the evidence depends are much less likely to have been common in East and West, as they are in no way essential to the subject. If we assume, therefore, as a tolerable working hypothesis, under all the necessary reserves, that the theory and practice of metallic transmutation, with some adjuncts thereto belonging, spread from Constantinople over Europe, and gave rise in several countries to a Latin literature which afterwards passed into the vernacular, the second step in the department of historical research would· be to ascertain the number and date of the earliest extant manuscripts. Their co-ordination would be the third step, and I suppose that herein I have already indicated a very serious labour. In neither case, however, has the step been taken, and as a fact we know utterly nothing as to whether the great and familiar Latin texts ever penetrated into Russia, into Southern Europe, with the exception of Portugal, Spain, and Italy, or—unless at very late periods—into northern countries like Sweden. There may be innumerable unknown superiors and masters of the art whose memorials lie entombed and forgotten far away from the great centres. Speaking generally, there is, so far as our acquaintance extends, no literature of the subject outside Germany, France, England, Spain, and a few great texts, with much that is late and negligible, in Italy.

Latin Alchemy arose about the tenth century and had an allotted life of seven hundred years ; it was slow in growth and it passed slowly into the vernacular of any country. An early example of the latter is furnished by the informal tract which Jean de Meung incorporated in his share of the *Roman de la Rose*. This is of the thirteenth century, and, whether or not it was actually the first text of its kind in the French tongue, its popularity set the fashion of writing on Alchemy therein, and some of the most valued and authoritative treatises on the Great Work belong thereto. As there is no very serious question that one of the memorials attributed to Nicholas Flamel, the wonderful scrivener of Paris, may be tentatively allocated to his period, our next date is at the close of the fourteenth century. But a curious set of monographs by Johannes Rupecissa, which move in a strange spiritual atmosphere, are near to the same epoch or earlier. They are earlier in high but not consummate probability. Bernard Trevisan followed in the fifteenth century ; and Denis Zachaire is another illustrious name which brings up the present unconcerted account of the literature in one country to the middle of the sixteenth century. I have mentioned the typical instances and have selected France, because it is with this country, as intimated, that—in respect of Hermetic High Grades—we shall be concerned in an especial manner. As Alchemy was a secret art represented by a secret literature, and as even in its most material aspects it claimed to be the gift of the Spirit or the gift of a Master abiding under the law of the Spirit, and as it confessed invariably to a religious motive, what I may be permitted to call the sacramentary of that art has great names to offer from the Middle Ages and onward in England and Germany. Though Écossais Hermetic Grades are fortunately not in evidence, I suppose that there are few adepts more illustrious in the catholic annals of transmutation than Alexander Seton the Scotchman at the beginning of the seventeenth century, or the pseudonymous Eirenæus Philalethes, an Englishman of the period of the Rebellion. I suppose also that Basil Valentine and Paracelsus are as great in Germany, though the latter had taken all secret science for his province, and—being supposed to have attained in all—is perhaps in a general sense the head of the whole body of occult adeptship. I have now mentioned three countries, though I have certified that our concern is with one, but my design is to make room for a particular distinction which is not without moment to my purpose. Between all the countries concerned in the great output of the literature, there grew up, as I have explained more than once elsewhere, two schools in Alchemy, the root-matter of which is to be traced from the assumed beginnings of the mystery among the Byzantine alchemists. There was the school of the physical work divided into two branches—one being that of transmutation, constituting the medicine of metals, which healed the sickness of reputed inferior elements in the mineral kingdom of Nature ; the other being that of the elixir, which healed sickness and senility in the kingdom of the natural man. Speaking broadly, the second of these schools did not, by the evidence of the texts, claim to confer immortality or literally to renew youth ; *ex hypothesi*, it healed disease and retarded the waste of tissue. But there was the school of a spiritual work, the claim of which was at once the most obscure and express that is to be met with in any of the concealed literatures. It used the veils and terminology of transmutation and the elixir to cover an experiment in the inward man, but that experiment is, I think, the last secret which yields itself up to research. In the words of Rupecissa, its initiates, or rather its proficients, are " enriched with an infinite wealth beyond all kings of the earth ; they are first before God and men, and are in enjoyment of the special favour of heaven." This statement is equally pellucid and hopeless, but this is not the place in which to carry the subject further and explain after what manner a student who is utterly prepared may follow this side of Alchemy into its deep recesses and behold from very far away how the closed eye of the secret does in fine open, and what light it diffuses.

The Secret Tradition in Freemasonry

I have shewn elsewhere that Thomas Vaughan
was an exponent in England of this side of the
art; Khunrath is an example in Germany, and there
are many Latin treatises of concealed or equivocal
authorship which might extend the list indefinitely.
In the early seventeenth century, Jacob Böhme
began (*a*) to rend the veils of the mystery, or
(*b*) alternatively to use the terminology of Alchemy
in a spiritual sense and to explain the art from
a standpoint particular to himself. It is for him
one of the works of regeneration, and is, I infer,
that consummation which is possible of attainment by the soul, wherein it may be said literally
and mystically that God wipes away all tears
from the eyes. And as I am entirely certain
that the pilgrimage of spiritual Alchemy was
in that undiscovered country of the soul from
which no traveller returns when he has proceeded
a certain great distance, and as it was in this
country that Jacob Böhme had received some titles
of freedom—not that I pretend him to have
undertaken the whole journey—so I think that
here and there he used some of the alchemical
language in its full and ineffable sense ; but I do
not think that he had the whole mystery thereof.
He remains, however, by his intimations, the
point of departure from which those may do
well to start in this quest who are in search of a
criterion for the literature. That criterion has
become a question of urgency ; the evidence for
the separation of the literature into two schools

has to be restated entirely and extended where no one has tried to carry it.

Even at the present day it would be difficult to estimate the extent of the influence which may have been exercised by Jacob Böhme on mystical philosophy in France. He began to be made known in that country under the auspices of Saint-Martin, and there is little question that the considerable vogue and the high appeal of the latter must have reflected in many quarters on the German theosopher, to whom such a throne of the inward life was attributed by one who had taken him into his heart of hearts. Still it was rather the fact of the influence, the testimony to greatness on the part of one who was obviously carrying very high titles himself, which provided the spiritual effigy of Böhme with something of a French nimbus. I cannot trace that Saint-Martin's translations of one or two Böhme texts made any conspicuous mark. There is reason, I think, to infer that they remained generally unknown, and their present excessive rarity is an indication that the original impressions were minute. However this may be, it does not transpire in the translations, nor in the independent appreciations of Saint-Martin, that Böhme had any place in the school of Hermetic tradition, much less that in him for the first time the veils of alchemical philosophy had begun to be lifted. Had the fact been much more conspicuous, had the revelation been much fuller,

I think that it would have spelled very little to the French mystic, who was not of the Hermetic tradition, and had, if anything, less patience for its obvious concerns and modes than he carried for theurgic processes out of the school of Martines de Pasqually. I question whether it had entered into his mind to conceive that there was a spiritual side of the adeptship which on the surface of its records was concerned with metallic transmutation. I almost question whether he would have entered into the side issue if he had met with testimony thereon ; his warrants were so much within himself; he was not a man of books ; he appealed little to tradition and less even to authority ; while he sincerely thought that he was not worthy to loose or to bind the shoes of the German cobbler, he carried his own implicits into the latter's writings and brought them out shining in no very new manner of expression. In a word, Jacob Böhme enabled him to look a little more clearly into his own deeps, but the pearls which he thus discovered were the same manner of jewels as they had been from the beginning.

The fact therefore remains, that the kinship in symbolism between the regeneration of metals and the work of regeneration in man did not materially trouble the dream of the French mind in respect of the *magnum opus*. When Johannes de Rupecissa affirmed, in the closing lines of his tract on *The Composition of the True Stone of the*

Philosophers, that the present order of the world would perish if the matter of the Stone were named ; that the possessor of this inestimable treasure was indeed born under a happy constellation ; that it was not the work of usury, of fraud or of deception, but was the special gift of God,—I conclude that the French mind, following the line of least resistance, understood in its simplicity that all this was the licence of adeptship—somewhat wider than the poet's licence. It had not really heard in its preoccupations about the doctrine of correspondences, which had scarcely been formulated—that is to say, in the French language ; but it knew something of occult sympathies, and it is probable that the analogy would appeal to the French student after this manner and as something instituted in the mind by way of artificial likeness. But it is even more probable that for practical purposes the French occult *literati* had heard nothing of the instituted analogy, by which I mean that they had not noticed the colophon added to one tract of Rupecissa, though it follows from Lenglet du Fresnoy that the work itself was prized.

There was, moreover, Jean d'Espagnet, whom I ought to have mentioned previously ; he also was a Frenchman, and, though there is very little doubt that he once worked in metals, he had occasional intimations, as from strange worlds of analogy, and some of records and glimpses are not precisely those of the kingdom of this world.

At the beginning of his *Secret Work of the Hermetic Philosophy* he makes it perfectly plain as to the nature and term of the quest and its wisdom : he says (1) that the light of the secret knowledge is a gift of God ; (2) that the postulant must be utterly dedicated to Divine things, and emptied, also utterly, of the concerns, desires and interests which have their root in this world ; (3) that the science is Divine in its nature, that it begins in the fear of the Lord and ends in love.   After such a preamble, coupled with the fact which is specified a little later, namely, that the student may be ignorant of practical chemistry, it would seem almost impossible to misconstrue the real subjects with which the author is dealing, to misinterpret his metals, his mercuries, his sulphurs, or the processes by which they are converted from one to another mode of manifestation or of being.   But, as a matter of fact, the mind of French Alchemy permitted the intimations to slide, overlooked the preamble, and continued its usual method of literalising the terms and processes.   D'Espagnet passed out of sight before the middle of the seventeenth century, and it will be remembered by many of my readers that about this time the belated rumour of the Rosicrucian Fraternity began to be heard of in France.   It was rumour only, and it was not until the middle period of the eighteenth century—when High-Grade Masonry was near the zenith of repute and power—that we get our first indications of the Mystery, its offshoots or developments, being at work in the country. One of its reformations was due to take place in Germany during the next quarter of the century, but there are French records which—if they are to be regarded as reliable in the historical sense—offer proof that its concern in 1750 was the same as that which is on record in respect of 1777. It was exclusively a society of Hermetists seeking the philosopher's stone on the material side. I have seen part of an exceedingly rare manuscript, written in French and dated 1763. It is entitled *The Practice of the Work of the Brethren of the Rosy Cross and their Key for the Extraction of Living Gold.* The extraction took place, by the hypothesis, from the subject-matter of minerals, and the fixation was by means of vulgar gold. I do not know whether the title which I have quoted is that of the whole collection or one of its parts only. There are two sections extant, the second treating of natural philosophy and the spagyric or Hermetic art. Five sections are missing, and it is in these if anywhere that specific information might be expected regarding the Society. So far as the surviving portions are concerned, the document is not of authority, as the anonymous writer speaks throughout on his own responsibility, recalls his personal discoveries and the marvels which he operated by their means. He does, however, affirm that the Brethren of the Rosy Cross were the first to recognise the existence, under the name of Living Gold, of a middle substance in metals and minerals, and that the first matter is gold. It is evidently, therefore, a record of little moment on the historical side, and in respect of its secret processes I have taken different opinions of old students as to their value, with the kind of enlightenment which is usually derived from experts ; that is to say, it was said on the one hand that more help could be derived from the collection than from almost anything else in the range of alchemical manuscripts. The alternative view is that no value attaches to the contents. I will only note in conclusion that the writer, unlike the general members of the Rosicrucian Order, would appear to have been a Catholic, and possibly even an ecclesiastic ; he mentions in one place that he had been in retreat for a period of four years at the *Abbaye Royale* ; he states, further, that he began his occult studies at the age of sixteen, or at the same period as in the case of Christian Rosenkreutz. If we are to accept this manuscript as a reflection of the Order, at however far a distance, it is interesting as a record of the Fraternity ; it registers the nature of its preoccupations, and shews that even in what may be tentatively called the high quarters of initiation there was then at least no horizon outside the physical work. I believe that the manuscript belongs to the date which is mentioned in one of its remaining sections, and it therefore follows that the Hermetists in France did not draw higher leading from the inmost circles than their particular dispositions helped them to extract from the prevailing texts of Alchemy.

Cagliostro and the Comte de Saint-Germain were the public advertisements of the subject at that period on the Continent of Europe, or at least of that part having France as the centre thereof. Both claimed to have been renewed by the elixir of immortality ; both could at need dispense it ; theirs also was the secret of wealth, and all power was at their demand. Saint-Germain is too doubtful and nebulous for any definite opinion to be formed concerning him ; he was little more than a portent, and might almost have furnished a case in point to the makers of historic doubts. But the impositions of Cagliostro are beyond all question, and the experience of Cardinal de Rohan, in search of the great palingenesis, at the hands of the dubious adept is evidence enough as to the kind of Alchemy which the latter practised.

There has been an attempt within recent times to redeem Cagliostro by indicating the very slight basis in fact which remains after a searching inquiry into the motives and circumstances of his identification with Joseph Balsamo, and I have recorded otherwise my feeling that there is at least a tolerable warrant for the suspension of judgment on the subject. The distinction, if it can be maintained, does not operate substantially towards the redemption of the Magus ; but it reduces the old charges by leaving his early life in a cloud of darkness. In another cloud of this kind the Comte de Saint-Germain remains throughout his whole career. He was a contemporary of Cagliostro, but the chief part of his pageant had passed across the stage of Europe some few years previously. It has been suggested that he was born in 1710, and he seems to have been first heard of in Germany about 1750. He visited England in 1760 on some kind of semi-political mission from the court of France. This was apparently arranged by Louis XV. personally, and did not prevent one of that king's ministers sending secret instructions to London for the arrest of Saint-Germain as a Russian spy. With the particulars I am not concerned, but two years later he was in St. Petersburg and was certainly involved in some kind of conspiracy. I mention this to shew that on the historical side he was rather a political personality, and his claims of the occult order, though in part they must have arisen from himself, are more largely of contemporary attribution and of romantic invention. Much in the latter respect is due to the Marquis de Luchet and to the imaginative writers who later on accepted his illuminated fables as facts. In 1774 Saint-Germain is said to have taken up his abode in Germany, there to live in retirement, and though he is heard of subsequently in Italy and Denmark, he had left the public stage. The date mentioned was two years before Cagliostro as such, and setting aside his time-immemorial identification with

Of *Alchemy* in *Masonry*

Joseph Balsamo, made his own appearance in London. Now in 1760 and thereabouts we know that Masonry was in the light of public evidence, both here and on the Continent, but the High Grades were at the dawn rather than the zenith and had not filled all men's ears. It has been said that Saint-Germain not only claimed initiation but a throne of Masonic adeptship, for which, however, I find no evidence ; no rite is connected with his name ; no Lodge is said to have received him. The explanation is probably that at the period when Cagliostro was in his high noon there was every reason why a person adopting the rôle of a travelling *illuminé* should identify himself with the Brotherhood, which was then in the glory of the High Grade fever ; but if there was some incentive from fifteen to twenty years previously, it was not in the same degree. The history of the Comte de Saint-Germain remains to be written in the light of first-hand knowledge, but in certain respects he may be called the precursor of Cagliostro, and it is for this reason that he is entitled to mention here. He is said to have resigned immortality in 1783 at Eckenfiorde. Having regard to his antecedents in Masonry, he is about the most unfortunate selection that could have been made by certain dreamers in the modern school of theosophy, when they were in search recently of a hypothetical adept to be installed as a guardian angel for the female Freemasonry which they have taken under their wing.

Whether the hypothesis accepts a comparatively old story that, despite his fatigue of immortality, and notwithstanding its alleged surrender, Saint-Germain continues to carry the load of the Christian centuries, I do not pretend to say ; but for our diversion in these matters of transcendental faith, it may be added that there is a person at this day resident in Hungary who affirms that he is the dubious Count *in propria persona*, that he is not as such re-embodied but perpetuated apparently in the flesh for ever and ever. It does not seem clear that he is the concealed guardian of the thing called Co-Masonry, and in the contrary event what attitude would be taken up by that doubtful body should the claimant appear in England is a question for those who are concerned.

I mention these trival matters to indicate the temper of the time, in respect of the present moment, but in respect also of the past. The evanescent but brilliant success of the personages in question at the close of the eighteenth century is an efficient touchstone for the predisposition concerning the occult sciences in general and things Hermetic in particular, and so it remains to-day. But that which prevailed in the world of adventure and trickery had then its parallel in more serious quarters. Baron Tschoudy and the Abbé Pernety, both in Masonic and in literary life, have left important memorials concerning their understanding of Alchemy—the first in his Catechism, which assumes a purely arbitrary and

COMTE DE SAINT GERMAIN

even fantastic air of Masonic connection and terminology ; the second in his interpretation of classical mythology as being the veils of the Great Work—which work, for all and sundry at that period and in that place, is rooted in earth and the material, carrying with it no suggestion of a deeper sense.

The century of revolution went, and I must not say that in France the sleep of Alchemy and the occult sciences generally was unbroken ; but I know of nothing—apart from Masonic Rites— that is worth mentioning, of nothing which belongs to our purpose for a period of sixty years. Thereafter, for another period, whatsoever was considerable, whatsoever was brilliant, whatsoever was attractive and plausible, was written over one signature, and the name was Éliphas Lévi. He was much too comprehensive and interpretative to see single phases only where more than a phase was possible, and if we question his oracle, it responds with no uncertain voice, as follows : (1) The Stone of the Philosopher is the foundation of absolute philosophy, the supreme, the immovable reason, which is the touchstone of truth. (2) It is also the certitude which follows conscientious researches. (3) The universal medicine is, in the soul, supreme reason and absolute justice ; in the mind, it is mathematical and practical truth ; in the body, it is the quintessence, which is a combination of gold and light. (4) Philosophical salt is wisdom ; mercury is skill and application ; sulphur is the fire of the will. I could multiply quotations like these, or I could select entire chapters, but I have made them available already by summarised or direct translation. Their sum total does not deny, or perhaps especially reduce, the hypothesis of the metallic work, but it offers the other side of the shield of Hermetic faith : it is Éliphas Lévi's presentation of spiritual Alchemy ; it is utterly unsubstantial, betraying no acquaintance with the root-matter of the literature ; but it has glimpses here and there.

III

MASONIC SYSTEMS OF ALCHEMICAL DEGREES AND, FIRSTLY, THE HERMETIC RITE OF ABBÉ PERNETY

THE travelling seeker, the travelling neophyte and the travelling adept went out in the sixteenth and seventeenth centuries like the knight-errant of earlier times, they seeking the high adventure of wisdom as those others the adventures of chivalry. Such offices, moreover, had not reached their term till the French Revolution abrogated the old order entirely in Europe ; they assumed, however, the veil of Masonry.

Some of the fantastic implicits of the High-Grade movement in the eighteenth century afford matter for very curious reflection, and few are more fruitful than those which depend from the integration of Alchemy in the general scheme of the Rites. As appears by the last section, I have looked about almost in vain for traces of the mystical work, and for evidences of the kind of adeptship which is connected with the assumption of success in the physical work of transmutation. If there is little of the one, there is assuredly nothing of the other. Yet there is abundant curious material ; there is evidence of ardent discipleship, and the Grades are sometimes the work of persons who have otherwise made contributions of importance, at least, to the archives of Alchemy. Things that are curious being set apart, I need not, however, regard it as a matter of regret that I cannot afford to the present consideration that full space to which on several considerations some might think that it is entitled.

Antoine Joseph Pernety, born in 1716, was, like Basil Valentine, a Benedictine monk, and he was first heard of in Masonry about the year 1760—if it is possible to trust my authority, who is French and doubtful, as usual. The two works by which he is known to collectors are, however, *Les Fables Égyptiennes et Grecques devoilées et réduites au même principe*, 2 vols. 1786, and *Dictinnaire Mytho-Hermétique*, 1787. In these he establishes the physical side of the subject, and it seems certain on their evidence that he had no horizon beyond it, so far as Alchemy is concerned. The Great Work had for him two objects in view : one of them was an universal remedy for disease in the three Kingdoms of Nature, the inferior metals—from this point of view—being in the pain and travail of imperfection, suspiring after the state of gold but attaining it only by the regeneration of Hermetic art ; the other was the transmutation of metallic substances into gold more pure than that which is found in Nature. It is obvious by the definition that these two are one. The terminology of alchemical literature, which is often so suggestive on the spiritual side, even when the spiritual intent is wanting, opened no doors for Pernety. The sensible soul for him is not the psychic part, but *sal ammoniac*, and the term Soul in its catholic sense is the Perfect Mastery at the Red, as the Ferment which animates the Stone for its conversion into elixir. So also the Universal Spirit is an element diffused throughout the atmosphere and impregnated with the virtue of the stars ; it is the food of natural life. It is not immaterial, but a very tenuous, subtle and penetrating substance, which enters into all composites.

This is sufficient on the point of view, and will determine *a priori* the department of Hermeticism which Pernety would represent in any Rite of Masonry that he established. Such an institution is said to have been the *Académie des Illuminés d'Avignon*, on the examination of which we shall find, however, that the whole subject passes into inextricable confusion. One alleged date of its foundation is that which I have already mentioned—1760, but another witness, equally definite and dubious, substitutes 1785. Whether the Academy was Masonic at all is the next question, for it is also affirmed to have been androgynous in character, and may simply have exacted as such the Masonic qualification from its members on the male side. Again, it may have been under the banner of Adoption, or an imitation of the revolutionary changes introduced by the Sieur Cagliostro. But these problems are to some extent extrinsic ; dates are essentially immaterial except on the historical side ; Masonic history has to dispense with them largely when it is concerned with the Continent of Europe ; and, lastly, at the general period on that Continent, the question of initiating women, though not favourably regarded, found no voice of authority to condemn it in an absolute sense.

There is, however, a more direct difficulty. The mysterious Staroste Grabbianka is said to have had a hand with Pernety in the inauguration or direction of the *Illuminés,* and their dedication was divided between Hermeticism and the visionary system of Swedenborg. Of the latter there is, I think, no question, on the evidence with which I am now dealing, which is that of my precursors in Masonry. Benedictine and alchemist though he was, Pernety had come within the influence of the Swedish seer, and it is probable that the twofold interest may have combined to render his monastic position untenable in respect of his personal sincerity. That he was anxious—and because of his sincerity—is made evident by the fact that he applied in an orderly manner to Rome for a dispensation from his vows, which he received ultimately. This was about 1765, and it was, as I should infer, thereafter—and not previously—that he became more fully identified with the Masonic and occult movement. The *Académie des Illuminés* might in this case belong— as it has also been suggested—to the year 1770, and could not well have been earlier. We shall reach, however, a different conclusion as this inquiry proceeds.

Pernety was, moreover, connected as a founder with the *Loge Hermétique du Contrat-Venaisin*, and in 1778, or later, he may have had a hand in establishing the *Académie des Vrais Maçons*, a system of six Degrees, also with a Hermetic motive, shewn by such titles as *Knight of the Golden Key, Knight of the Rainbow, Knight Argonautic* and *Knight of the Golden Fleece*. In the last two his interpretation of Greek mythology may have passed into the dramatic form of ritual. The *Illuminés du Zodiaque* is another of his fabled creations, and—for some writers—he is an alternative author with Baron Tschoudy of the Grade called *Knight of the Sun*, which still remains among us in the system of the ANCIENT AND ACCEPTED SCOTTISH RITE, as well as under other obediences.

I have had recourse so far to the sources of reference which are available in Masonic literature, but another light is cast upon the whole subject when the appeal is transferred to the records of the New Church and the research which has been instituted thereby into all that, directly or indirectly, is concerned with the mission of Emanuel Swedenborg, its connections and its history. They have something to tell us respecting Abbé Pernety and the school of Avignon ; it is new and direct to our purpose ; it is separable easily from accidental errors owing to unfamiliarity with the Masonic aspect of things ; and if it is not all that we could desire, I believe that from the same source there will be ultimately other materials.

It is now many years since Mr. R. F. Gould assured us that a society of Hermetists—whether formally incorporated or not—had existed at Avignon from 1740. I regard the date as doubtful, and I question the Hermetic interest in the exact sense of the term. It was, however, in that city, but more probably about 1760, that an unofficial and quite private association came into being, and the information regarding it comes (*a*) from a living contemporary witness in the person of Benedict Chastanier, and through him (*b*) from Count Thade Leszezye Grabbianka, Staroste de Lieve. The latter testifies that a certain Polish noble, who was a student of the Secret Tradition in Kabalism—but apparently on the so-called practical side—bequeathed a book of the occult art in manuscript to his nephew, together with a counsel that he should use it with great circumspection. The nephew went into consultation with a few friends, and they began to put in practice the information contained in the document. As a result they received several revelations of a serious and even terrifying kind—or, in other words, the shadows in Kabalistic language of coming events, social and political upheavals, and so forth. These things were to be kept secret, and as regards the mode of operation, it pretended to elicit " answers from the Word " to such questions as were put by the circle in accordance with the laws of the oracle. It is difficult on the information given to identify the particular process, but several things of this kind are known in debased Kabalism. The persons concerned in the practice included Count Grabbianka and Abbé Pernety, the other names signifying nothing to our inquiry.

It will be seen that the association received information in advance most probably concerning that Revolution which at the period in question may be said to have been already brewing. As is the custom of such revelations, it came to people who had neither power nor concern therein, but with peculiar fatuity certain Swedenborgian writers have jumped to the conclusion that the uninstructed tyros in Kabalistic Magic formed one of the forcing-houses of the great cataclysm, and helped, like the RITE OF THE PHILALETHES—as the same testimonies affirm— to prepare its programme. That which concerns us, however, is apart from such unreason, and is the curious occasion which caused the society to dissolve, at least for a period. The time came when, in answer to a specific question which does not itself transpire, the oracle is said to have affirmed that these things were declared already "to my servant, Emanuel Swedenborg," whom the little band were counselled to follow thereafter. The oracle on its own part spoke henceforth no more ; the associates dispersed ; and Count Grabbianka, who is still our informant on the subject, went, as no doubt did Pernety, in search of the new prophet. The so-called Mago-Cabbalistical Society, being the name attributed thereto by Benedict Chastanier, a Mason and ardent disciple of Swedenborg, was expected to reassemble in the North of Europe, but here memorials are wanting ; where it did so actually was at Avignon for a second time, and it was certainly in session before and perhaps after 1795. In 1789 it was visited by two Englishmen, and records have been left concerning it. They are illiterate productions and are otherwise difficult to disentangle, but it is obvious that the Society in that year was still occupied with the world of visionary prophecy and was concerned with the revelations of Swedenborg. To this the Abbé Pernety had added beyond all question something of his own concern in Alchemy and probably a Masonic aspect. The latter would have been rather fluidic, as there is no reason to suppose that the English visitors whom I have mentioned had qualifications of that kind, and yet there was no difficulty as to their reception. They made extracts from the Society's Journal and took part in its Eucharistic com- memorations ; they also witnessed its phenomena, some of which were akin to those of modern spiritualism. It is further stated definitely by my authorities that Count Grabbianka returned to Avignon in 1787, and there formed the *Société des Illuminés d'Avignon* in a Masonic Lodge. We have the authority of Kloss for the continued existence of this body in 1812.

It is colourable to suppose that Pernety may have had a hand in producing the Rituals. We are, in any case, now enabled to harmonise the conflicting statements of Masonic authorities as already cited. Something existed at Avignon in or about 1760. It was not Masonic, it was not an *Académie des Illuminés*, and it knew nothing of Swedenborg : it assumed these char- acteristics subsequently—that is to say, about 1785, the alternative date suggested. The year 1770 must be abandoned entirely, except in so far as some of the original members may have remained in their own city and watched events from afar.

The result of this summary research into one sequence of Grades connected with the Hermetic motive in Masonry brings these points into prominence : (1) they existed under the veil of Masonry, but were not of Masonic tradition ; (2)

in respect of Alchemy, Pernety was an amateur only, who is interesting and zealous as such, but he was not a Master on the physical side and his eyes had never opened to its higher aspects ; (3) the Staroste Grabbianka, though his name is like an occult talisman, was no itinerant adept, nor even an illuminated adventurer, like Count Cagliostro ; (4) with apologies to the faithful belonging to the Church of the New Jerusalem, he would not have been a disciple of Swedenborg if he had belonged to the Secret Tradition ; (5) the *Académie des Illuminés* was confused on its own issues ; (6) it followed Alchemy, against which Swedenborg uttered a warning ; (7) it followed Swedenborg, all of whose teaching was opposed to the Latin Church ; (8) and yet it is on record that the Academy enjoined devotion to the Blessed Virgin and the invocation of angels, which things were quite contrary to the revelations of the Swedish seer.

As a side issue hereto, supposing that the Benedictine Pernety, having been dispensed from his vows, consecrated the elements of bread and wine in the Lodge at Avignon, what would be the validity of that Eucharistic ceremony (*a*) in the opinion of the usual communicants ; (*b*) in that of the protestant visitors from England ; (*c*) in his own view ; and (*d*) from the standpoint of Rome ?

As regards the protestant brethren, the memorials concerning them shew that they were led by the spirit, but to some extent also under the advice of Benedict Chastanier, to undertake their strange journey to Avignon, and they performed most of it on foot. On their arrival they were well cared for, so that they wanted for nothing in the material sense ; they seem also to have received the communication of such knowledge as the Society was in a position to impart and they possibly to understand. I make this reserve because the visitors were little better than mechanics, to whom the Alchemy of Pernety would have been assuredly a dead letter. One of them, on his return to England, reduced his experience to writing, and it is from this source that we can obtain a tolerable notion of the matters which at times occupied the French brethren. Their chief concern was still with coming events and spiritual considerations arising therefrom. These are summarised by one witness in a schedule of prophecies relative to "the present times and approaching latter days" as recorded in the Journals of the Society. I will mention the salient features.

(1) Rome will be presently the theatre of great events and calamities. (2) The time is at hand when the living will envy the state of the dead. (3) There will be a purgation as if by fire. (4) The Mohammedan power will be destroyed. (5) The Pontiff will lose his temporal power. (6) After the terrors, the Incarnate Word will be acknowledged. (7)

Palestine will become once more the most fortunate country on the earth and the centre of that faith of which it was the cradle. (8) A great Temple will be erected to the true God — apparently therein. (9) The face of religion will be changed. (10) The serpent of the abyss will have power no longer over the race of man. (11) The world will be restored to its first estate. (12) The Eternal Himself will manifest ; He will assemble the elect of His new religion under the immovable ark of His love, establishing righteousness and peace.

It will be observed that these are the ordinary forecasts and reveries concerning the Second Advent in their crude and concrete form. From the spiritual instructions which follow the prophecies, it is impossible to extract anything in the nature of specific teaching ; much of it is vapid and commonplace, but a few maxims are lifted above the rest by the beauty of their spirit and, although outside my object, they are worth citing in a shortened form for this reason. (1) Confidence is the precept, love is the soul of life. (2) He who has only the eyes of flesh and blood takes the road to perdition ; but he who sees with the eyes of confidence and love follows the road of righteousness and walks straight to the light wherein the truth is attained. (3) With love and simplicity man has no snares to fear. (4) Nothing is useless to him who knows how to love. (5) The life of the soul is wisdom and the heart is love. (6) Docility is the road which leads to knowledge. (7) The Word is one only to him who can comprehend. (8) The ark of God is death to those who use false keys. (9) The Mysteries of God are the torches of His children. (10) He who knows how to preserve the Mysteries shall be blessed. (1-1) We cannot walk alone in the way of wisdom. (12) He who puts trust in God will no more be stopped in his course than the Son of Righteousness.

The brethren of Avignon had therefore a measure of illumination, though not after the manner of official *illuminati* ; most of their prophecies have been made void but a tongue did not fail them entirely, and though its utterances did not ring always so true as in these chosen maxims, I should be satisfied on their consideration, if I was not satisfied otherwise abundantly, that the visions and the oracles of Avignon, through the long watches, neither came out of revolutionary aspirations nor entered therein. That which I seek would not have been found among them, but I should not have counted it wasted time to have journeyed with the English visitors, or even at this day to proceed as far and hardly if I could obtain other records of Avignon.

I should add that Pernety was the first to translate some part of the revelation of Swedenborg into the French language, performing in this manner for the Swedish seer what was being done about the same time or later by L. C. de

The Secret Tradition in Freemasonry

Saint-Martin for the theosophy of Jacob Böhme. It is on record, for what it is worth, that Swedenborgian believers did not take kindly to his intervention, preferring, I suppose, a revelation without antecedents to the suggestion that Swedenborg was a Hermetic philosopher. The late Mr. E. A. Hitchcock had doubtless a similar experience when he revived or devised the thesis within the last forty years. It is just, however, to add that those who are entitled to speak on the text of Swedenborgian scriptures complain that the renderings of Pernety were (*a*) imperfect as translations and (*b*) contaminated by interpolations which represented the reveries of the French alchemist. Chastanier himself protested and assuredly spoke with knowledge. It is he who is credited with establishing the ILLUMINATED THEOSOPHISTS, as we shall see at a later stage. Antoine Joseph Pernety died in the Dauphiny about 1800 or 1801.

IV

Masonic Systems of Alchemical Degrees and, Secondly, the Hermetic Rite of Baron Tschoudy

BETWEEN the system of Pernety, the Benedictine, alchemist and convert of Swedenborg, and the Grades referred to Baron Tschoudy, alchemist and exponent of High-Grade theories which recall those of Masonic Templary, there is the correspondence by antithesis which may be held to subsist between the mystery of the New Jerusalem drawn into Ritual and the mystery of chivalry exalted into Grades of Adeptship. As in the one case we have learned something to our purpose from the literary memorials of Pernety, so in the other we shall obtain an adequate idea of Baron Tschoudy's particular dedications by reference to his chief work, called *L'Étoile Flamboyante*, which for two or more generations after his period was held in considerable repute and passed through several editions. It has been mentioned by writers in England, but without suggesting that there was any familiarity with the text. There is a good deal of extrinsic matter which can be set aside for our purpose, and the rest lies within a manageable compass. I propose to consider it briefly under three heads, being (*a*) its theory concerning the origin of Masonry ; (*b*) its connection *ab origine* with chivalry ; and (*c*) its Hermetic purpose and relations.

The theory supposes, but with no reference to authority outside the personal warrants of the author, that there existed from time immemorial an instituted body described—for purposes of concealment apparently — under the title of *Knights of the Morning and of Palestine*. They were ancestors, fathers and authors of Masonry. Their date is not specified and their secret is not to be betrayed, but their antiquity was such that they were witnesses of all the vicissitudes which the kingdom of Judah had successively experienced. They had long expected that a star of peace would, in the words of Saint-Martin, rise over their country, their life and the life of that afflicted, rejected nation to which, in some obscure manner, it would appear that they always belonged. For themselves, at the uncertain period with which the thesis is concerned, they were still for the most part under the obedience of the Old Law. They were, moreover, dispersed in different secret

54

retreats, wherein they awaited such a change on the face of things as would reinstate them in their ancient patrimony and would enable them there to erect a third holy Temple wherein they might reassume their original functions. These are not precisely intimated, but the scheme presupposed a restoration of sovereignty in Israel, and it is suggested that their work would be about the person of the king. They were not, therefore, a priestly caste, yet their particular liturgy is mentioned. A time came when they believed that the term of their exile was approaching ; this was occasioned by the preaching of the first Crusade, and more especially by the scheme for the safeguard of the Holy Places. The Knights of Palestine thereupon issued from their hidden retreats in the desert of the Thebaid, and they joined themselves to a remnant of their brethren who had remained in Jerusalem. The majority of these had abjured the principles of Jewish religion and followed the lights of the Christian faith. Their example led the others to adopt the same course ; they were, if possible, more anxious than ever for the restoration of the Temple, but now no longer to reinstitute the old sacrifices. Theirs would be the offices of mercy which the immolation of the Unspotted Victim had substituted for the old rites. It is said at the same time that they continued to respect those rites and to retain them in some obscure and seemingly modified way. The inference is that there is here a veiled reference (*a*) to some sect of Johannite Christians, (*b*) to the assumed perpetuation and conversion of a body like the Essenes, or (*c*) an independent presentation of Werner's strange story concerning the Sons of the Valley, who were the secret instructors and protectors at a distance of the Knights Templar till they were led at last to abandon them. The result of this was that the chivalry perished at the hands of Pope and King.

Recognising, as they are said to have done, that the rebuilding of the Temple was, under different aspects, the essential purpose of the first Crusade, the so-called Knights of the Morning, when the time came to make known their presence, represented that they were descendants of the first Masonic Craftsmen who had worked at the Temple of Solomon, and that they alone were the depositories of the true plans. It was in this manner that they were integrated in the alleged scheme of construction, that which they had in mind on the surface being a speculative architecture, which is said, however, to have disguised a more glorious intent. Presumably the suggestion here is that the Crusading Knights were drafted into a spiritual work in place of one which they had devised on the external plane. In any case, their instructors assumed the name of Freemasons ; the Christian chivalry was drawn towards an association which continued in a measure to subsist isolated and retired amidst the great hordes of ambition ; and for their further protection, as well as for the maintenance of their designs, the common cause adopted a fixed method of reception, of which Masonry is a reflection only. There were signs, pass-words and such modes of recognition ; of all these the three Craft Grades are the nearest remaining memorial.

It was in this manner that the Masonic institution arose ; the Knights of Palestine were therefore the first and the true Masons ; they seem to have been distinct from that system which the author of this thesis claimed to sustain and admire under the name of the *Écossais Grades of St. Andrew* ; it is said that the Order of Palestine is not in competition with these and is indeed quite independent—an intimation that in some form it had continued to modern times.

Such being the origin of the speculative art of building, it follows that it arose—by the hypothesis—in the midst of Crusading chivalry, but, while in it, was not fully identified therewith. The secret purpose in view is not so far disclosed, and the legend of the genesis breaks off at this point abruptly ; we are left to imagine what followed in respect of the entrance of Masonic art into Europe and all its subsequent history. It will be seen (*a*) that the hypothesis has a considerable unacknowledged debt to the Chevalier Ramsay ; (*b*) that, as I have shewn else-where, it is a memorial of Secret Tradition subsisting secretly in Palestine ; (*c*) that it makes no reference to the Knights Templar as such ; and I may add (*d*) that the only Order to which there is any allusion, and then on a single occasion, is that of St. John of Jerusalem— another derivation from Ramsay.

And now in respect of the hidden purpose, it is said without equivocation that the concern of the brethren in Jerusalem was research into Nature, profound meditation on its causes and effects, the design to develop and perfect Nature by means of art, for the simple purpose apparently of procuring resources which would enable the questers to prosecute that part of their design which has not passed into expression. The treatise attributed to Morien, which deals with the transmutation of metals, is said to be the work of one of the brethren, otherwise the ascetics, dwelling in the Thebaid. The inference is that, in the view of Baron Tschoudy, the art of Masonry is in reality the Hermetic art, behind which, however, there lies an undeclared mystery. We shall see presently whether there is any reason to suppose that this mystery corresponds to the spiritual side of the Hermetic secret. Regarded as a Masonic hypo-thesis, I suppose that in conception and expression it would be probably the worst of its kind, were it meant to be taken literally. It is obviously not, and my remaining point is to determine

what the author understands by Alchemy, if anything, outside the transmutation of metals.

I may mention, in the first place, that the
Thebaid solitary Morien is really Morienus
Romanus ; his description notwithstanding, he is
supposed to have written in Arabic, from which
language his tract was translated into Latin by
Robertus Castrensis. It is from this source that it
came within the horizon of Baron Tschoudy. The.
original is unknown, but the author is understood
to have been a Syrian monk whose proper name
was Morianos ; and the Latin text, though it is in
no sense really a translation, is considered a genuine
reflection of eastern Alchemy. It is entitled *Liber
de Compositione Alchemiæ*, and is a discourse between
Morien, Kalid the King of Egypt, and Galip the
King's slave, or captive. It is an account of the
search for the Hermetic Mastery on the part of
the monarch, and of the manner in which the
secret was communicated to him by the adept
hermit. The instruction reiterates the old story
that the matter of alchemical philosophy is one,
though its names are many. It is a substance that
is prized by the adepts, but is held as worthless by
common men in their folly. The method of its
treatment follows and a description of the vessel
which is used. It is idle to recite these particulars,
as the matter is naturally not specified, and though
the work appears to be physical, there is no real
criterion of judgment concerning its nature.

It is, however, on the basis of this tract that

The Secret Tradition in Freemasonry

Baron Tschoudy has raised the superstructure of an *Hermetic and Masonic Catechism* belonging to the *Grade of Adept*, or *Sublime and Unknown Initiated Philosopher*. He appeals naturally to other authorities, and was unquestionably acquainted with the texts which he quotes. The point does not concern us; we have only to ascertain the nature of the work which he envisages and its connection in his mind with Masonry. The work is physical; the matter is to be found everywhere; it is vile and originally is " without native elegance "; "should any one say that it is saleable, it is the species to which he refers, but, fundamentally, it is not saleable, because it is useful in our work alone." It contains Salt, Sulphur and Mercury, but these are not to be confused with the vulgar substances which are known under such names to the whole world; " it must be sought especially in the metallic nature, where it is more easily available than elsewhere." The three components must be extracted by a perfect sublimation, and thereafter follows " dissolution with purified salt, in the first place volatilising that which is fixed and afterwards fixing that which is volatile in a precious earth. The last is the vase of the Philosophers, and is wholly perfect." The practical instruction ends at this point; the Masonic analogies are remarkable as lights on the philosophy of the subject. They are hereinafter enumerated chiefly to indicate the horizon which they cover.

The object of research among Hermetic

philosophers is the art of perfecting that which
has been left imperfect by Nature in the mineral
kingdom, and the attainment of that treasure which
is called the Philosophical Stone.   In similitude
herewith, the object of research among Masons is
the knowledge of that art by which all that has
been left naturally imperfect in human nature is
brought to perfection and the attainment of the
treasure of true morality.   There is a sense therefore in which both arts are comprised in the first
instance by a process of purification ; the first
matter of Alchemy must be separated from all its
impurities, and this is symbolised by that which is
removed from the Candidate for the *Grade of
Entered Apprentice* before his admission to the
Lodge.   It is described as analogous to the
superfluities or *scoriæ* which are stripped from
the unknown matter in order to discover its
seed.

Alchemy is an experiment which is performed
on Nature, an experiment—that is to say—on a
volatile spirit which performs its office in bodies
and is animated by an universal spirit.   The latter
is veiled by the venerable emblem of the Blazing
Star or Pentagram ; it represents the Divine
Breath which vivifies all that lives.   The perfect
metallic state is found by the hypothesis in gold
only, and gold is a material symbol of the perfect
state in Masonry ; the latter is held to be attained,
in its fulness, either in the Master Grade or alternatively in some other Grade which is the crown

and end of any given Rite or system. The state of imperfection in the metallic kingdom is that of Saturn or lead ; the seed of this metal is one with the seed of gold, but it has been brought to birth in an impure region. The Candidate for Free-masonry, by the hypothesis, has also been born in a state of loss, imperfection and impurity, which state is summarised by the word " profane." On his initiation he enters the way of perfection, the way of transmutation, the golden way. The intention of Nature is always to produce gold in the metallic kingdom, but this is frustrated by circumstances, until the act of Adeptship intervenes and fulfils the design. The intention in the human kingdom is always to produce that which is understood by the idea of the perfect man, but this also is frus-trated by circumstances, until Masonic art inter-venes and fulfils the design.

From this point of view Masonry is an art of development, of building up, or of emblematic architecture, and it is the same also in Alchemy. The work in both cases is performed on a seed or substance pre-existing, which substance is life and the Spirit of life. It may be described in each case as the separation of the subtle from the gross, and this work is said to be signified by the number 3, "about which all Masonic science revolves." The original state of the matter—also in each case—is that of the rude stone, the rough ashlar, the superfluities of which must be removed ; in more Hermetic terminology, it is the primal chaos, the indiscrete and confused mass out of which a cosmos must be brought.

As the matter of practical philosophy is called by innumerable names, which are mostly those of well-known substances, it has to be understood by the student of art that there is here a veil or an evasion, because no material in its common or vulgar state is fit for the work of the Adepts. This again is signified by another use of the term Profane ; a profane person is disqualified for the work of Masonry, and as common quicksilver is out of court in Alchemy because it lacks the principle of life, so in Masonry the uninitiated or cowan, as such, is out of court, and is kept beyond the Lodge, because he also wants the essential or living principle. As regards the term of research in Alchemy, it is explained that there are three conditions of gold : (*a*) astral gold, the centre of which is in the sun, and the sun communicates it to all inferior beings ; (*b*) elementary gold, which is the purest and most fixed portion of the elements and of the substances composed of these : all sublunary beings have a grain of this gold at their centre ; (*c*) vulgar gold, the most perfect metal in Nature.

This triple state is said to be represented respectively in Masonry by the symbolism of the Sun as it is found in the earlier Grades, by that of the Moon, and by the compasses and kindred Masonic jewels. Finally, the number 4, which is of particular importance in the *Grand Écossais*

Grade of St. Andrew, represents the perfect equilibrium and equality between the four elements of
which the physical stone is composed. It represents also four processes indispensable to the
completion of the Great Work. These are composition, alteration, mixture and union. When
they are performed according to the rules of the
art, there is begotten the lawful Son of the Sun,
the Phœnix which is for ever reborn from its
ashes.

I have put these analogies in the simplest
language at my command, and as I do not think
that there can be any difficulty in following them,
so I incline to believe that their proper scheme
will be apparent to most of my readers. The
similitude at the root of the thesis is obvious
enough, and in its way it is legitimate enough
—the perfection of metals in the one case by
their conversion into gold, and the perfection of
humanity in the other by its conversion under the
graces of the moral law. It is not a comparison
which carries with it any particular force or
appeal, because it is the illustration of things that
are greater by things that are lesser, and it has
therefore no real office. It is faulty otherwise in
the way that it is expressed by the writer. It
does not suggest that metallic transmutation is the
term of Masonic research, and it is hence without
aim in practice. If, however, it were the intention of Baron Tschoudy to intimate that Masonry
is the spiritual side of the *magnum opus*, then he

has also and singularly missed his point. As he does, however, affirm that behind the imputed physical experiments of his so-called Knights of the Morning there lay concealed another intention, and as he states plainly that he was resolved to maintain the concealment, there is some warrant for considering the question a little further, by indicating certain points in the Hermetic Catechism in which the corners of the veil seem on the point of lifting. They are found in—

a. The statement that God is the end of Nature and, inferentially, that God and not physics should be the object of the investigators of Nature.

b. The reference to the Divine Breath, which is the life of all being.

c. The hypothesis of the development of substances beyond the point of perfection which they attain in the natural order.

d. One mystical interpretation of the term "centre of the earth," which is said not to be the common earth.

e. The analogies established with the ethical allegories of Masonry.

f. The fact that the substances made use of in Alchemy are distinguished from any of an ordinary kind, and, in particular, that the Mercury of the Philosopher is no earthly thing, even as Christ's Kingdom was not of this world.

g. The use of mystical numbers.

h. The application of the so-called metallic

elixir to the body of man as a principle of universal reconstruction, when the writer could not have ignored that the physical reconstruction of humanity can only be accomplished from within, or, as mystics would say, by a spiritual elixir.

i. The definitition of the chief agent in the Great Work, which is described as a single corpuscle, and is obviously the Rosicrucian *minutum mundum*, the Microcosmos, or Man himself—*i.e.*, his inward and essential principle.

k. The transliteral interpretation of alchemical literature which is openly recommended.

l. The concluding references, which seem to stand at the end of the treatise like a key to unlock the whole.

I do not intend to dwell upon these points unduly, or to suggest that, because of any force which they possess, the Catechism is not in the main concerned with a dream of material transmutations and renewals. But the fact that there is something which the author has kept to himself, and his confession hereto, puts him in the same position as Elias Ashmole, the amateur of Hermetic philosophy, who saw that there were great things undeclared therein, about which he knew only enough to hold his tongue. They were also renewals and transmutations, but of another kind. The mystical side of Alchemy is in this sense the search for a Great Elixir, which is the Great Elixir of all, the quest of the Phœnix-state of life, of rebirth from the ashes of the simple life in Nature, and of the lawful Son of the Sun. The beginning of this work is a glorious spiritual dawn, its perfection is a high noon, and the sun does not set for ever. In this sense the closing lines of the Catechism are not without suggestion :—

Q.∴—When must the Philosopher begin his enterprise ?

A.∴—At the moment of daybreak, for his energy must never be relaxed.

Q.∴—When may he take his rest ?

A.∴—When the work has come to its perfection—(that is to say, in the Sabbatic repose which the spirit attains at the centre).

Q.∴—At what hour is the end of the work ?

A.∴—High noon, that is to say, at the moment when the sun is in its fullest power, and when the Son of the Day-Star is in its most brilliant splendour—(noon of the summer solstice being taken to typify the Divine in its utmost manifestation to the self-knowing spirit, the state of self-knowing being the consciousness that the spirit is indeed the Son of that Sun, lawfully begotten).

Q.∴—What is the password of MAGNESIA— (in other words, what is the electrical attraction by virtue of which the centre draws back those who came out of the centre) ?

A∴—You know whether I can or should reply—I reserve my speech—(the reason being that this is the Great Secret).

Q∴—Will you give me the greeting of the philosophers — (signifying the inward certitude with which those who have attained the union recognise all others who have also attained) ?

A∴—Begin ; I will reply to you—(but it is noticeable that the challenge changes at this, the initial point).

Q∴—Are you an apprentice philosopher—(this is the Masonic substitute for that which is termed the greeting) ?

A∴—My friends and the Wise know me (an evasion : the true question and answer concern the state of knowing even as we are known, but it is not asked).

Q∴—What is the age of a philosopher ?

A∴—From the moment of his researches to that of his discoveries, the Philosopher does not age—(because the Great Experiment, in so far as it is undertaken in the time of this life, is made in a suspension between two chronological points, representing the mystic space of—say—half an hour, or any other duration, and

between the two points a door opens
into eternity).

Between (*a*) the legend of the Knights of the
Morning—which seems to summarise in a single
thesis all that was dreamed of the Holy Wars
in Palestine and their Masonic possibilities ; (*b*)
the serious, critical standpoint taken up in the
work on the subject of the cloud of High Grades ;
and (*c*) the Hermetic Catechism, I believe that
L'Étoile Flamboyante created a great impression.
We shall see that the Catechism was imported
into late Masonic Rites ; it was regarded by
Éliphas Lévi as the most luminous and unmistak-
able presentation of the alchemical Mystery that
had been ever put into words ; and, reflected
from him, some of its material passed into the
lectures attached to the ANCIENT AND ACCEPTED
SCOTTISH RITE by the illustrious Albert Pike. I
think, on my own part, that it has a considerable
and permanent value in the proper understanding
of its materials.

In the course of his work, two Masonic High
Grades are separated from all others for especial
commendation by Tschoudy : (*a*) the *Écossais de
St. André d'Écosse*, and (*b*) *Knight of Palestine* ;
the first is said to be the antecedent of the second,
which emanates from it directly. He is supposed
to have collected these, with other chivalrous
degrees, into an ORDER OF THE BLAZING STAR,
but the evidence is doubtful. When a certain

obscure Parisian instituted his COUNCIL OF
KNIGHTS OF THE EAST, in opposition—as it is
said—to the COUNCIL OF EMPERORS OF THE EAST
AND WEST, Tschoudy was by repute the author
of the rituals, but with this fantasy it will not
be necessary to deal. They are said to have been
a combination of Egyptian and Jewish doctrine,
with some Christian elements. We have already
met with *Écossais de Saint André* as the 29th
Degree of the ANCIENT AND ACCEPTED SCOTTISH
RITE. The authorship has been always referred
to Tschoudy, and as I have no special ground
for disputing it, I will only recall that it was
one of the additional Grades superposed by the
SCOTTISH RITE on the collection of the COUNCIL
OF EMPERORS.

The Grade of *Sublime and Unknown Apprentice
Philosopher* appears to have rested in theory, for I
find no trace of its existence. The author of the
Catechism was, however, attracted by the notion
of Unknown Philosophers, derived probably from
the Concealed Superiors of the STRICT OBSERV-
ANCE, and he published their Statutes, shewing
that, on the hypothesis of their existence, they
were willing to admit persons of all religions, but
could only communicate the Mysteries of true
Philosophy to those who were awakened in
respect of the Mystery of Faith. Members were
supposed to adopt a Kabalistic name. If any
such member pursued the Hermetic work to its
perfect, fulfilment it would be his duty to certify

the fact to his chiefs — an old Rosicrucian regulation.

The association, whatever its nature, was therefore one of research and not of adepts in possession. It gave preference to those who could affirm their earnest desire for an acquaintance with the mysteries of chemistry, even "a curiosity concerning them which goes down into the very depths of their souls." On the one hand, however, they were to beware of sophistic experiments, an inclination to which, if discernible, would disqualify a Candidate for reception, and, on the other, it is obvious from the Statutes that the operations of the art were those of an exotic chemistry rather than of an ordinary kind. They were concerned with "the wonders which can be wrought by fire." The association on its own part promised nothing definitely to aspirants, though—contrary to Masonic rule—it was considered proper to imbue persons who were prepared with a desire to enter its ranks. It transpires at the same time that there were existing archives and that on the occasion of his reception the Candidate was placed in possession of an important secret which is termed in the Catechism "the password of MAGNESIA." It was communicated in the "tongue of the Sages," and it revealed "the true and unique matter of which the Stone of the Philosophers is composed."

The Statutes contain no suggestion concerning a Masonic aspect ; the method of recruiting was by means of a patron, who took his own sponsor into a kind of unofficial consultation by putting a hypothetical case, in which the name of the possible postulant—at least in the absence of some special understanding—was rigidly suppressed, an Unknown Philosopher having not only his identity concealed from the world without but, by a convention or presumption, if not in actual practice, from the world within the circle. The object was to protect by all measures of prudence those who should ultimately succeed in composing the mystic Stone. In the absence of such precautions, not only the particular vessel of high alchemical election but the Society at large might after a short time be " brought to the brink of ruin."

When it was decided to receive a Postulant, it was ordained in the first place that " the light which enlighteneth from the Eternal " should be invoked in a public service, held in a consecrated place of religion, " according to the Rites of that faith which is professed by the person to be received." In France this would obviously mean the offering of a votive Mass for that person's intention, but in other cases, as difficulties were foreseen, the observance was so relaxed that it probably passed into desuetude. In the second place, the Candidate was sworn to preserve the Statutes inviolable, the secrets, " whatsoever may befall," as also to keep faith with his brethren, with the laws of his land and with the sovereign who ruled over it. On his part, the patron who imposed the obligations, speaking in the person of the Order, assured the Neophyte of its friendship, its fidelity and its protection. An imputed disclosure of the great arcanum—enigmatically or otherwise—concluded the cermony, which obviously took place between Patron and Aspirant only ; after the reception it was open to the new member to become himself a patron. He was known, as I have intimated, by a Kabalistic name, and was made acquainted with the Kabalistic characters used in the art. On the anniversary of his reception, should he be of the Catholic faith— and a Candidate of this kind seems more likely to have proved a *persona grata*—he was to offer the Holy Sacrifice to God, as an act of thanksgiving, and that he might " obtain from the Eternal the gifts of knowledge and illumination."

I believe that this curious document represents a scheme in embryo and not the regulations of an actually incorporated body ; and if, as I also believe, it was the unaided work of Baron Tschoudy, the presumptive inference therefrom is either (*a*) that his studies and experiments had, in his own faith at least, placed him in possession of the problematical First Matter of the Physical Work ; or (*b*) that he had received a communication concerning it from a secret source of knowledge. It does not follow, and I see no reason to think, that in consequence of such knowledge he had performed what is called the Great Work in the particular department which concerned him.

So also—whether communicated or discovered by his own efforts—there may have been mistake or deception concerning the First Matter.

It is just to add in qualification of my previous statement, that the statutes, here analysed briefly, do contain a single casual allusion to the Grand Architect of the Universe, but it is made under such circumstances that it scarcely carries with it any Masonic suggestion ; but, on the other hand, we have seen that the Catechism belonging to the Apprentice Grade of the Order is obviously and persistently Masonic. It is therefore a matter of speculation how in the mind of the author it was proposed to bring the procedure of reception as delineated into consonance with ordinary procedure according to the mind of the Craft or the High Grades. This is one problem left over, and it will be seen that I have no pretension to deal with it. Another concerns the title of Unknown Philosophers, which I have sought to explain by the antecedents of Unknown Superiors in the RITE OF THE STRICT OBSERVANCE. It is not altogether adequate, and we have further to remember that the RITE OF ELECT COHENS was in existence at the period of Baron Tschoudy, though I question whether it can be regarded as in open evidence till after the appearance of Pasqually at Bordeaux, and even after *L'Étoile Flamboyante* was published. It may, however, be to this source that the title should be more correctly referred, but I suppose that in the last resource the question is not vital. It is more important to distinguish between the society described by Baron Tschoudy in 1763, when *L'Étoile Flamboyante* was published, and another alleged ORDER OF THE UNKNOWN JUDGE-PHILOSOPHERS, the particulars of which are confined to a work of Ragon which did not appear till 1853. He calls it Jesuitical, Templar and a part of that system which was perpetuated in the ORDER OF CHRIST. The last allegation does not need refuting, and, if I speak my whole mind, I question whether the mysterious Judges had any corporate existence outside the perverse brain to which we owe the treatise called *Orthodoxie Maçonnique*. However this may be, Ragon affirms that the Order was divided into the two Grades of *Novice* and *Judge Commander*. The condition of reception was the possession of the Grade of *Rose-Croix* and the reception in the first instance took place in a vault. The Order claimed to be the *ne plus ultra* of Masonry, and to unveil its entire meaning. The Candidate was pledged, in the name of the most Perfect and Holy Trinity, to work for the triumph of the Order, for the regeneration of society, the liberty of all Brethren and the destruction of superstition—together with all usurpation of the rights of man. With this object, the character of man was to be made his special study. The noviciate lasted for three years, during which time the initiate knew only his sponsor and the officer by whom he had been received. At the end of his probation he was qualified for admission to the Second Grade of *Commander*, in which he was pledged to the practice of mercy, and was informed that the purpose of the Order was the reintegration of the Judge Philosophers in their true rights as the successors of the Temple. He was made acquainted with the analogy between the central legend of the Craft Grades and the martyrdom of Jacques de Molay, and with the vengeance sworn by the Order against the traitors in chief —being the papacy, the principle of royalty and those who had profited by the conspiracy, namely, the Knights of Malta. In what manner the vengeance was to be accomplished does not appear in the Ritual, but in a general sense the Candidate undertook to protect innocence against the superstition, usurpation, tyranny, hypocrisy and savagery by which it was threatened. In some obscure manner these dedications were connected in the mind of Ragon with the study of the secret sciences, more especially on the Hermetic side. He published the Statutes of the Order, which in certain respects recall those of Baron Tschoudy, though it would be an idle task to specify the examples of analogy.

There are now only a few points to complete the considerations of this section. The connection which *L'Étoile Flamboyante* sought to establish with the Secret Tradition in Israel through the so-called Knights of the Morning, and with Alchemy as a part of the tradition, suffers comparison with an alternative hypothesis which was current about the same period, and traced the Fraternity to another secret association, under the name of the Dionysian artists. These, in the mind of the hypothesis, arose in Syria, and in some occult manner were acquainted with the Essenian sect, which constitutes the claim of this particular dream to a word of notice here. I will put its chief contentions in the words of the witness. "It is advanced that the people of Attica went in quest of superior settlements a thousand years before Christ, that they settled in Asia Minor, the provinces which they acquired being called Ionia. In a short time these Asiatic colonies surpassed the mother country in prosperity and science; sculpture in marble and the Doric and Ionian Orders resulted from their ingenuity. They returned to instruct their mother country in a style of architecture which has been the admiration of succeeding ages. For these improvements the world is indebted to the Dionysian artificers." By the scope of this hypothesis, the persons in question were, however, something more than builders of the ordinary kind. They carried with them their Mysteries into Ionia, and these were the Mysteries of Bacchus. They were further an association of scientific men, who possessed the exclusive privilege of erecting Temples, theatres and other public buildings in Asia Minor. "These artists were very numerous in Asia, and existed under the same appellation in Syria, Persia and

India. They supplied Ionia and the surrounding countries, as far as the Hellespont, with theatrical apparatus by contract, and erected the magnificent Temple at Teos to Bacchus, the founder of their Order. About three hundred and sixty years before the birth of Christ, a considerable number of them were incorporated by command of the kings of Pergamos, who assigned to them Teos as a settlement, it being the city of their tutelary god. The members of this association, which was intimately connected with the Dionysian Mysteries, were distinguished from the uninitiated inhabitants of Teos by the science which they possessed, and by appropriate words and signs by which they could recognise their brethren of the Order. Like Freemasons, they were divided into Lodges, which were distinguished by different appellations, . . ., and each separate association was under the direction of a master, or president, and wardens. . . . They used particular utensils in their ceremonial observances, some of which were exactly similar to those that are employed by the Fraternity of Freemasons. . . . If it be possible to prove the identity of any two societies from the coincidence of their external forms, we are authorised to conclude that the Fraternity of Ionian Architects and the Fraternity of the Free-masons are exactly the same ; and as the former practised the Mysteries of Bacchus and Ceres, it may be safely affirmed that in their internal as well as their external procedure the Society of

Freemasons resembles the Dionysians of Asia Minor."

We are not at this day so learned or perhaps so readily convinced as some of our precursors in the past, and we are not therefore so familiarly acquainted with the procedure, external and internal, of building guilds in Asia. The hypothesis is of course negligible, and if it were worth while to say so, it is not even in tolerable harmony with its own assumptions. The claim is (*a*) that the work of these Craftsmen was to be found in Judea prior to the period of the Temple, which was erected in the Ionic style ; (*b*) that they can be traced through the Fraternity of Essenes, though the Essenes were a contemplative Order ; (*c*) that they were continued through the Templars, though the Templars were not architects, notwithstanding their attributed design of restoring to despoiled Zion the glories of its emblematic Temple ; and (*d*) that they are ultimately brought down—partly through Eastern perpetuation but in part also through the architects of Byzantium—to " that trading association of architects " which appeared during the dark ages under the special authority of the See of Rome.

The inference is that in addition to the literal art of building, the emblematic mysteries of Greece and Asia were also handed down, under whatever changes, and that thus—through Orders of Chivalry and even through contemplative Orders

—there has been derived to symbolical Free-masonry some part of that mystery which is still at work among us.

Baron Tschoudy died at Paris in 1769, but I have dealt with him subsequently to Pernety, that I might remove an alchemist from the con-sideration in the first place whose hand in the Hermetic Degrees is not so clearly indicated as is that of a contemporary who happened to die earlier, and indeed before his time.

V

MASONIC SYSTEMS OF ALCHEMICAL DEGREES AND, THIRDLY, THE RITE OF MIZRAIM

THERE was a time in the High Grade movement when each particular interest, concern and school of thought which drifted into the Masonic encampment was represented by a specific Rite or group of Grades ; it attracted those who responded to its appeal ; it was not in competition with any other kindred interest ; and the motley crowd of all these brothers in Ritual dwelt together in harmony. The great Rites and the great collections incorporated from there and here, but for some reason, which it is a little difficult to assign, they did not annex, as a rule, anything from a few special proprietors already in possession of their field. The COUNCIL OF EMPERORS, the *Écossais* systems, the ingarnerings of Philosophical Rites and of Mother Lodges so-called, drew all things into their archives, excepting, however, generally the things that were of Alchemy, the things of

Magic and Kabalism. The RITE OF PASQUALLY suffered no depredation ; no one borrowed from Egyptian Magic ; the ILLUMINATI OF AVIGNON performed their mysteries in peace, apart from serious encroachment.

The instinct of the period recognised two domains, in which, however, all was common property ; no one could expect to produce a Grade illustrating or extending some historical or symbolical period under the Old Alliance and claim to hold copyright, so to speak, because this kind of thing was thought much too important in the catholic side of the subject. It was the same with the Chivalrous Grades ; to whomsoever it was given to produce a new Knightly Degree, it was made evident that he had entered into the liberties of all Masonry ; it was no sin on his part to reflect, to borrow, to adapt, and he extended apparently—or was at least supposed to extend—the same licence towards all who came after. Baron Tschoudy or another might institute a Knighthood of the Sun and might incorporate it into a system of his own, but before long it was taken over in other directions, where it seemed to fall, reasonably or not, into a totally different sequence. He was content, no doubt, on his part, and his debtors were content on theirs. There came, however, another time when it was deemed desirable to constitute encyclopædic Rites, containing whatsoever had entered into the Masonic field, to say nothing of supplementary inventions.

Of Alchemy in Masonry

Thus were produced the RITE OF MIZRAIM and soon after the RITE OF MEMPHIS. Mizraim is *de omnibus rebus* and Memphis *de quibusdam aliis*. They would not have been encyclopædic—containing all things and supplements to all things—had they left out (*a*) Magic, (*b*) Alchemy and (*c*) Kabalism. Avignon, Montpellier, Bordeaux, Lyons, Paris, did not offer sufficient materials for their purpose, and there was consequently a spur to invention ; the inventions and the borrowings from all quarters were classified into great series, some of which I will proceed to codify briefly. The ninth class in the RITE OF MIZRAIM, and the tenth class also in that Rite, is more or less alchemical in its character, but the supreme power of the Order, as represented by its Absolute Grand Sovereign and the 90th and last Degree, must have been ruled by the sovereign unreason, if I may venture to assume that the Heads of the Rite were responsible for the mode of classification. The Hermetic system may be taken to begin with the Grade of *Chaos Discreet*. To understand this title, it must be remembered that the first matter of the Stone in Alchemy is sometimes represented in the terminology of the old literature as unformed and chaotic, like the matter of the world before it was brought into order. The next Grade was called *Chaos the Second*, or *Wise*, and involves the suggestion that a cosmos had begun to be produced in the vessel of the philosophers.

Perhaps in the mind of the Rite the vessel

represented the Candidate, though it is rather by implication than expression, and to exemplify his cosmic condition he is made in the 51st Grade a *Knight of the Sun,* in which he is permitted to forget that he has become a *zelator* of Alchemy. We have met with this fantasia already in another system, but here his experience with Brother Truth, and encompassed by Cherubim and Sylphs, is prefatory to a greater dignity, for he becomes in the next Grade a *Sovereign Commander of the Stars.* We have heard of this also at a distance, but not that the Candidate re-enters therein the occult sphere of Alchemy and is made acquainted with a new interpretation of the Craft Legend, which may be summarised under the following heads : (*a*) The Master Builder represents the First Matter of the Wise ; (*b*) that Matter must pass through the stage of putrefaction, and hence the death of the Builder ; (*c*) after putrefaction it becomes the source of life and is ripe for reproduction ; (*d*) this truth is symbolised by the sepulchre of the Master ; (*e*) the Master of the Lodge represents the First Matter when it is in the stage of putrefaction, and he is therefore the Builder, also in that stage ; (*f*) it is evident at this point that the interpretation has blundered in respect of its own canons, but a public explanation of the reason cannot be given ; (*g*) according to the truth of the symbolism, the Master or President of the Lodge typifies the Builder in a far different and higher state ; (*h*) let those who have passed through the Grades of Craft Masonry recall the experience of the Candidate towards the term of all, and they may see a certain light ; (*i*) recurring to the discourse itself, the ornaments of the Lodge include a Pentagram, in which the word Force is emblazoned, and this word signifies the First Matter in the Black Stage, which again is that of putrefaction ; (*k*) another symbol is the Moon, inscribed with the word Wisdom, signifying the Matter at the White or the first purified state ; (*l*) a third symbol is the Sun, inscribed with the word Beauty, and this is the Matter at the Red Stage, which is the source of all good things.

It remains only to say that if a Mason acquainted with a few of the Books of Alchemy will remember the attributions of certain inferior Masonic lights, he will see how and why this interpretation has gone astray quite naturally. It is, for those who can appreciate it, a very curious instance of the fact that Masonic symbolism cannot be transferred to another plane of ideas until it has been suffered to assume a corresponding change in its vestures. I know exactly how they should reappear when they have passed through the tingeing process of Alchemy, and it is not after this manner. The maker of the Grade was not therefore one of the Hermetic Masters, though I admit that he has produced a curious and at first sight colourable artifice.

There is another form of the Grade which offers several variations from that which I have been so far following. Having been clothed in a black garment and hoodwinked, the Candidate is laid upon an embroidered carpet—which represents a tomb—and passes symbolically through the state of alchemical putrefaction. He represents the body of the Master, and is in fine raised for the purpose of taking the obligation. It is obvious that a very curious symbolism could be developed along these lines, but it is of course missed by the Ritual. The Catechism says that the First Matter is a crude stone, which is the germ of the seven metals, and it is nurtured by the fire of heaven. This Matter is unknown. The President of the Lodge is in red vestments because such is the colour attributed to the powder of projection. The apron is black, white and red, for so must the crude stone of the Candidate pass through three stages, in correspondence with these colours, to arrive at wisdom.

It is beyond my province to suggest after what manner the person who suffered the experience which I have thus outlined was held to command the stars, but it is at least certain (*a*) that if he brought no alchemical knowledge to the Temple in this Grade, he derived none therefrom, and (*b*) that if he possessed any it was not increased by the ordeal.

These Degrees did not therefore carry the philosophical research to a definite term, and the RITE OF MIZRAIM thoughtfully recurred to first principles. It remembered that the metals which

Of *Alchemy* in *Masonry*

Alchemy seeks to transmute are liable to be found in the mines, and it therefore instituted four Grades, classified as the Key of Masonry, being (*a*) *Miner*, who brings up the necessary materials from the bowels of the earth ; (*b*) *Washer*, who, by the hypothesis, separates the foreign substances ; (*c*) *Blower*, who purges the matter by fire ; (*d*) *Caster*, who moulds the purified matter of the Wise. In this manner the Candidate who has passed with success through these searching tests is held qualified to become a *True Mason Adept*, which he does in the next Degree. It will not prove surprising herein that he has ceased to reckon his age, the fact notwithstanding that, according to Baron Tschoudy, from the moment he sets his hand to the work the philosopher does not age.

The discourse puts forward, with native modesty, the claim that the science of the Grade is the most ancient and primal knowledge, of which the source is in Nature itself, or—more accurately—it is Nature made perfect by art as established on the ground of experience. The adepts of this science have existed in all ages, and if there are those at the present day who lay waste their substance, their toil and their time in vain, it is because they forget that *Sigillum Naturæ et artis simplicitas est* and have gone aside from the straight path. This expatiation is only an enfeebled reflection of recurring complaints and counsels in alchemical literature. So also is that

87

which follows, being a reference to the scorn and the ridicule to which the errors of such uninstructed enthusiasts have brought an honourable and sublime subject. It has come about in this manner that the audacity of hostile criticism has relegated Hermetic Science to the rank of fabulous invention and popular superstition. The Candidate is recommended to leave the children of darkness and haters of holy light to their proper vanity and folly, and to share, on his own part, the advantages reserved for those who are Sons of the Doctrine. This notwithstanding, it does not appear that he enters into the substantial enjoyment of any hidden treasure, for Hermetic Masonry, according to the mind of the Grade, is built upon three pillars—the faith which goes before work and constitutes its condition ; the hope which carries it forward ; and the charity which should follow its success. It is no part of my province to reduce the theological virtues from their high estate, but the *True Mason Adept*, who has mined and washed, who has blown also and cast, is now justified by the terms of the symbolism in expecting a formula of transmutation to recompense the faith and hope of eight and fifty Grades, and I conceive that his sense of charity must have been raised from the plane of a theological virtue to that of a counsel of perfection, should he feel that he has received his reward.

The Lodge or the Temple is then, so to

speak, called off, that one who has suffered so much may receive a few titles of honour, such as Sovereign of Sovereigns. It is not till the 2nd Grade in the eleventh class that he is made a *Knight of the Rainbow*, or *Perfect Alchemical Master*.

Although J. M. Ragon detested the High Degrees, it is evident that he had always a certain tolerance and even a favourable leaning towards the RITE OF MIZRAIM. In respect of the present Grade, he describes it in his curious terminology as *philosophale et philosophique*, and explains that the hues of the rainbow are assumed by the matter of the alchemists when it is approaching the stage of perfection. I therefore consulted an old codex of the Ritual in the expectation of finding at least some shadow of the Hermetic work ; but it is only the old vanity of a purely ethical Degree and, though longer than most of its class, it has no greater mysteries than vapid discourse on the religion of Nature, the love of virtue, charity and courage. In the Catechism there is a legendary account of Noah. Perhaps this is why Ragon says that it has been marred by a biblical presentation.

So culminates, so passes and so dissolves in clouds the Hermetic Masonry of this particular Rite, which seems in the palmary sense to have existed for the pretended communication not only of that which it did not possess but which it could not even simulate.

There is believed to have been a detached Grade under the name of *Knight of the Rainbow*, so it is difficult and unnecessary to say whether that of Mizraim was annexed by Marc Bédarride, who was one of the founders of the Rite, or is a novelty under an identical title.

MARC BÉDARRIDE

VI

Masonic Systems of Alchemical Degrees and, Fourthly, the Hermetic Elements in the Oriental Order of Memphis

THERE is no question that the Abbé Pernety and Baron Tschoudy were alchemists of their period, and more especially as regards the first, he deserves to be regarded as a most serious student of the art. If, therefore, the specific knowledge which they brought to the composition of Hermetic Rituals is so slender in result that a lover of the art might be well cautioned to avoid the paths which they open, in the ratio of probability, there is less still to be expected (*a*) from the fortuitous collection of detached Grades into a classified list ; (*b*) from their incorporation after this manner into a Rite ; or (*c*) from the compilation of Hermetic Rituals by persons who have exhibited otherwise no titles to recognition as proficients in the particular subject. The process of examination for the discovery of treasures in such inchoate heaps is the rummaging of Pandora's box with a very slender chance of discovering truth, or one of its colourable substitutes, at the bottom.

THE ORDER OF MEMPHIS has a tolerably entangled history which it would serve very little purpose to disentangle in this place. It was first heard of in Paris during the course of 1838, though there is a legend that it was established at Montauban in 1814. The point does not signify. In either case it had the glory of 95 Degrees, its stars of the first magnitude being of wide knowledge and repute in other systems. They were classified into three series, reclassified in 1849, and again in or about 1862, while—some four years later—they were reduced to 33 under the ANTIENT AND PRIMITIVE RITE OF MASONRY. It has been said further, that they have been re-edited of recent years for the purpose of expunging the Christian elements—an appeal, I suppose, to the Jew and the apostles of something called Theism. As a fact, I believe that the charge is without foundation, since the original compilers of the Rite were really those who excluded the vital Christian elements from the Grades which they borrowed, while into those which they seem to have invented the elements did not enter. The skeleton which remains of a Grade like that of *Rose-Croix* is, in any case, rather weird as a spectacular effect, but "much too naked to be shamed." In the present connection, however, it is again scarcely my concern.

Of Alchemy in Masonry

Through all its variations a Hermetic element has been preserved to the Order, and is represented in the ANTIENT AND PRIMITIVE RITE by a *Senate of Hermetic Philosophers*. Its five Grades are immediately reducible by four, which are neither Hermetic in the wider nor alchemical in the narrower sense. The Degree which remains is *Knight Hermetic Philosopher*, and the elements of its instruction are as follows : (*a*) The planetary qualities—so-called—of exploded occultism and science ; (*b*) the symbolism of numbers, referred to Pythagoras ; (*c*) that of the Hermetic—but not apparently the Fylfot—Cross ; (*d*) alchemical notions concerning the four elements ; (*e*) a description of Alchemy as a branch of learning cultivated by the Egyptian priests ; (*f*) the reduction by Moses of the golden calf to powder, considered as an example of their proficiency in the art, the thesis being, I infer, that he was skilled in all their science ; (*g*) a so-called lecture embodying certain excerpts from Baron Tschoudy's *Hermetic Catechism*, which I have dealt with in the previous section.

These matters may be described as the first part of the Hidden Mysteries of Nature and Science, as understood by the genius of the Grade. The second may perhaps be held to include its grand principles as follows : (*a*) Fixity and regularity have always existed in the universe ; (*b*) matter has a limit in respect of weight and volume but not in respect of immensity ; (*c*) a new world is—or is at least liable to be—created every instant ; (*d*) action is necessary before a result can follow. These things being certified, the final discourse of the Grade offers a legendary account of the origin of pardon and repentance. This is a result which does not seem to follow from the points of the previous instruction.

It has taken seventeen Grades of Masonry to reach this height of illumination ; it would be easy to say that comment is needless, if I were content with stereotyped phrases : it is needed badly enough, but it would not confess to the reasonable limits of space. The Rituals of the ANTIENT AND PRIMITIVE RITE are a portly collection in themselves, but—as we have seen—they are only a third of the treasures which the ORDER OF MEMPHIS offered to its original disciples. It gathered them from all quarters, as we have also seen ; it edited those which were good and those which made for glory—more is the pity thereof ; but even after such a process something remained. Then there were the things which never in the world before had come within the Masonic horizon —*choses inouies* indeed. Between the one and the other I know not whether to be the more sorry for a few fools who followed such masters in the high craft of ritual, or for the masters themselves —patriarchs of Isis, pontiffs of the Mystic City *et hoc genus omne.*

To the Chapters, Senates and Councils of the ANTIENT AND PRIMITIVE RITE there are certain lectures attached in the form of catechisms, and in one of them there is a further and indeed exhaustive levy on the *Hermetic Catechism* of Baron Tschoudy, though he also has had the dubious advantage of an upside-down editing. When this comes to an end there is an ingarnering from Éliphas Lévi—which is rather curious on the question of date, and shews the intervention of another and later hand. It is also said that when the alchemists speak of a Brazen Sea, in which the Sun and Moon must be washed, the reference is really to the cleansing waters of spiritual grace, which does not soil the hands but purifies all leprous metals. The Alchemy of physics is one thing, and the mystic side of the art is another and very different ; but here the images of both are confounded inextricably. It is further said that the Spouse of the Chemical Marriage and the six virgins are the seven metals, but they are also the seven virtues. Which among the latter responds to the Bridegroom—or the Christ-Spirit—does not appear, but as the contribution in this case is levied on the parable of the wise virgins, it seems permissible to point out that the analogy does not subsist.

What follows next in the lecture may be a quotation from Marconis, one of the founders of the Rite. " When the Sun shall have visited his twelve houses, typified by the twelve chambers of a Hermetic philosopher, and has found you attentive to receive him, matter will no longer

have power over you ; you will be no longer a
dweller on earth, but after a certain period will
give back to earth a body, which belongs thereto,
so as to take up an altogether spiritual body.
Therefore "— with apologies to logic—" the body
must be revivified and born again from its ashes,
which must be effected by the vegetation of the
Tree of Life, symbolised by the Golden Branch
of Eleusis and the sprig of myrtle."

I may assure my readers that this is not
spiritual Alchemy, either in the substance or the
shadow ; it is rather the blundering of a pretender
who does not know the language that he is
attempting to use. Let us see, however, the
testimony in conclusion concerning the Hermetic
quest as it is understood by these records. It is
the discovery of the principle of life "shut up in
the profoundity of matter and known by the name
of *alkahest*, which has the generative virtue of
producing the triangular cubic stone, the white
stone of the Apocalypse." I do not know who
is responsible for this definition, but he has not
heard the voice of Christian Rosy Cross speaking
from the tomb of the universe.

The ANTIENT AND PRIMITIVE RITE is the last
evolution in reduction of a consummate folly.
It is not undeserving of the reprobation which it
has received everywhere. It is Memphis and
all that it meant by the wisdom of an Oriental
Order in a comparative nutshell of thirty-three
Degrees, and so numbered to parade its piracies

Of Alchemy in Masonry

from the ANCIENT AND ACCEPTED SCOTTISH RITE.
I am far from acknowledging the titles of this
Rite, considered as a collection ; but whatever
its antecedents, and whatever the logic of its
sequence, it has been long in possession of its
particular field ; it has at least the squatter's
right, and the rival claims are imposture.   If this
may appear in view of any possible interests—
though I think that these are few and mostly
negligible—somewhat too hardly put, then the
ANTIENT AND PRIMITIVE RITE is at least like a
competitive bishop allocated, under another obedience, to a see which is in occupation already by
the delegate of a different Rite.

VII

WE owe as much to our enemies occasionally as
we owe to some of our friends ; and amidst their
fantasies, their wrested facts, their tortuosities of
construction and their determined ill-will, a few
trifles are to be placed to the credit of writers like
Abbé Barruel. Even when they set us upon a .
wrong track—to do which is their particular
office—we may find something in the course of
its measurement which proves serviceable to us
unexpectedly. I know of no more interesting
books on their particular thesis than the *Proofs of
a Conspiracy* and *Memoirs Illustrating the History
of Jacobinism*, unless indeed it be *Le Tombeau de
Jacques de Molai*, which was afterwards recanted
by its author, Cadet de Gassicourt. By the first
of this triad—which is the work of Professor
Robison—I was put upon the track of a little
book-collecting which I followed for several years
without reaching a term. He had held that *Des*

PROFESSOR ROBISON

Of Alchemy in Masonry

Erreurs et de la Vérité, by L. C. de Saint-Martin, was a kind of inspired Talmud for the High Grade Lodges and Chapters at its period in France. From his forms of expression and reiteration it might be concluded that " water was all Bible-lore," but that this *Mishna* was " strong wine " and prized above " all the prophets." The suggestion is decorative exaggeration, but I knew quite independently that it had a solid heart of truth. The text in question created a great impression, especially at Lyons, and much more especially still at the Masonic centre therein, the *Loge de Bienfaisance*, of which we have heard already in connection with the Lyons Convention and that of Wilhelmsbad. There was no more important High-Grade Lodge in France, unless it was that of the Philalethes at Paris. Saint-Martin was one of its members, and about his great personal influence I have no need to speak. On its own merits and the great consideration of its author, the book was sure of success among those to whom it appealed.

I was therefore prepared to take, with reasonable reserve, the intimations of Robison when he became eloquent and even alluring in his account of another text under the title of *Archives Mitho-Hermétiques*, and I went in quest of this work. That quest bade fair to be extended over the third part of the earth and sea—if not of the stars of heaven—on account of its utter rarity. When out-wearied by my personal adventures and researches, a copy was at last found in the *Bibliothèque Nationale*, and I obtained a transcript in full. I think it likely that I am the sole person who at this day is acquained with the text in England.

Having thus recited my own story concerning it, in contrariety to all my precedents, I will speak of Professor Robison's testimony in respect of its content and position. He affirms (*a*) that it is considered an historical and dogmatical account of the procedure and system of the Lodge which I have named at Lyons : he misquotes the title of the book, and he is in error as to that of the Lodge at the date in question, but these things are details ; (*b*) that the work is a strange admixture of mysticism, theosophy, real science and freethinking in religious and political matters ; (*c*) that it is the annals of the proceedings of the Lodge, but at the same time is the work of one hand. It is obvious that on none of these considerations, if taken literally, would it call for any notice in my pages, but long before it came into my hands I was prepared to find that most of the statements were not to be taken literally —an inference fully confirmed at length by the event of its discovery.

Leaving now my dubious authority, with gratitude for an introduction to the text, it is obvious that if, in conformity with the title, it is really an Hermetic work, and certainly or possibly Masonic, then it has full title to our concern. There is nothing to bear out the connection established with the Lodge of Lyons, but I can see how this error arose. Robison, being acquainted with the writings of Saint-Martin, could not fail to see that *Des Erreurs et de la Vérité* had influenced deeply the anonymous author of *Archives Mitho-Hermétiques*, who quotes the alleged Talmud with marked approbation. Robison must also have known the connection of Saint-Martin with Lyons, and he effected an imaginary marriage. There are no Masonic references in the text whatever, but it is dedicated to Savalette de Langes, founder of the Lodge or RITE OF PHILALETHES at Paris, and the rest was inference. That Lodge was tinctured deeply with Hermeticism ; de Langes was not especially noted outside Masonic circles—though he was a well-placed man—and from the terms of the dedication I think it highly probable that the author belonged not only to the fraternity itself but to the particular centre. It is needless to say that it is not the annals of the proceedings of any Lodge, but it is a presentation of exactly the kind of doctrine and hypothesis with which the Philalethes were permeated. That Lodge is said to have been based on the principles of Martinism, which was not, however, Hermetic, while the statement is otherwise untrue ; it counted among its members Court de Gebelin, Cazotte and the occult *literati* of Paris—as we have seen indeed already. It was disposed to theosophy and what Robison would have called mysticism ; I am quite certain that the *Archives* must have appealed widely to its members. There is no printed book more likely to have emanated unofficially from that quarter. It may thus be taken as, in high probability, representing a phase of Hermetic Masonry at its period. It was the direction, in other words, in which such dreams were turning.

In approaching the text itself we shall do well to put aside the fraudulent charge brought against it by Robison in respect of freethinking on questions of religion and politics. It is a · treatise on the Universal Medicine, and though, as such, it is completely unfinished—for it was published in parts, and the parts came to an end abruptly—there is no mistake possible as to the principles from which it depends. It separates Hermetic philosophy from all chemical manipulation, as from that which was never its intention ; and in the light of such philosophy it proceeds to consider (*a*) the first estate of man, (*b*) the circumstances of his Fall, and (*c*) the means of his rehabilitation by the mediation of that Medicine, " the mystery of which has been put on record by many hundreds of Masters who are in perfect agreement with one another." The *Divine Pymander* of Hermes is the root-matter of the instruction concerning the nobility of our original nature, the concupiscence by which it was brought down and the means of its rehabilitation. I do not think that I am warranted in laying out the scheme of the subject, and will

JACQUES CAZOTTE

therefore say only that the primordial envelope of the soul was a most pure quintessence of the elements ; that its sustenance in this state is symbolised by the fruits of the Tree of Life ; that man sought another food, symbolised by the Tree of Knowledge ; that he thus forfeited his birthright, entered into degradation and exchanged incorruptibility for death. It is obvious that this is the old story, and I summarise it only because the hypothesis of the *Archives* is that a Medicine exists—and it is also the quintessence of the elements —by which man can be restored to his primitive integrity and the work of the Fall undone.

The question that arises is whether this Medicine, in the mind of the writer, is to be understood physically or mystically. Is the quintessence the result of a laboratory process, and therefore contained in a vial, or is it the operation of the Christ-spirit within ? If it be the former, it departs altogether from the *Divine Pymander*, which it claims to illustrate and expound ; if it be the latter, it offers the same answer to the recurring problems of our lapsed estate that High-Grade Masonry offers to those of the Craft. The answer is I.N.R.I., and if this be interpreted as *Igne Natura renovatur integra*, we know that the fire referred to is a Divine Fire, and the correlative is *Jesus Nazareus [est] Rex Judæorum*, Jewry being the four parts of the human personality, corresponding to the four elements, and the archetypal *Jesus* being the eternal quintessence. There is a school of symbolism which allocates the four elements to the four letters of the Sacred Name of Jehovah—יהוה —and here again the quintessence is that letter *Shin*, of which we have heard previously, which intervenes in the centre of the Tetrad, as the quintessence works upon the natural elements, and the result is יהשוה or *Jesus*. If it be said that— by the Hermetic hypothesis—the quintessence is, strictly speaking, the four elements in a state of occult correlation, the analogy remains on the understanding that *Jesus Nazareus* is *verbum caro factum*—" the only begotten of the Father, full of grace and truth."

The text, however, is unfinished, as we have seen, and the intention of the writer does not issue clearly. Some of his extensive citations are intelligible only on the simple material side, but when he speaks on his own warrants the intimations are of a different kind. For him the Hermetic Philosophy seems to be concerned with an inward process ; the work is a work of self-knowledge, in the interior and essential nature, and its term is to restore a Divine Nature within us. This restoration is rebirth in the perfect similitude of the Eternal Word. At the same time, the memorial of these things is not in the proper sense of the expression a mystic text, for in his purest and most primitive state it does not contemplate the spirit of man in Divine Union but rather in the condition of the Earthly

Paradise. Had he remained among the incorruptible and virginal elements of that prototypical Garden, he would have been animated through eternity—that is to say, in unending separation, in Eden truly but not in the Beatific Vision, and not in the hypostatic oneness.

I do not therefore find in this curious text the presence of those seals and marks by which we recognise the Secret Tradition, but there are things on its skirts and fringes if the real elements are wanting. Some allowance must also be made for the conventional cryptic style which is inseparable from alchemical writings, as well as for a text that is unfinished. The part that is most to our purpose occurs towards the end, and may be described as a fuller statement concerning the origin of the soul, its emanation from the Divine Principle and the infinite capacities which it possesses by virtue of that origin. The thesis of course is that its powers have been arrested by the traditional fall of man as a consequence of which its environment is matter in corruption, but there is a way of escape open described as a reactionary movement on and within itself, by which it can be restored to primitive integrity. Though not after an adequate manner, because it is somewhat hindered by the crude language of its place and period, there is no question that here there is some attempt to give expression to traditional mystic doctrine, and the terms of the intimation suggest

that, had the experiment of the *Archives* been
carried to its proper term, the process of reaction
would have been set forth more fully under the
veils of the Universal Medicine, if not indeed
more clearly. As it is, and confessedly vague as
they are, indications are not wanting regarding
the way of the research as a path in the untrodden ground of consciousness, the possibility
of entering which distinguished in the mind of
the writer the state of man from that of the
animal world. The searcher after wisdom is
recommended to strip from himself those vestures
by which he has been clothed in his corruption,
and to recall within him that internal light apart
from which he is far from the self-knowing state.
It is therefore difficult to interpret his allusions
to an Universal Medicine except as an intimation
of that renewed life which follows from consciousness in the spirit, while as to his understanding of the spirit there is still less question.
That which he regards as the Divine in the
universe and the Divine behind the universe is
that which is all in all and abides at the centre
of all. Man has come forth therefrom but after
such a manner that he remains essentially therein,
not simply as some part or emanation of that
which was once the all, because in manifestation
itself it still remains the all, the end as well as the
beginning. The analogy is drawn from that mysticism concerning numbers which regards the unity as
their principle and all numeration as its content.

Of Alchemy in Masonry

This doctrine is elaborated on the basis of the
Trinity in man and its correspondence with the
Divine Trinity. It assumes in such manner the
more especial phases of Christian mysticism,
though the implied ideas have suffered a certain
change and indicate a line of development which
approximates at one side towards Neoplatonic
philosophy and on the other towards the peculiar
theology by which the *Zohar* is characterised in
respect of this same teaching. The eternal and
Divine unity is the principle of all things ; in the
wisdom thereof lie all the treasures of the Father ;
eternal understanding is engendered within its
own essence as the Son, by a first operation of
Divinity, without departure from unity. The
Third Person is the Love relative to the Father
and the Son, still in the bosom of Divinity, and
understood as the term reached by the action of
Divine Will. Thus the Father engenders the
Son eternally ; the Son is the essential image of
the Father ; and the Holy Spirit is the eternal
agent which operates between them. In respect
of manifestation, the Father is essence of all
things, the Son is their essential form ; and the
Spirit is the activity of all, which operates all in
all. These are the three which give testimony
in heaven, but there are three also that bear their
witness on earth, in the likeness of that which is
above, and these three are one in the nature of
man. The likeness is resident, however, in his
higher principles and not in the corrupted and

sensual form by which we are here and now manifested. It is a likeness which has to be recovered and the path of such recovery is that which the writer understands by the mystery of resurrection.

This is the substance of the thesis in that part with which we are chiefly concerned.

It has served, I think, a purpose to make known for the first time to English readers a Hermetic commentary which is not without interest after its own kind. It signifies, as I have said, the preoccupations of Hermetic Masons at that period in France ; it is one of a family, and has the marks of likeness to its kinsfolk.

BOOK VI

Of Magical and Kabalistical Degrees

THE ARGUMENT

I. The Horizon of Ceremonial Magic

The answer of Jewry to Christendom—Putative distinctions concerning Ceremonial Magic—The Key of Solomon—The traffic with good and evil spirits—Diabolism in the Literature—Folk-lore elements—Pagan remnants—Ceremonial Magic in France—The Continental literature of the subject—Importations by Great Britain—French occultism in the eighteenth century—Vestiges of the science of the soul—Mesmer and Puységur—Of Magic in Masonic High Grades.

II. Of Certain Isolated Systems claiming Derivation from Magical and Kabalistical Sources, and of the Rite of Schrœder

Correspondence in the Masonic substitutions for alchemical and magical secrets—An illustration drawn from the genuine and forged books of Cornelius Agrippa—The existence of an expert criterion in such subjects—Vain offices of Magical Rituals of imputed Masonry—An example of their instruction—Certain detached Grades—Hypothetical Grades—Schrœder

The ·Secret Tradition in Freemasonry

and the Rectified Rose-Croix — Confusion of this
person with another of the same name—Paucity of
our knowledge concerning him—His character and
intentions must be left an open question.

III. THE MASONIC RITE OF SCHRŒPPFER

*Further concerning the permutations and fatalities of
the Rose-Croix Grade — Its rectification in the
interests of Magic—A Café-Keeper and his Lodge
of Mysteries—A concise list of possibilities in respect
of his Rite — Confusions between Schrœder and
Schrœppfer—Pursuits followed in the Lodge at Leipsic
—Phenomena of evocation and the testimony concerning them—Schrœppfer and his Unknown Superiors
—Their hostility to the Strict Observance—Of treasures
promised to disciples — Alchemy and Magic as
alternative aids to riches—A false claim and its
discovery—Another invention—The Last Supper of
Schrœppfer—His suicide—A side-light on the event.*

IV. THE EGYPTIAN MASONRY OF CAGLIOSTRO

*Alternative judgments on Joseph Balsamo—Voice of the
Holy Tribunal—Expert opinion on his Rite—A
possibility which lies behind it—Rag Fair of Magical
Masonry—A general apology for minor Rites in
respect of their sincerity — The mythical George
Cofton—The hand of Cagliostro in the Grades—
Points in defence of Egyptian Masonry—The three
Degrees of the Rite—An androgynous system—The
Legend of Elias and Enoch—An impartial con-
sideration of the ascription—Comparison with other*

112

The Argument

Masonic inventions—The imputed connection with Egypt—Magical character of the Rite—Its elements of this Order—A debt to Mesmer—Its chief operative process compared with the skrying experiments of Dr. Dee—Partial sincerity of Cagliostro—General content of the Grades—Qualifications of Candidates—A System of three Degrees—The Neophyte .in Egyptian Masonry—In the Grade of Adoption—The Companion or Fellow Craft—The Egyptian Masonry —Conclusion on this system.

V. THE RITE OF MARTINES DE PASQUALLY

Of legitimacy as a political opinion in the occult schools of modern France—Their opinion concerning Masonic conspiracies of the eighteenth century—The Templar interest—Kadosh Grades—Offences of the Chapter of Clermont—Hostility of Pasqually in respect of this Rite—His Order of Theurgic Priesthood—Rite of the Elect Cohens—Question as to the date of its foundation—A brief biographical sketch—Pasqually and the mystic term — Practices of a magical character—A particular order of manifestation— The Unknown Agent or Philosopher—Rosicrucian connections imputed to Pasqually—His alleged connections with Swedenborg—The Grades of his system The instruction in that of Apprentice—The Elect Companion Grade—Legends and symbolism of the Particular Master Grade — The Grade of Elect Master—That of Grand Master Priest—Grand Elect of Zerubbabel—The antecedents of Pasqually— Further concerning the practical part of his system —Affirmations of Modern Martinism — Masonic career of Pasqually—The story of his Rite—Its

BOOK VI

Of Magical and Kabalistical Degrees

I

THE HORIZON OF CEREMONIAL MAGIC

THE answer of Jewry to Christendom as a counterblast to centuries of scorn, proscription and exile, centuries of persecution and even of torture, was the gift of Ceremonial Magic, as it is understood at this day in the kingdoms which are ascribed by imputation to the rule of the Prince of Peace. It did not give Black Magic, the counsels of perdition and the pact with Satan—as distinguished from magic of another tone and tincture. It did not give White Magic exclusively, to the exclusion of Goëtia or Infernal Necromancy and the other arts of the abyss—as one who after ages of suffering should heap coals of fire on the head of his tormentors. It gave Ceremonial Magic simply, and in the plenary sense—as one who put]poisoned counters in the hands of children, every combination of which was likely to spell destruction. It was the recipients who made their distinctions after their manner, and so I incline to believe that the old rabbins, within the limits of their own law, had a sense of eternal justice, even in the course of a visitation which was not meant to repose lightly on the heads of the designed victims. I conclude also that the importation of Christian doctrine into the processes was no part of the heritage which they conveyed.

The Ceremonial Magic to which I refer here depends from formal rituals, being processes of evocation, compulsion, entreaty and the other devices by which spirits of the height and the deep, spirits of the four quarters, spirits of the elements, were rendered, *ex hypothesi*, subservient to the will of man.

I am not prepared to say that the memorial which is extant under the mendacious title of the *Key of Solomon* is demonstrably the oldest of its kind, but alternatively it depends from the common source of all such products, and is of all the most approximate thereto. I do indeed think that it bears the palm of antiquity from the ragged cohort of its competitors, and if I confess to a sense of reduction in certitude on the specific point, it is solely because the cause of its antiquity has been championed by the last persons who are entitled to speak about anything whatsoever in the world of scholarship. The matter which concerns us, however, is really no question of date ; it is more especially one of fact. The *Key of Solomon* responds neither to the title of a key of white or of black magic, and, as I have exhibited more fully elsewhere, there is no such distinction possible in the whole circle of the literature. From the standpoint of Ceremonial Magic in its original understanding, and in consonance with its own mind, it was equally lawful for the operator to be occupied with the traffic in evil spirits or with those who were good—by the hypothesis concerning them. The attempt to produce a purely innocuous and efficiently safe-guarded variety proved so difficult to those who were practised in the art, that there is no extant example of the fulfilled distinction. It is satis-factory to establish this point, because it facilitates our comprehension of the root-fact which follows in history—namely, that practical magic, in so far as it is reduced to the communication with worlds of spirit, has been always diabolism more or less thinly veiled, as the extant literature proves.

There are, of course, a great many practical processes which, taken as things separable from their general environment, may seem to enter the deeps by the side of idiocy, rather than by the side of Satanism. So also there are many which belong more properly to the department of folk-lore, and are not in any sense referable to the persistence or the express circulation of Jewish tradition. These include procedures of the lesser ceremonial kind. There was a senility and decadence of the rites of old religions all over Europe long after the conquest of the West by Christianity ; it means that they died hard and, in certain sporadic cases, that in respect of their memorials and vestiges some of them have never died. There is very little question that some pageants of the Sabbath—black or white, as predisposition may determine — were remnants of the old religions ; but herein also we can, I think, trace the withered hand of intervening Israel, for the Sabbath was more especially indigenous to France and Spain, and the South of France was a centre from which went forth much of the base occultism of Jewry as well as its theosophical dreams.

There is a feeling in several quarters that the natural disposition of the French mind towards vain, evil and unclean offices is likely, as a general rule, to exceed anything that is alleged concerning it rather than to fall short ; but if the literature of Satanic practice according to occult art has been exported to England more especially from this centre, it is perhaps just to say that it is rather a question of proximity than of extraordinary dedication or concern. If France had its indigenous collection of the villainous little *Grimoires*, so also had Italy and Germany ; while if we know comparatively little of such interests in Spain, our unfamiliarity is not its exoneration.

Of Magical and Kabalistical Degrees

One certainty emerges which is to the credit of Britain, and this is that in the matter of Ceremonial Magic and its abominations — under whatsoever guise and cloak of pretended palliation, or in whatsoever naked horrors and follies—there is nothing indigenous to these islands. The literature of the subject—printed or unprinted—is all imported matter.

The eighteenth century in France was moderately productive in respect of works belonging to the department of what is called the occult arts, though there were never any which were less occult in their nature, seeing that their motive and procedure have been always utterly transparent. But it was also, within limits, a period for the opening of the psychic sense, the fact of which lies within the whole circle of such arts as the mystery which is behind all and the explanation which is within all, so that something of the science of the soul began to emerge into knowledge. Mesmer and Puységur had touched the skirts of this mystery and believed that they had seized the goddess, but the *Atalanta fugiens* eluded them. In this manner there was a striking of "the electric chain wherewith we are darkly bound." There was a feeling of the soul awakening and a sense of its wonder everywhere.

So it came about that some makers of Masonic Ritual had dreams of occult adeptship, and even dreams of Magic, as one of the paths to knowledge concerning the soul and its powers. As usual, however, the subject fell into the hands of persons who were no better than impostors, and in approaching this branch of Masonic development there is one section only in which we shall find material that is curiously arresting within its own lines.

II

Of Certain Isolated Systems claiming De-
rivation from Magical and Kabalistical
Sources, or Working their Particular
Mysteries, and of the Rite of Schrœder

THE secrets of Alchemy which are conveyed in
Masonic Grades are highly substituted secrets,
and the *Knight of the Golden Fleece* at the term of
his quest may become an adept in name, but his
knowledge of the tingeing Stone is worth as much
and as little as the cosmic power allocated by
another Grade to the Sovereign Commander of
the Stars. The substitutions of real Masonry are
priceless in their symbolism ; these are a hollow
pretence, and in Rites like those of Memphis
they enter into the lowest deeps of banality.
The recipient, however, in most cases of the past
probably experienced no disappointment, because
he expected and knew nothing, even by report.
Being blind, and led by the blind, the proverbial
ditch was only that of folly, and when they reached

it together at the close it may even have seemed to them the abyss of wisdom.

As it was with the Grades of Alchemy, so also with those of Magic ; there is nothing on their surface or in their roots to suggest that the pitiable mastery of occult art had been acquired by the makers of the Rituals—always, however, with that single curious exception which I mentioned at the close of the last section.

It is a little difficult to extend this statement so that those who are themselves unproficient will be able to appreciate the fact in a comprehensive way. We know absolutely that the *Three Books of Occult Philosophy*, by Cornelius Agrippa, are the work of a student who—in the sense and within the limits of his period — grasped his subject absolutely on the intellectual and theoretical side ; but there is not the least trace in all their length of an acquaintance with the so-called practical workings. He knew how to cast horoscopes, but he did not cast them, and—according to one story concerning him—he perished of want rather than yield to the solicitations of an exalted lady who desired to be acquainted with her future. He has told us precisely in virtue of what theoretical principles—from his standpoint and the claims of the subject—he regarded magical art as a thing feasible ; but he did not evoke spirits, or confect talismans, or gaze in crystals. We know as certainly, on the other hand, that the forged *Fourth Book* of Agrippa is a work of practical

Magic ; it is the theory of the others drawn into realisation, and this is why (*a*) it is so exceedingly like its prototypes and (*b*) why it is quite certain that Agrippa did not write it.

This is my case in point, to indicate that there is a sort of expert criterion or touch-stone in these matters, and as it enables us to distinguish the scholar and licentiate who philosophises, who in that field deserves and wins his laurels, from the man who is at work on the operative side of the subject—psychic or what not—so it helps us very readily to separate the amateur into his proper place and the pretender into his world of vapours.

The Masonic Rituals into which some elements of magical art are reflected represent neither the shadow of an instructed theory nor the *simulacrum* of a practical method. We find barren enumerations of planetary spirits, lifted from one of the familiar ceremonial texts—as, for example, *Arbatel of Magic* ; but we do not find a single luminous intimation to justify or excuse their presence, or a single interesting analogy, such as that which is established in the Grade of *Heredom of Kilwinning* concerning the mysticism of the number 9 and the Hierarchy of the Blessed Angels. The doctrine of intermediaries is not in the last resource of any vital consequence to the term of the Secret Tradition, but its place in the Tradition exists, and had the makers of the Grades in question possessed any notion of the subject with which they were pretending to deal, there were opportunities enough in cases of this kind for the exhibition at least of their warrants. But they dreamed as little of these as they did of the Higher *Magia* and the Wisdom of Adeptship as it is understood in these days within the occult circles, or in the courts of such particular tabernacles.

Several detached Grades, and others which have been incorporated into Rites, are mentioned as containing some elements of the occult sciences, for example : (*a*) The *Brethren of the Grand Rosary*, with Rosicrucian implications, in the PRIMITIVE RITE OF NARBONNE, which belongs to the year 1780 ; (*b*) *Master of Paracelsus*—a lordly and pretentious title in the particular connection, but heard of only in the private archives of Pyron, which we do not know otherwise than by name in England ; (*c*) the three alleged Grades of *Occult and Philosophical Masonry*, affirmed by Ragon to have emanated from the Greater Mysteries of Antiquity, but it is obvious that they existed only in the mind of the writer in question ; and (*d*) THE EXEGETICAL AND PHILOSOPHICAL SOCIETY of Stockholm, about 1787, which gave a course on the secret sciences, as *Diabolus Magnus* is said to have done at the University of Salamanca. The Prince of Lies was cheated in the end by his students, but it is probable that the institute of Stockholm tricked its disciples by the distribution of colourable imitations for real knowledge on the dubious subject. In any case, nothing remains at this day of these things—and others innumerable—but the fact of a casual report.

In the year 1776 a certain F. J. W. Schrœder, who was an ardent seeker after occult mysteries, is reported to have established a Rite, under the name of the RECTIFIED ROSE-CROIX, at Marburg. He has been called an impostor, a German Cagliostro, and so forth, but there are no particulars forthcoming to justify the charge, except that, by the hypothesis concerning him, he instructed his disciples in Magic, Theosophy and Alchemy. The Rite had seven degrees, but they are not particularised by name after those of the Craft, which were the basis. It is said that in 1844 the system was at work in two Lodges under the obedience of the Grand Lodge of Hamburg; and in 1877 an English writer certified that it was acknowledged as legitimate by that governing body. It is doubtful whether any credence should be given to either statement. It is indeed much more probable that the personage in question has been confused with F. L. Schrœder, who was alive at the same period, was an eminent Mason and ultimately Grand Master at Hamburg. He recognised only the three Craft Degrees and exercised great influence upon Masonry within his jurisdiction.

It is said that F. J. W. Schrœder was born at Bielefeld, Prussia, on March 19, 1733, and that he died on October 27, 1778, but on what authority I am unaware. We know nothing concerning him, and, as we shall see in the next section, it is a little difficult to distinguish between him and a personage of similar interests under the name of Schrœppfer. Curious enthusiasts and transitory impostors flitted across the proscenium of Masonry while the High Grades were still in the course of their development. Whether this particular interest was of the one or the other class must be regarded as an open question, and the benefit of the doubt is due. Schrœder—if indeed he was more than a shadow begotten of mere confusion—was probably an adventurer, on the understanding that the term is not of necessity used in an invidious sense. His counterpart in name is said, probably on better authority, to have been born at Schwerin on November 3, 1744, and to have died near Hamburg on September 3, 1816. Certain considerations arise out of the name attributed to the Rite, but they are reserved till the next section.

III

The Masonic Rite of Schrœppfer

We have seen that the *Grade of Rose-Croix* has suffered interventions and the wild life of many variations. It has been reduced, extended, catechised and transformed out of all knowledge ; it has lost everything but its name, while even its name has been borrowed and transferred to things of which it knew nothing. It has communicated the Lost Word in the Christian sense of salvation, but the interferences have changed the word and have offered some dubious notion of an arid Justice, some substitute of Philosophical Fire and a score of questionable vanities to replace the Name of Christ. The straight staff of the Grade has been so bent in these pools that it must have turned in disdain from its own distorted likeness. Perhaps none of the affronts which have been offered it can have exceeded that of Schrœder, or alternatively of Johann Georg Schrœppfer, who opened a café at Leipsic on October 29, 1768, and turned it into a Lodge of the Mysteries. Those which he communicated to his initiates are, however, in that state of glorious uncertainty in which the peculiar genius of High Grade Masonry is so continually shrouded, apart from any conscious intention on its own part. It comes about in this manner, that we have a choice among the following possibilities : (*a*) That Schrœppfer was a member of the Rosicrucian Fraternity prior to its reformation in 1777, the inference being that—as he was himself an impostor—he was likely to have a hand in an association which, *ex hypothesi*, was incorporated by rogues for the better advancement of roguery ; (*b*) That he was, or pretended to be, an Écossais Mason, and that he founded an Écossais Lodge at his café ; (*c*) That he added thereto certain Rosicrucian degrees ; (*d*) That the Lodge was simply a spurious Scots Lodge, into which he introduced magical and alchemical pursuits ; (*e*) That it was . Rosicrucianism purely and simply of the kind already indicated ; (*f*) That it was a particular transformation of *Rose-Croix* Masonry in the interests of Magic and Alchemy, in which case the maker was either working the same scheme as Schrœder or the same personality has been presented under two names ; (*g*) That Schrœppfer was an *Illuminé* who practised occult illuminism under the guise of Masonry ; (*h*) That he was a self-styled reformer of the Order of Freemasons generally ; (*i*) That he was an emissary of the devil; but this, I think, is negligible.

There is thus—among other confusions—that kind of superincession in the mind of some writers between this personage and the putative adept Schrœder which I have mentioned in my previous section, and it is not unlikely that the transformation of *Rose-Croix* Masonry has been allocated to the former at the expense of the latter—or alternatively. The question signifies nothing. They were alternatively figures of the same period, in the same country, with the same predispositions. I decline to call Schrœppfer's system Rosicrucianism in the proper understanding of that term, because the attribution has almost certainly arisen by an error of ignorance from the nature of the pursuits followed in his Lodge. These were the evocation of the dead, with which no branch of the Fraternity, genuine or otherwise, was ever concerned —at least, by the evidence of its history. We will say, therefore, with a recent French writer, that he founded a new Masonic Order for the objects in question. An anonymous letter, appended by the Marquis de Luchet to his *Essai sur la Secte des Illuminés*, gives some account of the evocations from the description of an eye-witness, who passed his hand through one of the spectral forms which appeared at a certain *séance* and experienced an electric shock, so that—whatever their source and origin—apparitions of some kind were manifested.

It is further suggested (*a*) That Schrœppfer claimed to have Unknown Superiors behind him who were at feud with those other equally Unknown Superiors of the STRICT OBSERVANCE, and had ordained that the Rite of Von Hund should be destroyed by their own Magus : for this I find no evidence ; (*b*) That Schrœppfer taught Alchemy as well as evocation, and, between spirits who could transport treasures or indicate the places where they were hidden and the art which could produce them in quantity by a cheap process, it would seem that he promised great wealth to his initiates ; (*c*) That he became famous by his demonstrations for a period, and converted his café into a hotel, where he received only persons of distinction ; (*d*) That he paid a visit to Dresden, and convinced or duped some exalted personages of that city ; (*e*) That, on account of a false claim made by him in respect of his previous position in the French Army, he was driven to fly from the place ; (*f*) That he wandered about for a period, but returned ultimately to Leipsic ; (*g*) That he gave himself out as the natural son of some French prince and assumed the title of Baron von Steinbach ; (*h*) That on October 7, 1774, fearing the consequence of his impostures, he called his disciples together, told them that he was acquainted with the scandals which were being spread abroad concerning him, but that he had his answer. As a matter of fact, he gave it—after entertaining a

considerable company at a supper. That is to
say, he invited them to take a walk to Rosenthal
in the suburbs of Leipsic on the following morning, and there, retiring among the trees, put an
end to his difficulties by shooting himself.

There is nothing in the depositions to shew
that he was in such straits as to make this course
likely, but what seems to have been unknown by
my informants is, that the frequent practice of
evocation and the pathological conditions which
it induces have a tendency in this direction ; it is
l'attrait de la mort mentioned by Éliphas Lévi.   I
am inclined, on the whole, to believe that
Schrœppfer may have had certain psychic powers,
which he eked out by the usual kinds of imposture
that tend to intervene in such cases ; at the end
he was to some extent his own victim.   It is one
of the consequences of following the path of
delusion.

IV

THE EGYPTIAN MASONRY OF CAGLIOSTRO

LIKE Abraham Cowley—master of many measures
—the alleged Guiseppe Alessandro Balsamo—who
was master of many putative mysteries—"flamed
the comet of a season"; and as somewhere in the
world of literature there may still be a few who
consider that Cowley was really great in the royal
and divine art of verse, so in the occult circles,
and such curious houses of life, there are some
who believe that the self-styled Count Cagliostro
—whatsoever may have been his true name—was
one of those great adepts who had attained to
be more than human. It matters little that the
catholic voice of history has risen up against him
with a great *dossier* of records; they are incon-
venient to deal with, and they are permitted to
sink out of sight: it matters much more, however, that the Holy Inquisition pronounced
against him and inspired the Italian life by which
he is perhaps more fully known to infamy than

by any other single document. That judgment
and that motived memorial are sufficient by their
bare fact to exonerate him before any tribunal of
secret and indicible arts. I think, on my own
part, though it happens seldom enough, that the
Holy Office and its findings are not in this one
case essentially and antecedently worse than the
occult tribunals, whose rulings are like their
science—a thing of vanity which is always re-
voked beforehand.

The most temperate and detached statement
which can be made on the general subject is perhaps that the characteristics of those who devised
the magical Grades — Cagliostro, Schrœder and
Schrœppfer — were precisely what might be
expected from their dedications, which belong,
intellectually and spiritually, to the deep purlieus
frequented by maniacs and impostors. Masonry
on its magical side was allocated to the second
rather than to the first class ; there are alternative cases, but for the most part it was the Rag
Fair of intellectual roguery, and the rogues had
every needful knowledge of their subject ; it came
about in this manner that the purlieus found their
voice. I shall make an exception, as will be seen,
regarding the Rite of Pasqually, who belonged to
neither class, and it is partly for want of a better
working classification that his Order must appear
in the list of magical Grades ; let me say that it
belongs at least to a very high plane of the subject,
for the secret of this Rite was the ecstasy of

prayer. I do not intend for such reason to appear as its apologist, and I ask, therefore, for the present statement to be regarded as of fact only. Outside the Grades of this section, I feel almost inclined to affirm that there are no Masonic Rites which are the work of conscious imposture ; and even for Egyptian Masonry something remains to be said from another standpoint. Some of the Rites are trivial and some are foolish ; some offer preposterous considerations to the rational understanding ; and some, which otherwise might hold up certain lights, are confused beyond hope on the issues of chronology. But among those which are not great there are at least a few which have served a good purpose. We may say of them what can be said sometimes of us, and of many like us, in the world of daily life : Do not let us despise any instrument which God sees fit to use, more especially if it be ourselves. We also serve, and those above others who do not stand and wait, though we have heard on other warrants that a certain waiting is not apart from service.

It is not only the indiscriminate enemies of High Grade Masonry, nor those only who can distinguish in that department between the things which stand for value and things of no worth whatever, who have spoken with disdain of Cagliostro and his EGYPTIAN RITE. When so doing, they have indicated unawares a possibility, at the back of their minds, that it included something perhaps not entirely negligible ; for they have taken uncommon pains to point out that he was not its author, that he picked up a curious manuscript at a London bookstall which furnished him with material that he worked up later on into the form of Grades ; or alternatively, that to the discovery in question he owed the actual Rituals. I do not know how or with whom this legend originated ; as it stands, there is no trace of evidence concerning it, and I set it aside therefore—not that the question signifies to us in either sense. It is obvious, on internal evidence, (*a*) that the ceremonial was fantastic in character ; (*b*) that it was devoid of Masonic elements ; (*c*) that it was a product of Cagliostro's period and had therefore no trace of antiquity. The "Sicilian" was naturally a person of mean education, nor was the Count as such a scholar, and it is thus antecedently unlikely that he should have written the books of the words with his own hand ; but I am of opinion that it was written under him, because it embodies precisely the kind of materials and the *mise-en-scène* which he wanted ; while, apart from this, the last place in which to come across such a production was London, and this will obtain whether the alleged manuscript was preserved in archives or hawked in streets.

Having thus disposed of the unknown George Cofton, who is supposed to have possessed or written the root-matter of the work, a second point which arises is whether Egyptian Masonry was actually so contemptible a device as ordinary

criticism suggests. I have called it fantastic, but
not of necessity in the sense of a judgment pronounced against it ; I have said that it is devoid
of Masonic elements, but the statement applies
equally to a great mass of Grades which are not
for that reason without interest along their own
lines. An unbiassed review of the Rituals should,
I think, lead us to conclude that, while apart from
any real value, they were decorative, dramatic and
withal sufficiently suggestive to have obtained the
prominence which they did for a short period in
the jumbled Masonry of France.

There are several descriptive accounts available, and I have myself cited one of them elsewhere.
What follows is, however, a summary of information drawn from several sources.

Egyptian Masonry was comprised in Three
Degrees, passing under the Craft titles, and it was
conferred upon both sexes—apparently in separate
Temples. It was intended to replace the Craft,
which offered a vestige only of the true mystery
and a shadow of the real illumination ; but in
order to secure the end more certainly, according
to the mind of Cagliostro, the Masonic qualification was required of his male candidates. The
Reformed and Rectified ORDER OF THE GOLDEN
AND ROSY CROSS, as established in 1777, said
exactly the same thing—that Masonry was a
brotherhood of " the appearance of light " in the
natural world only, and that the true light was
shining in the centre of the Mystic Cross. This

institution also exacted the Masonic qualification, but did not initiate women.

The imputed founders of Egyptian Masonry were Elias and Enoch, the most mystical among the prophets of the Old Alliance, well chosen for this reason, and more especially as they left nothing in writing, some reputable apocrypha notwithstanding. Elias connected through Paracelsus with the tradition in Alchemy, and his rebirth in an artist of that name, seems to have been expected ; great things were promised to the City of Hermetic Triumph when Elias Artista should come. Enoch and the pillars on which he perpetuated the knowledge of the world before the Flood have always stood up as beacons on the more external side of the Secret Tradition.

The ascription which I have thus mentioned has been naturally placed to the account against Cagliostro, but I should like to understand in what sense it is more culpable than any other legend of the High Grades. On the literal surface, and in that kind of understanding, they were each and all mendacious, and if one or more of them—as I have tried to shew—are to be understood symbolically, and as affirmations of the Secret Tradition perpetuated in Masonry, I know of no form of the parable which—*cæteris paribus*—is better or more suggestive than the fable concerning the two pre-Mosaic prophets. The view usually taken depends of course from the known antecedents of

Cagliostro, for whom in other respects I am making no apology. He had assuredly no part in any one of the holy traditions, but the existence or possibility of these has not been present to the mind of the criticism under notice, and I see no reason for condemning the " Sicilian " *illuminé* in respect of a most patent fiction when historical theses like that of the *Red Cross of Rome and Constantine* have been suffered to pass unassailed —almost as if the vanity of such claims went without saying.

The legend—whatever the verdict—goes on to affirm that Elias and Enoch instructed the priesthood of Egypt in their form of Masonic art ; but I do not find that the line of transmission from these seers of old to the day of Louis XVI. is clearly, or at all, indicated. Cagliostro indeed pretended to have drunk at many Oriental fountains of wisdom, but there is nothing in his history to indicate with any clearness that he had even crossed over from Sicily to the northern coast of Africa. This is perhaps too clearly accepting his disputed identity with Balsamo. But if we set the ascription aside, he is without known antecedents and there is utterly nothing in his career which would justify belief in his own unsupported story, had it no fabulous elements.

So far in respect of his Rite in its dubious origin. The next point to establish is that it was magical in character, but the elements were exceedingly simple, being confined to a dramatic *mise-en-scène*, accompanied by extravagant personal claims. I shall not speak of the debt which the maker owed to Mesmer, or of the high probability that he possessed some proportion of that semi-occult power which was spoken of as magnetism at the period. It was perhaps from Mesmer's method, rather than from Cagliostro's recollection concern-. ing the communication of apostolical succession, that it was his custom to breathe upon his disciples when they were made Egyptian Apprentices. For this purpose the Neophyte knelt before him, while the fumes of swinging thuribles entranced his senses. For the rest, the most magical operation which took place at the Masonic *séances* was identical with one that was followed by Dr. Deé during several decades of years. This was the induction of vision in crystals by the mediation of boys or girls who were in a state of maiden purity —according to the hypothesis, at least. There is evidence to shew that the magus believed in this simple process and seriously attempted thereby to establish communication with thc prophet Moses. That experiment was, however, always a failure. It is very difficult to dabble in the occult arts — as the common spiritist medium knows, among many others—without discovering that there are ungauged possibilities in the psychic side of our human personality ; and I believe that Cagliostro may have had just enough casual experience in this direction to give him a certain air of seriousness over his Egyptian Masonry.

He did not exactly know when certain phenomena might occur spontaneously with his lucids ; he hoped that they would occur, but he prepared by fraud against failure.

By a collation of sources of information among Masonic authorities of the past and by the history of Cagliostro otherwise, we learn that he promised his followers both physical and moral regeneration. He claimed that by the First Matter when it was changed into the Philosophical Stone, and by the Acacia, symbol of immortality, they would enter into the state of eternal youth. By the pentagram, on which angels were said to have impressed their ciphers and seals, they would be purified and restored to that primitive innocence of which man has been deprived by sin. The qualifications on the part of Candidates was a belief in the immortality of the soul and, as I have intimated, in the case of men, the possession of the Craft Degrees. The statutes and regulations of the Royal Lodge of Wisdom Triumphing, being the Mother Lodge of High Egyptian Masonry for East and West, specify three Grades as comprised by the system. These were *Egyptian Apprentice*, *Egyptian Companion* or *Craftsman* and *Egyptian Master*. At the end of his experience the Candidate is supposed to have exterminated vice from his nature, to be acquainted with the True Matter of the Wise, through intercourse with the Superiors Elect who encompass the throne of the Sublime

Architect of the Universe. These intelligences are seven angels, who preside over the seven planets, and their names, most of which are familiar in ceremonial magic, were said to be as follows : Anael, the angel of the sun ; Michael, the angel of the moon ; Raphael, who was allocated to Mars ; Gabriel, referred to Mercury ; Uriel, the angel of Jupiter ; Zobiachel, attributed to Venus ; and Anachiel, the ruler of Saturn.

In the Grade of Neophyte, the Candidate was prepared in a vestibule containing a representation of the Great Pyramid and the figure of Time guarding a cavern. He was introduced into the Temple in virtue of his ordinary Masonic titles and as a seeker for the true Masonry possessed by the wise of Egypt. He knelt before Cagliostro, who posed as the Grand Copht, founder and Master of the Rite in all parts of the globe, and the Master breathed, as I have indicated, upon him. This took place not only amidst the swinging of censers but the recital of exorcisms to effect moral regeneration. He was instructed in seven philosophical operations : (1) in connection with health and disease in man ; (2) on metals and the medicine thereof ; (3) on the use of occult forces to increase natural heat and that which the alchemists term the radical humidity of things ; (4) on the liquefaction of the hard ; (5) on the congelation of the liquid ; (6) on the mystery of the possible and impossible ;

and (7) on the means of doing good with the utmost secrecy. Moral regeneration notwithstanding, the so-called knowledge of the Grade dwelt on the physical side of Alchemy, though it was presumably concerned with the search after God and the examination of Self, all work undertaken being in view of the Divine Glory. The other subjects recommended for study during the period of the noviciate were natural and supernatural philosophy. Of the second there is no explanation, but natural philosophy was described as the marriage of the sun and moon and knowledge of the seven metals. The maxim was : *Qui agnoscit martem, cognoscit artem*—the significance of which is dubious. As connected with Alchemy, the discourse dwelt upon the First Matter, which is said to be an unveiled mystery for those who are elect of God and to be possessed by them. It is symbolised by the Masonic acacia, while its mercurial part is denoted by the rough or unhewn stone. It is this which must suffer the death of philosophical putrefaction and then the Stone of Philosophy is made therefrom. The Blazing Star represents supernatural philosophy and its form is that ot a heptagram, signifying the seven angels about the throne of God, who are intermediaries between God and man. In correspondence with the divisions of philosophy, as here stated, the term of the system was dual, being (1) moral and (2) physical regeneration, but the word morality

must be interpreted rather widely. Divine aid
was necessary to the progress of the Candidate,
and he was recommended meditation daily for a
space of three hours.

In the case of Female Apprentices who, if
they were not received—as I have suggested—
in a separate Temple, were initiated alternatively
at special meetings, the Grand Copht said : I
breathe upon you, that the truth which we
possess may penetrate your heart and may
germinate therein. So thall it strengthen your
spiritual nature and so confirm you in the faith
of your brothers and sisters. We constitute you
a Daughter of the true Egyptian Adoption, to be
recognised as such by all members of the Rite
and to enjoy the same prerogatives.

There were, at least by the hypothesis, three
years of noviciate between the first and second
Degrees, during which the Candidate was supposed
to put in practice the counsels of his initiation.
The Ceremony of Reception took place in the
presence of twelve Masters, and the presiding
officer said : By the power which I hold from
the Grand Copht, Founder of our Order, and by
the grace of God, 1 confer upon you the *Grade
of Companion* and constitute you a guardian of the
new knowledge which we communicate in virtue
of the sacred names, *Helios*, signifying the sun ;
Mene, which referred to the moon ; and *Tetragrammaton*. The Candidate was made acquainted
with further symbols of the First Matter in the

form of bread and wine. He was given red wine to drink, and this is a clear issue on the symbolical side, but it is confused by the further indication that Adonhiram is also the First Matter and that this must be killed. There is here a reflection from the system attributed to L. G. de St. Victor, wherein this name is attributed to the spurious Master Builder. There are also analogies with the Grades of Memphis, which therefore drew something from EGYPTIAN MASONRY. There is finally an intimation that the Sacred Rose gives knowledge of the First Matter. The discourse is concerned with moral and spiritual regeneration, and the Candidate is advised to purify himself within.

It was only in the *Grade of Master* that the so-called magical aspects appeared, for it was there that the dove, being a clairvoyant girl or boy, was shut up in a tabernacle and, prior to the introduction of the Candidate, was interrogated as to his fitness. This ceremony was performed with great reverence, beginning with an invocation addressed to God by all present, who solicited that the power possessed by man before the Fall might be communicated to the instrument thus chosen as a mediator between the seven planetary spirits and the Chief of the Lodge. The dove demanded on her or his part the grace to act worthily. The Grand Copht also breathed upon the child. If the answer were affirmative in respect of the Candidate, he was brought into the

COUNT CAGLIOSTRO

Temple and into the presence of two Masters, who represented Solomon and the King of Tyre. They sat upon a single throne, reproducing an arrangement which we have met with previously. One of them was clothed in white and the other in blue bordered with gold, while on either side of them were the names of the seven angels. Twelve other Masters were present, and these were saluted as the Elect of God. The Candidate saw also the symbol of a phœnix rising from a bed of fire. The procedure at his reception owed comparatively little to the culminating Degree of the Craft. He renounced all his past life and was directed to prostrate himself on the ground with his face laid against it. Prayers were recited over him ; he was lifted up, created a Master and decorated with the insignia of the Grade. The dove was finally interrogated to ascertain whether that which had been done was agreeable to the Divinity. The obligation of a Master included blind obedience as well as perfect secrecy. The discourse of the Grade turned again upon the symbol of the Rose, as representing a further type of the First Matter. Some additional explanations were given concerning the two regenerations which I have described as constituting the term of the system. That which is called moral depended on prayer and meditation continued for a period of forty days and followed by a specific rule. That of the physical kind lasted for the same time, and it is this which the Cardinal de Rohan is supposed to have undergone, but without much profit to himself, at the instance of Cagliostro.

When a woman was made a Mistress, the acting Mistress, or Chief Officer of the Temple, represented the Queen of Sheba, and she alone remained erect during the invocation of the Supreme Being which first took place. The Candidate, lying prostrate on the ground, recited the *Miserere mei*; she was then raised up; the dove was consulted; three sisters sang the *Veni Creator* and burnt incense about the Candidate. The Worshipful Mistress scattered gold leaf with her breath, and said: *Sic transit gloria mundi.* A symbolical draught of immortality was drunk by the new Mistress before the Tabernacle, and the dove prayed that the angels might consecrate the adornments with which she was about to be decorated; Moses was also invoked to lay his hands in blessing on the crown of roses which was placed about her head.

Recurring to the regeneration of the Rite, that of the moral kind was begun only by the ceremonial procedure and the physical was scarcely initiated. The first was, by the hypothesis, continued in a pavilion placed on the summit of a mountain and was supposed to result in the power of commanding the seven spirits. The physical regeneration was far more complicated in its design, and I do not propose to speak of its procedure or of the results, except that the end was vanity.

Of Magical and Kabalistical Degrees

I do not question that the sense of pageantry
— almost the showman's instinct — which un-
doubtedly was a marked feature of Cagliostro,
would have insured the communication of his
Grades under the best ceremonial auspices, and
I can imagine that the Mastery of the system
may have produced a signal impression on its
recipients.   In the Rituals there is otherwise
very little ; they represent, from my point of
view, another opportunity missed.   It is, however, a satisfaction to have determined for the
first time that, although classing as magical, they
are more especially Hermetic in complexion.

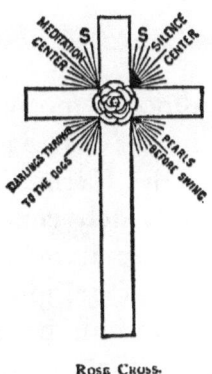

ROSE CROSS.

V

THE RITE OF MARTINES DE PASQUALLY

M. JOLIVET F. CASTELLOT is of opinion that a modern French alchemist who would hold the plenary warrants should belong to the Legitimist party in politics. I infer that this is a high counsel, even a counsel of perfection, being the last cleansing of the heart when it is seeking the gifts of grace, in which connection it should be understood that even the art of metallic transmutation—with which the author is concerned only—must be characterised as *Donum Dei.* I introduce by this statement of a curious fact in occult feeling at the moment a generalisation on the subject of an attitude which now, or until recently, is or was a little conspicuous in French schools of thought. They are in the party of law and order, and they have formulated their faith in the hierarchy. They are not political schools, and even in the respect which I have stated there is almost a motive of religion, as this is understood in the Parisian circle which confesses broadly to the Hermetic Tradition.

As in things which concern the government of nations the circle is no centre of conspiracy, so in the matter of religion I suppose that its imagined hierarchy will be established when the adepts come into their own, for in that of the Roman pontificate it has no part whatever. Now, we can refer everything in modern French occultism to Éliphas Lévi, the reverence for the hierarchic method included. The feeling goes back upon history, and this is the point which brings me to my proper subject. The circles, in the persons of their chief spokesmen, are reasonably and laudably severe upon the imputed dedications of certain Masonic Rites—at the end of the eighteenth century—to the revolutionary movement. They believe, further, that the Templar interest, culminating in the *Kadosh Grades*, represented the delinquency in chief.

The question, however, is more involved than might appear on the surface from the simplicity of this net statement. It does not apply, nor is it intended to apply, to that revival of the chivalry wherein one celebrated but dubious name—that of Fabré-Palaprat—stands out as more especially prominent. Certain testimonies notwithstanding, this section knew nothing of *Kadosh Grades* in the odious sense which is sometimes attached to the term ; it knew also nothing of revolutions, for it was not in manifest or perhaps in any form of existence when all Grades indifferently were for a period swallowed up in that vortex. Its dream was of nobility, of courtliness, even of esoteric religion, as we have seen fully in its place. It was above all things Christian, though leaning to the apocryphal side. On the other hand, the RITE OF THE STRICT OBSERVANCE should be equally free from suspicion, though it has been attacked on this ground; it had a Templar hypothesis, as we know, and one of the most advanced kind, but there was no vengeance motive, and hence again the *Kadosh Grade* is wanting to its system, though insufficient knowledge in a state of aggression has attempted to find it (*a*) in its Templar degree generally or (*b*) in the more exotic and advanced sections thereof. I have said sufficient already on the blunders and misconceptions which have been multiplied concerning this part of the Rite, and I may be content here with registering a simple denial as to what has been alleged, both new and old, in connection with the present issue.

The part major of the odium is fastened by a general consent on the CHAPTER OF CLERMONT, regarded as a Templar system, and as there is contemporary evidence, not indeed of the political fact or of the Rite in question, but of the suspicion in which the Templar system was held in a quarter that I regard as important, I must be content to let it remain. The simple and undefined odium is free from the element of arbitrary attribution such as might be and is made at the present day in the purlieus of Parisian occultism, in the boulevardier quarters of spurious Neo-Rosicrucianism, and among the intellectual sinks of pseudo-Gnostic schools. It is further not a derivative from the phantom hierarchies of Lévi, which breathe a far other atmosphere than those of Dionysius ; it goes back, in a word, to the time of Martines de Pasqually, with whose work in High Grade Masonry we are concerned in the present section. He carried his strange Rite of Theurgic Priesthood from Toulouse to Bordeaux, from Bordeaux to Lyons, from Lyons to Paris, seeking its recognition every-where at the centres of Grand Lodges and Chapters, imposing everywhere its overruling claims, but everywhere evincing its opposition to all that was expressed and implied, done and thought by the systems presenting the claims of Templar Masonry.

Let us look in this light a little more closely at the question of dates. The RITE OF ELECT COHENS was founded, according to one story, in 1754 at Montpellier, and was taken to Paris in 1767. The first of these dates is entirely mythical and, as it happens occasionally in attributions of this kind, we derive a certain help from an ex-cluding alternative. It is said also that in the same year and at the same place a Rite under the name of JUGES ÉCOSSAIS was established by the same person ; of this institution no one has heard anything, and I believe that it is another fantasy, like that which is almost its synonym, the JUDGE PHILOSOPHERS of Ragon. It serves, however, to indicate the nebulous condition in which the origin of Pasqually's Masonic activity is involved. Pasqually was born somewhere in the parish of Nôtre-Dame, belonging to the diocese of Grenoble, but the date is unknown. He is first heard of in the year 1760, which I have already mentioned, but he was then located at Toulouse, not at Paris, which city, however, he had left recently, evidently with his theurgic Rite already formed in his mind, though it is impossible to speak certainly concerning the stage of its development. He was making serious claims as a species of Inspector-General of Masonry, and he exhibited certain titles from an unknown source. He did not in this year establish any Rite whatsoever at Paris. It is stated by Dr. Papus that the ORDER OF THEURGIC PRIESTS or ELECT COHENS was inaugurated at Lyons in 1765, but this is also untrue. Five years later he had visited this place and had initiated six persons only, among whom was Willermoz, who became subsequently very prominent in the Order.

It is important to bring down in this manner the date of establishment, as the years 1750 to 1754 already shew an incredible list of High Grades, most of which on examination prove of a later period. It follows that 1760 was the year in which Pasqually began to emerge on the Masonic horizon of France, and the period of his activity was only about twelve years. He left his country ultimately for St. Domingo in the West Indies on personal business, and he died at Port-au-Prince in 1779.

I have intimated that the RITE OF ELECT COHENS is one which redeems the magical side of Masonic inventions, firstly, from utter fatuity and, secondly, from the prevailing motive of imposture. A sense of justice has led me to place Cagliostro's Egyptian Masonry under a more tolerable light than it has been presented heretofore, but it was merely a decoration, an impression, while its magic was of the elementary kind utterly. Of Schrœppfer and Schrœder we know quite as much as we need, and it is to be questioned whether their supposed evocations and necromancy were not extrinsic to the dubious Rite which is allocated indifferently to either. Pasqually comes before us with a system which responds somewhat definitely to the term theurgic ; there is no question that his Grades were Grades of practical working and of the kind which is called magical in the common convention of terms. Whatsoever fresh evidence comes to light concerning him makes it additionally clear that he is not to be classed as an impostor but as a man with conspicuous psychic gifts, and although he was continually in financial difficulties, even sometimes in extreme need, it cannot be said that he was exploiting Masonry for his personal advantage or as a mere means of livelihood.

Having cleared the issues in these respects, it is next important to certify that the quality of Pasqually's theurgic ceremonial differed essentially by its motive, though not unfortunately in its procedure, from the common and familiar intentions and concerns of practical Magic. It was not the evocation of demons as such, of demons under the guise of angels, of familiar spirits, or any of the foul traffic represented by the ceremonial literature of the past. The hope, the attempt and the supposed result were to establish intercourse with Christ under the name of the Repairer, and the thesis was that the Master came in person and instructed his disciples. I do not propose to debate the question whether such a manifestation was antecedently impossible, or what actually appeared under the form of the Unknown Agent, as It was also termed ; I set aside further the question of collective hallucination ; we have insufficient material—as there should be no need to say— for the determination of the latter point. I desire only to put on record my personal assurance, after an anxious review of all the facts available, (*a*) that manifestations of a very marked kind did take place and (*b*) that they were characterised by the high distinctive motives which I have mentioned, as well as by results in teaching, which, whether satisfactory or not to us at the present day, were extraordinary for their period, and, as I think, suggestive for all time.

The first consequence is that Pasqually, his

practical work notwithstanding, comes before us in his written remains as one who was conscious, almost in the plenary sense, of the mystic term : the second consequence is that he prepared his school unawares for the purely mystical mission of his pupil L. C. de Saint-Martin, of whom we shall hear something in the next section. He prepared him to such purpose that albeit Saint-Martin left the theurgic school, he did not leave that especial phase of theosophy which is represented by Pasqually's treatise on *La Réintégration des Êtres* ; he carried it much further, but the root remains and his books are its branches.

The intimations concerning Pasqually's theosophical doctrine are found in the Rituals belonging to the Grades of his Order, concerning the numerical capacity of which there is some doubt and not a little confusion. It is said to have comprised (1) *Apprentice,* (2) *Companion,* (3) *Particular Master,* corresponding to the three Craft Grades ; (4) *Grand Elect Master,* apparently a Grade of transition ; (5) *Apprentice Cohen,* (6) *Companion Cohen,* (7) *Master Cohen,* being the priestly Grades of the Order ; (8) *Grand Master Architect,* and (9) *Knight Commander,* identified with *Knight of the East.* As it is certain from the remains of the founder that there was a Grade of *Rose-Croix,* being a kind of capstone of the edifice, it has been suggested that this is really the last of the nine Grades enumerated above. For this I believe that there is no foundation and the notion derives from a source which does not as a rule put forward speculations that prove of value. However this may be, there are genuine documents available which certify to the classification following : (1) *Apprentice Elect Cohen*, (2) *Companion Elect Cohen*, (3) *Particular Master Elect Cohen*, (4) *Master Elect Cohen*, (5) *Grand Master Cohen*, otherwise *Grand Architect*, (6) *Grand Elect of Zerubbabel*, otherwise *Knight* or *Chief of the East.* Of these the first three are so far thinly analogous to the Craft Grades that the latter could have scarcely preceded them, while there are points in the Ritual of *Apprentice Elect Cohen* which make that which is unlikely impossible. The *Rose-Croix* was probably a seventh Grade in comparative concealment — a reward of merit and distinction in the practice of the peculiar work imposed by the Order on its members. That work was, as we have seen, magical, having a considerable ceremonial apparatus, not especially distinguished from other processes except by the intention which I have stated. There. seems to have been also an elementary part which did not aspire beyond communication with the angels and spirits of the planets, or intelligences of similar order, but this I have regarded as negligible in speaking of the work as a whole. The particulars concern us in neither case, and I pass therefore to a summary analysis of the Rituals.

Speaking of course within exceedingly wide

limits, the first Grade has a certain correspondence with that of the Craft. The preparations
are almost identical, the implements are some of
them the same, the interpretation of the Lodge
itself is in the terms of an identical symbolism,
and there is a marked correspondence in what is
understood by the technical expression of "the
Lodge furniture." Some of the explanations,
however, depend from certain philosophical
aspects of Alchemy. Salt, Sulphur and Mercury,
which are the three alchemical principles, find
their correspondence in the human body considered as the Microcosm, and are reflections of
greater principles in the Macrocosmic world. A
distinction of importance from my standpoint is
found in the claim that there is a true building
plan of the symbolical kind and that it rests in
the heart of the Master, meaning the presiding
officer as a type of the whole Order. He is in
his official capacity the epitome of the Secret
Tradition and of the powers concealed therein,
as derived by a Rite which claims to be the
essence of true Masonry. In the manifest sense
of things, there are five Temples recognised, one
being the archetypal body of man, but apparently
understood in what I must call the archnatural
sense ; the others are the body of the universe,
that of the earth on which we live, that of the
inferior and material part of man as here and now
manifest, and finally the apocryphal body which
is that of human conventions, including apparently

the outer and artificial side of Masonry itself. The instructions which are given to the Novice during his probation as an Apprentice are described as a perfect knowledge concerning the existence of a Grand Architect of the Universe, the principle of man's spiritual emanation and the mode of his direct correspondence with the Master of all. I do not know whether this teaching which, for the most part, is obviously theoretical and dogmatic, passed into some form of practice in the third of these categories ; something would depend on what was meant rather than expressed by the reference to the Master. As regards the origin of the Order, it was a wisdom which came down originally direct from the Creator, and its institution, so to speak, took place in the Adamic age, being perpetuated from those first days of human chronology to the modern world. The possibility of such perpetuation was owing to the pure mercy of the Great Architect, Who raised up successively, by the operation of His Spirit, those who were suitable to preserve the life of the Order and to manifest it in the midst of concealment. The meaning is that the law of attainment can be put to work and will reach its term, at any period, in those who are properly prepared. The chief epochs of the Order were from Adam to Noah and from Noah to Melchisedek, Abraham, Moses, Solomon, Zerubbabel and Christ. More curious than anything is the affirmation that the Order has no limits, for it embraces the four celestial regions, however understood, together with the three terrestrial regions and therein all nations of the world.

I suppose that this is a recurrence to the old idea of the three known continents in correspondence with three recognised worlds of occult philosophy. The fourth great continent has never been allocated in symbolism, though—for what such arbitrary devices may be worth—it would be quite easy to arrange in symbolism the rough tetradic division of the material globe. The instruction of the first Grade concludes by the communication of the official secrets belonging to the Craft and certain High Grades of external Masonry. After the same manner, as we shall see shortly, that the Rosicrucian Fraternity of 1777 described ordinary Masonry as merely the Appearance of Light, so here, but after a more drastic manner, it is denominated apocryphal. The High Grades included were *Knight of the East, Knight of the Sun*—otherwise *Knight Commander*—and *Rose-Croix*. It will be observed that these were important Degrees belonging to the Council of Emperors and the unnecessary communication of their verbal and other formulæ was part of the hostile attitude adopted by Martines de Pasqually towards this system. It offers to my own mind the proof· positive mentioned previously, that the ordinary Craft Grades did not enter into the Rite of the Elect Cohens.

It is equally certain that the Masonic qualification was not exacted from Candidates, as the Order existed to communicate it on that which, *ex hypothesi*, was a far more exalted plane.

At this point, let the Masonic reader recall the kind of occupation which is ascribed to the *Entered Apprentice* while he remains in that initial Grade. According to the corresponding Degree of the ELECT COHENS, he is employed in a work of symbolical demolition, which is preliminary to emblematic building, according to the law of Masonry ; he is undoing the work of the Fall. In the terms of the Ritual itself, he is expiating his own prevarication ; and at this point an insight begins to be obtained into the root-matter of theosophical doctrine professed by the Order. The Master whom he has never seen, the Master Builder of the universe, has been put to death by the Candidate's crime, into the consciousness of which he enters in the *Fellow Craft* Grade, for reasons which should be understood by every Master Mason. He has crucified the Lord of Glory, and through him it is that the Lamb has been slain from the foundation of the world. The precious blood still cries to the Eternal for vengeance. Of that which lies behind this bizarre reflection of Christian symbolical teaching there is no explanation whatever, and I can understand it on my own part only by assuming that what is called in another form of symbolism the cosmic event of the Fall is taken as re-enacted by each one of us in his own person ; it is against his own higher nature that the crime has been committed by the Candidate, and it is in this sense that the blood, so poured out mystically, is described in the Grade as superior to that of human nature. But the Fall was, as I have intimated, cosmic besides personal and successive through all generations ; and hence the Candidate—in common with the whole world—is in pain and dereliction and travail, waiting for the manifestation of the Son of God within him. It is a toil and groaning of body, soul and spirit, and because of it the creation at large cries out in chorus. The expiation imposed upon him constitutes the service of his apprenticeship, leading towards perfect reconciliation ; and in the symbolism it is a purgation by fire, for which reason his place as a Craftsman is said to be in the South of the Temple. It is added, however, that this quarter is that of the Fall of man, as to which I confess that there is no law in symbolism by which such an allocation can be justified. In comparison with the mode in which the celestial quarters are understood by the Craft itself, the entire design is not only confused but arbitrary in a high degree. The same must be said of the circumambulations performed in the Rite which, in this Grade, are from East to North and thence by a horizontal progress to the South, the last being a pausing point. Finally, there is a mystic understanding of numbers which is contrary to the accepted systems ; five is the number of the Fall ; six is that of emancipation ; and seven is that number in virtue of which the Candidate, but in another Grade, will enter into the reconciled state. It is said also that the Craftsman's state of privation is indicated by the prison of his body, and that his business, as part of his purgation, is to know the legend of his soul—its ambition, its lapse and its punishment. So in the RITE OF ELECT COHENS did he explore the Mysteries of Nature and Science.

My information concerning the Grade of *Particular Master* seems to shew that the veiling was especially heavy in this Degree. It may mean that in some sense the Candidate completes his expiation therein. He enters the Temple like a criminal and is sealed with a secret name which is said to be that of one of the officiating members, representing apparently some great mystic principle, as if he were to be saved thereby from the wrath to come. There is, however, no explanation and any attempted interpretation can be only tentative. He is received in the West by a Worshipful Master of the West and two Wardens, and the Temple is traversed from West by North to South and thence to the East, as it is said, with trembling steps. Among the duties imposed upon him there is—still more strangely— that of research into sciences prohibited by Divine Law, at which point the whole subject seems to pass into utter unreason. He receives the number

9 as particular to his present state, and this signifies his subjection to material labour, while the incertitude of his spiritual and temporal operations seems to intimate, but as something that would not follow in any ordinary course, the reintegration of the principles which constitute his corporal individuality. In this sense it is certain that he has not expiated and that the Grade ends in a state that approximates to darkness visible, as we know of it in the Craft Grades. If we could interpret the earlier Degrees of the Rite as belonging to the history of man's spirit before it entered the body and the Master Grade as that of material life, we could reach a better understanding of the system regarded as a whole; we might see also, through whatever dark glass and darkly, why the Master and Wardens receive the Candidate in the West.

In the Grade of *Elect Master*, the Candidate is represented to himself rather as a knight in warfare, a position which corresponds with that of the Novice in the *Masonic Order of the Temple*; he is held to be in perpetual combat with the enemies of Divine Law and with those of man on earth. But the Ritual is again concerned with the crucifixion of the Macrocosmic Christ, represented on the manifest side by the Christ of Nazareth. Those who receive him are conscious on their part of a mission which is analogous in the divinity of its nature, being the reconciliation of profane humanity by attracting those who are prepared within the sacred circle of true and transcendent Masonry. The labours of the Grade are opened at the ninth hour, in allusion to the time at which the Reconciler finished His work on behalf of human nature and uttered those words of consummation which were the sign of His deliverance. The Candidate is sealed (*a*) upon the head, signifying the reconciliation which takes place when the justice of the Creator has been satisfied ; (*b*) on the left hand, signifying the price which is still paid to that justice by those in the reprobate state signified by the Southern quarter ; (*c*) on the right hand, to typify the tribute offered by the dwellers in the North as the price of their affiliation in the spiritual sense ; (*d*) on the feet, representing the mystic signs which the Creator impressed upon matter to render it susceptible of those forms which His will required it to assume ; and (*e*) in fine upon the heart, to designate the different spiritual agents which God sealed and sent out to co-operate with the spiritual essences of primeval matter. It is obvious that this is an interpretation which stands badly in need of an interpreter, and though again it might be possible to assume this office, the value of the result attained would remain entirely speculative as I am certain that a part alone of the doctrinal elements has been placed in our hands. I will therefore say only that as the result of his experience, the Candidate learns (*a*) that there are two classes of *Elect*

Masters, who are (*b*) the Perfect and (*c*) the Temporal Elect ; (*d*) that the mystic name of the latter is Man-God of earth, but (*e*) the first Man Elect derogated from his august position and by this means (*f*) was rendered man of the ordinary kind, in place of man the unseen. I conclude that Martines de Pasqually suffered, like some other symbolists, from an incapacity to co-ordinate and give a logical expression to the notions which dwelt in his mind.

The Grade of *Grand Master Cohen* is a Grade of light and also one of priesthood, for the Candidate is ordained therein, in virtue of the thought and will of the Eternal, and of the power, the word and intention of His deputies. The officiating adepts are four Wardens, who represent the four symbolical chiefs of the four quarters of the heavens, recalling the occult mystery of the Enochian Tablets, according to the *Faithful Relation* of Dr. John Dee, with whose posthumous work it is barely possible that Pasqually may have been acquainted, either at first hand or through the mediation of his own instructors. The Postulant is dedicated henceforward to the purification of the material senses, that they may be rendered fit to participate in the operations of the spirit. He is further engaged, in common with his peers, upon the work of constructing new tabernacles and rebuilding old ones, that they may be fitted to receive the different words of power which govern the operations of every created thing.

The Secret Tradition in Freemasonry

In the Great Universal Temple there are four tabernacles, being (*a*) the body of man, (*b*) that of woman, and these are of the corporal order ; (*c*) the tabernacle constructed by Moses, and (*d*) the spiritual sun. The ark of Moses was a reproduction in analogy of that which was built by Noah, containing material tabernacles as a testimony of the justice exercised on the children of God when they became sons of men by their alliance with the daughters of Cain. The ark of Moses, on the contrary, was intended for the deliverance of Israel from the law of demons and to place it under that of the Eternal. It had four doors, corresponding to the quadripartite nature of the Divine Essence, the four potencies of man and the four celestial quarters. The Grand Master Cohen can open the door in the North and close that of the South, but over the portals of the East and the West he has no power, because at present he is a temporal creature only. The doors further correspond to four principles operating in the universe : the principle under Adam was Rhety ; Enoch under the posterity of Seth ; Melchizedek under that of Abraham ; and Christ in favour of every created being. To these principles four high priests are allocated : Zalmun among the people of Ishmael ; among the Egyptians, Rharamoz ; Aaron in respect of the Israelites ; and, curiously enough on the whole, Paul among the sons of Christ. In fine, it is said that the efficacious names and words by which the Grand Masters are consecrated are those which the Creator delivered to His priest Moses for the dedication of his kind to spiritual and Divine works. But it is affirmed that in this Grade the meaning of the first Tables of the Law and their destruction by Moses is not communicated to the Candidate ; it belongs to the dispensation of a higher mystery.

The Grade of the *Grand Elect of Zerubbabel*, having regard to all that has preceded, offers a confused symbolism, but this is on the surface, for it is so adapted that it is made to serve the end which it declares only by intimation. The end, I conclude, would be found in that Grade of *Rose-Croix* which is the term of the whole research. The symbolism is based on the liberty which was granted by Assyria to the tribes of Israel at the expiration of their captivity, and it is compared to that which the Eternal will grant to all created beings after the expiration of time and by their entrance into perfect reconciliation. Zerubbabel is, in this sense, regarded as a symbol of Christ and his work as a type of our redemption. The Grand and Elect Brethren are not of the tribes which went into captivity in Babylon, but are the descendants of Ephraim and his successors, a little company of the elect which has been always in the world, the custodians of the Secret Tradition. In the symbolism of the Grade this company stood therefore apart from humanity, apart from the common limitations and darkness of material life, signified by the seventy years of exile : they were of the true priesthood. Furthermore, they were not to be counted among those who worked at the building of the Second Temple. The explanation is that the latter was only a sign of that material edifice of ours which is destined to be restored by the spirit, and this work exceeds the capacity of man. As it is intended to shew that it was reserved for the efficacity of the Christ-spirit, the change of name by which Jacob became Israel is treated as signifying that alteration in the Divine Law whereby it was transferred from the Jews and communicated to the other nations of the world. The same event was predicted by Moses when he broke the Tables of the Law and afterwards imposed upon his followers a rule which was of the conventional and ceremonial kind. The root of this intimation is in the *Sepher Ha Zohar* and is not contained—so far as my knowledge extends —in that part of the vast text which at the period of Pasqually had passed into the Latin tongue. The point is more curious than it seems, because neither he nor his pupil Saint-Martin owed anything substantial to Kabalism. At the end of his reception the Candidate took his proper place among the friends of God, protectors of virtue and professors of truth.

Hereof is the philosophical substance of the RITE OF ELECT COHENS, so far as I have met with materials concerning it which come within the scope of my purpose ; it will be agreed that I have justified my view in respect of its utter distinction from all other Grades of Magic which, at one time and another, have been enrolled under the banner of Masonry. We know nothing regarding the early life of Martines de Pasqually, nothing of the antecedents of his system. It offers here and there certain sporadic analogies with earlier theosophical reveries, but the root-matter seems so far to be almost without father or mother. Its maker has been described as a disciple of Swedenborg, but those who instituted the companion could have known little of the imputed master and nothing of the pupil as he was. He has been accounted an emissary of the Rosicrucian Fraternity, that forlorn hope of occult explanation which reminds me of China, when it looms in some minds as the last resource for the origin of all things that have their roots in obscurity. There is nothing Rosicrucian in the Rite of Martines de Pasqually. It must thus be taken simply for what it is worth in itself, recognising that it is almost without precedent in the domain of transcendental thought. As it is married to an occult practice, and as it is not concerned directly with the Divine term recognised by the mystics, it must be called occult rather than mystic, though I conclude that there are gates and posterns which might open strangely into the higher regions of research. Whether they had opened for Pasqually is another question, but I doubt whether he had ventured far in directions where the psychic powers of our nature count for nothing ; his elections were too clearly from the intermediate world.

I should add as regards the practice, that it was an attempt to communicate with that Active and Intelligent Cause to which the order of the universe is committed. This Cause is called otherwise the Repairer and signifies Christ. When Saint-Martin issued his first work, *Des Erreurs et de la Vérité*, he was still so far in sympathy with the theurgic work that he put on record his belief that certain men have known this Cause in the immediate sense which is usually called physical, adding that "all might know Him in this manner did they . . . take more pains to purify and fortify their will." He said also, but at a much later period, that in his share of the communications established with the unseen world by his occult school of the past, "every sign indicative of the Repairer was present." The fact that, this notwithstanding, he was still unsatisfied is again another question, and his reasons—which do not now concern us—I have given elsewhere.

The French school of Martinism has put forward within comparatively recent years the thesis that a Being whom it designates as (*a*) the Agent and (*b*) the Unknown Philosopher, by whom it unquestionably intends us to understand the Active and Intelligent Cause, or Repairer, of

Pasqually and Saint-Martin, appeared in the theurgic circles and dictated mystical knowledge ; that part of the record was destroyed by the communicating intelligence for the rather commonplace reason that it might fall into the hands of Robespierre ; and that other part was incorporated by Saint-Martin in *Des Erreurs et de la Vérité.* The evidence of these things is wanting and, without desiring to be invidious, it is requisite to say that on all subjects connecting approximately with Masonry in itself, or its connections, my experience leads me to regard what comes from this source — in the absence of stated warrants—as open to profound suspicion. The RITE OF ELECT COHENS is much nearer to Masonry than are its compeers in the Grades of Magic ; it is the result of an attempt to place it on the plane of occult thought and practice, and, whatever our view of the intention or the result in a particular case, the aspect in which it comes before us is recognisable at least by all who are within the bonds of the Brotherhood. The school of Martinism is specifically wrong in nearly everything that it has put forth in good faith on Masonry, and its motive has not been invariably of that kind which connotes good faith of necessity.

There are two senses in which the present account is deficient to my own mind, extended as it has otherwise been. I have explained that the antecedents of Pasqually are unknown in respect of his earlier life and the school of thought in which he was, so to speak, trained before his appearance in the Masonic arena. Light on these subjects will never perhaps be forthcoming ; but it has been said that when he appeared at Toulouse in the year 1760 he presented himself at a Masonic Lodge, bearing a certain hieroglyphical chart and claiming to exercise the functions of an inspector-general, derived apparently from some unknown Lodge in the interests of the Stuart legitimacy. There is no one in this world who had less of political bias, and we have seen already that the question of Jacobite Lodges is a pitfall of deception and fable. At the Toulouse Lodge there is no question of his appearance as there is none about his general claims ; but it is just possible that the Stuart warrant may be a point of phantasy brought into an otherwise faithful relation. He did not obtain recognition, largely because he offered certain practical demonstrations of an occult kind to enforce his titles, and —whatever the operations were—they proved a failure. He took therefore elsewhere his perfect plan of Freemasonry, his interpretation of the first and second Temple and his mysterious intimations concerning an elect priesthood. He had a better experience at Foix, where he was received with honour and the Lodge of Joshua accepted his system so far as High Degrees were concerned. At Bordeaux he was also recognised and was affiliated to the *Loge Française*, where he appears to have given evidence of what is termed his powers, meaning obviously those of an occult kind. In the year 1766 Pasqually carried his various titles to Paris, with the object of establishing in that city the Sovereign Tribunal of his Rite. Here was his centre henceforward, though it was not frequently, or for long periods, under his immediate guidance.

In 1767 he was again at Bordeaux, and there by the year 1770 he had a large number of adherents, as well as subsidiary Temples at Montpellier, Avignon, Foix, la Rochelle, Versailles also and Metz. It was not till 1771 that he returned to the Sovereign Tribunal for a brief period. He was afterwards yet again at Bordeaux, which he left in 1772 for the West Indies and there died, as I have mentioned. It is clear from all the evidence that his various deputies and adepts, theoretical or practical, regarded themselves as only partly instructed in respect of his theurgic system, and although his absence in the West Indies did not mean the entire cessation of his activity, it was committed to the uncertainties of the post, and in the end it must be confessed that his work, from his own point of view, as from that of others, was left unfinished.

Those who are acquainted with the history of occult practices which, whatever their motive and end, must follow certain lines of broad resemblance, will understand that any experiment of the kind is foredoomed to failure, seeing that the powers of a Magus are not communicable, and unless there were others in his circles who also possessed such powers, all the Lodges and Temples depended from his personal demonstrations only. It was those which were in request ; when therefore he was in session at Bordeaux Paris was in widowhood, and when he was taken across the seas there was a suspension of nearly everything. Some of his Princes *Rose-Croix* were not without experiences on their own part, but in his absence everything flagged and it is easy to see that at his death the RITE OF THE ELECT COHENS was near its dissolution. At Lyons, where I suppose that it had been established during Pasqually's absence, it went over to the STRICT OBSERVANCE and other Temples lapsed into their former Masonic obediences. The fact that this was naturally gradual may be registered but does not concern us. The Sovereign Tribunal appointed a successor to the Master, Pasqually on his own part having transmitted his powers to another. Some kind of existence in a decrepit manner was thus maintained there and here until the period of the Revolution.

The second point about which this account is so far insufficient regards the Secret Doctrine communicated by Pasqually to his adepts as an extension of that which is found in the discourses belonging to the Rituals. It is a difficult subject to approach because of its innate obscurity, and because it represents a version of the Secret Tradition which is only a reflection at a great distance. It is therefore likely to prove a source of confusion to my readers rather than a light on the path. I must say something concerning it but it shall be the least that may be possible, having regard to these circumstances. Franz von Baader, a German mystic of the late eighteenth and early nineteenth century, is perhaps the one person who has made Pasqually's doctrine the subject of a serious study and has almost taken it into his heart; his faculty was however of such a quality that what is comparatively clear in his author becomes almost unintelligible under the light of his presentation, while that which is involved in the original passes beyond comprehension. He suggests that Pasqually was at once Jew and Christian, which may be an allusion to the old idea that the Magus belonged to the stock of Israel, but more probably that his system effected some new kind of marriage between the two dispensations. As Christian, he was Catholic and Roman, but beyond the fact that he was married in the Catholic Church and that his child was baptized therein, I do not find much evidence of dedication in this particular respect, so far as his writings are concerned. As a Magus, it is said that he revivified the old covenant by his occult powers, and here again I think that the intimation only darkens counsel. The ceremonial magic of

Pasqually followed that type which I connect with the debased Kabalism of Jewry, but it was simply because there was no other form of practical working ready to his hand in the ceremonial order of things, and it is ridiculous to suggest that the old covenant was restored, much less revitalised, thereby. The Kabalistic Magic prescribed for use by the Elect Cohens was of course of a Christianised type, having regard to its imputed object, but most of the old Rituals are of this kind, though their purpose was either the discovery of hidden treasure or the opportunity for some illicit indulgence. Franz von Baader is nearer to the truth when he speaks of Pasqually's epoch as one in which the light of Christianity was eclipsed and when he regards the Magus rather as a ghost of the departed appearing on the horizon. He is right also when he says that Christian obscuration was an opportunity for the revival of Magic, whether pagan or Jewish. I think, however, that credit must be allowed to Pasqually for attempting at such a period, by means of his occult practices, to get direct revelation from the source of revelation in Christendom ; the proposition was preposterous, even to the insensate grade, but it was redeemed by the motive, and I do not question that he regarded it in two aspects : (*a*) as that medicine which the age most needed, and (*b*) as leading up to a new and fuller realisation in the light of Christ. According to von Baader, who reflects

MARTINES DE PASQUALLY

herein the mind of his original, the dealings of
God with man involve a triple covenant, corresponding to the past, the present and the time
which is still to come. There is, firstly, that of
Israel ; secondly, that which was established by
Christ ; and, thirdly, the covenant under the
light and grace of the Holy Spirit, after which
there will be the rest of the Sabbath. But the
last is not a dispensation ; it is rather a fruit
of the three overpast periods, and it is the
great epoch of union. The correspondences in
Masonry are in the three Craft Grades, but
the Mason may rest assured that the similarity
is utterly forced and apart from all likeness in
symbolism, ritual or imputed state of initiation.

If we turn from such points of criticism to
Pasqually himself and to the information which
can be drawn from his *Traité de la Réintégration
des Êtres*, we shall find in the first place that he
makes reference to certain teachers, from whom
he learned on his own part. He describes them
as faithful friends, cherished by truth and pro-
tected by wisdom. He says indeed that his
explanations are made with the same clearness
with which they were dictated to him by the
truth of wisdom. That which was communicated
on his part had been received therefore from an
anterior source, but, as there is no further intimation concerning it, we must determine for
ourselves on the general grounds of likelihood
whether his instructors were living custodians of

a secret tradition or whether he received teaching through his astral practices. I am inclined on the whole to the latter view, because the essence of his system lies in its claim that there was a communion possible with powers unseen, who could and did instruct under given conditions. The nature of the teaching is a much more important point, and as regards the treatise in which it is embodied, it is very curious in respect of the form. It constitutes a commentary at large on Genesis and Exodus, and thus covers a considerable part of the field which is occupied by the *Midrash-Ha-Zohar*, which itself embraces the entire Pentateuch.

It should be understood that there is no sense in which the Christian text can be said to follow from the great work of Jewry in exile, though there are certain points of correspondence ; there is nothing or next to nothing which indicates an acquaintance with Kabalistic tradition on the part either of Pasqually or of those from whom he learned. There is a system of numerical mysticism, for example, in both cases, but it is not the same system ; there is an interpretation offered in both of the same events recorded in the Biblical narrative, but it is not the same interpretation. On the more external side, an important distinction between the two works is that the *Zohar* cleaves almost with literal exactness to the Scriptural accounts, howsoever it may at times obscure them, and at times illuminate, in the course of its vast commentary; but the tract on Re-integration offers at every point some departure from the sources on which it depends. The histories of our first parents, of their immediate descendants, of Noah, Abraham and Moses, are new stories written on the basis of the broad facts concerning them. It follows that, by necessity, the force of the interpretation is reduced, supposing that it has any within its own measures, for the simple reason that there is a fatal facility attaching to any Commentary which begins by varying the text that it pretends to explain. With the variations themselves we have no concern here, my object being to exhibit after what manner, and to what extent, the tradition of Pasqually and his Masonic priesthood offers correspondence with other Masonic traditions on the same subject.

To summarise it at the beginning in a single sentence, the concern in particular is with the Fall of man and the way of reconciliation in Christ, and the intention throughout is to shew that every important epoch and history found in the two first books of Scripture are in some way a foreshadowing of the New Dispensation and Covenant. With this kind of exegesis we are acquainted to our distraction and weariness in the old and accepted commentators; but to these Pasqually owes little, even when some of his system follows the same lines. Prior to any manifest existence all spirits were in the bosom

of the Divinity, and at the beginning of manifestation they were emanated therefrom. The
emanation of the angelical hierarchies preceded
that of man and so also did the Fall of the
Angels, which came about by the perversion of
the will. The physical universe was a consequence of this lapse, and it provided a field
within which the malice of fallen spirits should
be contained and should exhaust itself. The
emanation of man was ordained that he might
have dominion over all beings in perversity, and
behind this general thesis there lies the notion
that his government was intended ultimately to
restore those who were cast out to their first
estate. In the language of Pasqually, man prevaricated, however, on his own part ; the glorious
body with which Adam was clothed at first was
exchanged for a material form, and he was
precipitated from the Edenic world—exalted
above all things of sense—into the abysses of that
earth whence came the fruit of his prevarication.
The path of his redemption is now that of the
life in Christ, and the rest of the thesis is concerned
with such a delineation of that path as an exceedingly forced method of construction can extract
from the various events of Genesis and Exodus.
As a delineation, the treatise falls so far short of
its term that I regard it as an unfinished experiment, by which I mean not that it is a fragment
but that the writer had in his own mind intended
to carry it further.

Of Magical and Kabalistical Degrees

Like all others who have claimed to put forward some part and substance of the Secret Tradition in Christian times, Pasqually provides a warrant for his system by assuming (*a*) that some of his primeval knowledge and wisdom remained with Adam after the Fall and was from him perpetuated ; (*b*) that one of its custodians was the prophet Enoch ; (*c*) that it subsisted till the days of the Flood ; (*d*) that its witness at that period was Noah, by whom it was again handed on ; (*e*) that it was with Abraham at a later period and so came down to Moses, whose original intention in respect of the Law delivered on Mount Sinai was different from that which he did in the end establish by the Second Tables of the Law.

The connections with official Masonry are thinly maintained by such allusions to the Temple of Solomon and that of Zerubbabel as happen to be found in the treatise ; but these events of Jewish history were evidently held over with the intention of completing the Commentary by its extension to the other books of the Pentateuch.

There is, I suppose, no need that I should express on my part an opinion as to the value of the system here summarised baldly ; in so far as it is old, and to that extent familiar, it is not a true part of the Secret Tradition in my understanding thereof, while in so far as it is new, it is of arbitrary invention. I have left for the end of this section one intimation which I regard personally as more curious than any, and this is where Pasqually says that those who have heard him will see clearly how the true Messiah has been always with the children of God, but always unknown. It is behind this statement that the true Tradition is concealed. The witness who uttered it stood, I think, at the gate which opens into that secret world, but he did not go in.

VI

THE SCHOOL OF MARTINISM

THE Masonic and theurgic mission of Martines de Pasqually, with which the mystic Louis Claude de Saint-Martin was identified by the fact of his initiation in the days of his youth, has created unawares a predisposition to confuse the master of strange occult arts with the disciple of Divine Science who entered later on more fully into the degree of certitude than did ever the most zealous Mason of that period enter into the Grades of innumerable dedications conferred in the various Rites at the end of the eighteenth century. The name of Saint-Martin will be so familiar now to many of those whom I address more especially, and the chief source of information in England is so near to every one's hand in my study of *The Unknown Philosopher*, that I can assume either some knowledge on the part of my readers or a willingness to seek it where it can be obtained most readily. He came out of all the orders and sodalities, but not as one shaking the dust off his feet, as one rather who had found a more excellent way, and had entered into the inward life. He did not scale all heights or sound all deeps therein ; but he opened that unknown world and brought back a report concerning it which, in several respects, will remain in permanent memory. The records thereof are in his books, and beyond them other record there is none, as it is antecedently unlikely that there should be any. But because of his early Masonic and occult connections, and because it is my fantasy to think that Martines and his Rites were mixed up with Saint-Martin and his Mysticism, there has been a kind of interpenetration in clouded minds between two tolerably distinct worlds of activity, and the mystic emerges first of all as himself the Reformer of a Masonic Rite, originally established by Pasqually, or the founder of one upon his own part. Both notions are rooted in misconception. But in the second place, and outside these intimations, it has been proposed for our acceptation that he at least founded a school—that is to say, an occult school—and it is with this notion and all that has been developed therefrom that I must say a few words first of all in the present section. The memorials of his influence are said to have remained in Russia, as the result of a visit concerning which we have few particulars, and which perhaps—though not indubitably for this reason—may be almost legendary rather than historical in its aspect. The rumour concerning him was certainly conveyed into that country at a period which must be marked as receptive to such influences in such a place. I do not believe in the least that he left one single trace which can be constructed in the sense of a school, even in the most informal manner, either there or elsewhere. I doubt above all whether the materials would have come into his hands at that distracted period in the land which he called his own. In the comparative refuge of Switzerland, and in the vicinity of the Baron de Liebistorf, he might have found another *entourage*, or in that part of Germany which connects with Eckartshausen, but not in France at the Revolution, in the dictatorship, or in the long struggle of the Empire. The confusion has arisen, to my mind, in the persistence of that exotic interest of Masonry which centred at Lyons in the days of Pasqually, which survived the death of this master, which survived the Terror and the Empire, and had not wholly perished at the close of the first quarter of the nineteenth century. In other words, therefore, that which remained over was the school with its roots in the theurgic processes of Pasqually's Masonic priesthood, primarily in the care of people like Willermoz and then of their successors. There has been an attempt in recent times to connect this school with an occult hypothesis concerning an Unknown Philosopher whose manifestation was a theurgic product, and I know not what authority can be ascribed by sober criticism to the documents offered in the evidence. But if they belonged to the period, and drew from the origin which is claimed, we can understand more fully how Saint-Martin, the Unknown Philosopher of a mystic literature, came to be connected by imagination with a school not only long after he had ceased to belong thereto, but long after its disintegration. For that which was perpetuated and brought over into the nineteenth century was not of the incorporated order, but rather the records or memorials of something that once had been. The fact remains that in respect of Saint-Martin that which persisted in connection with his name was and could only be a sporadic disposition towards the inward life during a clouded period in the outer world. Some of the memories were persistent, some of them must have been exceedingly sacred. I set aside now all that concerns the theurgic school of Lyons and Bordeaux. Jean Baptist Willermoz, though not the titular or in any sense the acting successor of Pasqually in the Masonic group, never quitted the path of things phenomenal which had been followed by his master, and he could have remembered Saint-Martin, his early and, for some period, his intimate associate, only as one who had passed into another region which was very far away from his own. One cannot help speculating as to what memories abode in the mind of the Abbé Fournié during some twenty or more years of exile in London, after all those wonderful experiences which rewarded by sensible consolations the hunger and thirst after God and Divine things, about which I have written elsewhere. He also, like Willermoz, was connected with Saint-Martin during a time of active work and under the eyes of their common teacher. Of the most precious, most intimate, most direct memories there are, however, no records ; they were those which centred at Strasbourg, the Zion of the Unknown Philosopher's mystic life ; they were those which were gathered into the hearts of beloved and elect women, like Madame de Bœcklin, the Marquise, de Lusignan and the Duchesse de Bourbon ; they were those of chosen men like Rudolph Salzmann and the Comte d'Hauterive. Among these, and those like them, were the germs which he said in his last moments that he had endeavoured to sow and that he believed would fructify.

There is no opportunity here to trace how this purely mystical influence, which must have passed more and more into that which Saint-Martin bequeathed in his books to the world, has grown up into the hypothetical and semi-instituted warrants of the modern ORDER OF MARTINISM, with a Supreme Council located at Paris, an almost vast membership and sporadic branches—I was about to say everywhere, but certainly in several countries, including the United States. It has certain titles to consideration and has already produced its dissidents, being branches which have segregated of their own accord from the parent tree. It is, however, essentially anti-

Masonic in character, because it is a kind of *voile levé pour les curieux*, which publishes to its members the so-called secrets of Masonry, and though, as English Masons, it is impossible for us to recognise the Grand Orient of France and the Lodges which depend therefrom, it is obvious that this proceeding is a blow struck at Masonry of all denominations, even under the legitimate obediences. The fact that it is of no effect, and that those who possess nothing but a few elements .which have long been public property can communicate nothing, makes no difference to the nature of the policy or to its intention. The ORDER OF MARTINISM is an axe which has been ground, and ground well enough for that matter, in the interests of those who established it, and it is mentioned here more especially to affirm (*a*) that it is anti-Masonic, in the sense which I have just defined ; (*b*) that it has no part in any tradition whatsoever ; (*c*) that the name which it has assumed should and can deceive no one who is properly informed, as (*d*) it has no connection with Martines de Pasqually and the RITE OF THE ELECT COHENS, or (*e*) with *le philosophe inconnu*, Saint-Martin, except a literary and philosophical interest in the work of both, but perhaps especially that of the former ; and (*f*) that Saint-Martin, for his own part, would indubitably have denounced all its ways, had it arisen at his own period.

There is one more task to perform in the present section, and that is to make an end more definitely

COMTE D'HAUTERIVE

Of Magical and Kabalistical Degrees

of the old mendacious myth which represents Saint-Martin (*a*) as the reformer of the Masonic Rite of Pasqually, or (*b*) alternatively as the inventor of an *Écossisme Reformé*. According to the first story, he established two Temples, one of which conferred the Grades of (*a*) *Apprentice*, (*b*) *Companion* or *Craftsman*, (*c*) *Master*, (*d*) *Ancient Master*, (*e*) *Elect*, (*f*) *Grand Architect*, (*g*) *Mason of the Secret*— possibly *Secret Master* ; and the other, (*h*) *Prince of Jerusalem*, (*i*) *Knight of Palestine* and (*k*) *Kadosh*, or sanctified man. The alternative story usually represents the Écossais Rite as a reduction of the first into seven grades, as follows : (*a*) *Apprentice*, (*b*) *Companion*, (*c*) *Master*, (*d*) *Perfect Master*, (*e*) *Elect*, (*f*) *Écossais*, and (*g*) *Sage*. It will be seen that, over and above the Craft Degrees, both nomenclatures represent ingarnerings from several sources. The first account originated possibly with Clavel and the second with Ragon, but there might be earlier sources discoverable, if the question were worth the pains. Ragon says that the Grades were full of ridiculous superstitions and absurd beliefs, which is probable enough ; but as regards the first foundation he stultifies himself in a later work by attributing precisely the same series to Baron Tschoudy.

There is abundant evidence in the correspondence of Saint-Martin to disprove that he ever went in search of a Masonic reformation, whether of his own device or another's, but it is only of recent years that the true nature of the misattribution has transpired. Among the materials laid before the Convention of Lyons in 1778, it is said that there were (*a*) the *Écossais Rectifié Suisse*, the production of a certain De Glayre, and (*b*) the *Écossais Rectifié de Saint Martin*. The first does not especially concern us, but the second is affirmed to have been practised since 1770 by the Chapter of St. Theodore at Metz. The name, however, had reference to that canonised Archbishop of Tours who divided his mantle with a beggar and not to the theosophist and mystic. If the date which I have named is reliable, it is certain that in 1770 Saint-Martin, the Unknown Philosopher, was then unknown to fame.

THE RITE OF SAINT-MARTIN and its particular *Écossais* system passes therefore into the same category as the RITE OF RAMSAY. It is said that the Metz compilation was used by the Convention of Lyons to assist in the fabrication of *Novice* and *Knight Beneficent of the Holy City*, but those who have the opportunity of comparing these Grades with their direct correspondences in the RITE OF THE STRICT OBSERVANCE will be aware that the statement has no foundation, except in the sense that both systems laid the usual stress upon the Masonic virtue of beneficence.

ADONIA.

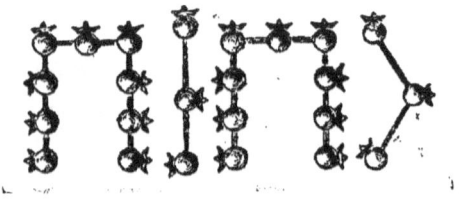

VII

THE GRADES OF KABALISM

WE have seen the content of the later Rites so far as the elements of *Magia* are concerned : there are detached Grades, known by their titles only, which suggest more express intentions and perhaps a fuller realisation, but it is impossible to speak concerning them. The position of Kabalistic Grades is similar in all respects. I set aside those which convey intimations in their titles but have nothing corresponding thereto in the Rituals themselves. The office of some collections seems akin to that of creating large expectations in the names of Degrees, but they furnish a morality only or a laboured discourse on an aspect of the philosophical kind, as this was understood at its period. In the RITE OF MIZRAIM there is a considerable show of communicating the tradition in Israel through the medium of certain Grades. One of them is *Sovereign Prince Talmudim*, which is a Grade of erudition in doctrine ; there are others which speak a similar language of vague and delusive promise ; nothing follows therefrom, and the recipient is left with a doctrinal illumination which is of much the same value as his licensed rank among the Supreme Commanders of the Stars, in the 52nd Degree of the system, already cited. It would be waste of time to speak of these inventions or others of the same order which would enter into a classified list. In a work on the Kabalistic Tradition I have mentioned a Degree entitled *Knight of the Kabalah*, and have shewn that its speculative thesis is concerned with the mystery of numbers, developed rather curiously. I recur to it only that I may put on record one point which was then omitted. As may be expected, the Grade does not represent even a reflection of knowledge concerned with its supposed subject. It illustrates, however, the prevailing sentiment of the period about which I have spoken otherwise. Those who were thoroughly indoctrinated respecting things Kabalistic approached the tradition of Jewry, as we have seen, solely as an instrument for the conversion of Israel, and this rumour of its assumed office filtered down into regions where there is no trace of acquaintance with texts at all. The anonymous compiler of the Kabalistic Grade under notice presents his thesis on numbers so that he may enlarge upon Christian aspects. For him the unity of numbers corresponds to the notion of the *Logos*, and for some purely arbitrary but not expressed reason he lays down that this

Word is incarnate in the bosom of a virgin. That virgin, also inexplicably on the hypothesis, represents religion. The triad in numbers recalls naturally the three theological virtues and the mystery of the Trinity in Unity. The number four is above all things the cardinal virtues. Six in some mysterious manner conveys an intimation regarding the coming of the Liberator, in consequence of the Fall of man; and seven is the instituted Sacraments of the Catholic Church. Twelve is in correspondence with the twelve Articles of Faith into which the Creed or symbol of the Apostles may be divided; it is also the Apostles themselves, and it is the twelve stones of the Mystic City of the Apocalypse.

The ceremony, which is held in an apartment termed a Sanhedrim, opens symbolically at midnight and closes at dawn of day, the Master or President being saluted as Most Profound Rabbi. The Candidate is announced as a *Knight of the Golden Fleece*, so that it is neither a detached Grade nor part of a rational sequence, as the qualifying title belongs to Hermetic Masonry. His aspiration is to be initiated in the Sacred Mysteries of the Kabalah and he undergoes an extraordinary ordeal corresponding to the four elements. Having been hoodwinked outside the Lodge, he is stripped naked and thus is plunged into water, which accounts for that element in a drastic manner; his forehead is marked with ashes and the equivalent of *memento homo quia pulvis es* is recited over him, this being the trial by earth. He is then suspended in the air, and finally his right hand is passed over a brazier of burning coals. When he is reclothed and the obligation is taken, it has to be signed with his own blood, and he is then restored to light. As the reward of this terrific experience, he is informed that a Kabalist is one who has learned by tradition that the sacerdotal art is also the royal art. He is further recommended to study the mysteries of religions and the harmony between them ; if he chance to succeed, he will arrive at the summit of true felicity, which is the sole end of Masonry. It seems just to say that even in Memphis and Mizraim no Candidate has fared so far and hardly to attain less or as little.

There is, however, the *Knight of the Kabalistic Sun* and it combines Alchemy with the forlorn substitute which it has to offer as the Secret Tradition in Jewry. Here also Jewry is Christianised, and as there is no Ritual whatever I will classify a few points from the two catechetical instructions as follows : (1) Soul, spirit and body are in correspondence with Salt, Sulphur and Mercury. These are the three catholic substances of which all things are formed. They result from the influence of the planets poured upon the four elements. (2) Art is superior to Nature in bringing things to perfection, but it depends on a knowledge of the quintessence and the fire of the philosophers.

The result is a Sovereign Medicine and the Stone. (3) The Cross is salvation to man, and the Stone is the perfection of the three kingdoms. (4) In the main, however, the Alchemy is of a moral kind, for the seven planets represent the seven modes of human passion. (5) The Kabalism is confined to an interpretation of the seven Cherubim, whose names are inscribed in a great circle which is exhibited for the study of the Candidate. (6) They typify, however, only the five senses, repose and thought, being seven forms of felicity with which man has been endowed by God. (7) This being so, there is a recommendation to trust in the Creator's goodness, exercise fraternal love, and do nothing of which one is likely to repent hereafter.

There is a bare possibility that we might carry the question of Masonic Kabalism a few paces further, if it were possible to speak about the Grade of *Kabalistic Mason* in the private collection of Peuvret, but nothing can be verified concerning it.

We have now finished our inquiry regarding the institutes of Masonry in respect of those secret sciences and philosophies which, on the surface, might be supposed most plentiful of all in the matter of Secret Tradition. The result is interesting in its way, though it may seem scarcely satisfactory to some readers ; it is in perfect conformity with my root-thesis, that occultism, generically understood, has been at no time the channel of a tradition which itself has been always purely mystic. I therefore at least, and those who are in harmony with myself on this question, will set aside the consideration of Magical and Kabalistic Degrees with a sense of relief that the result has been so slender ; yet the investigation has served its proper purpose to establish the point of fact.

I conclude here my examination of Rites and Degrees incorporated under the ægis of Masonry and, by their titles and claims, connected presumably in a certain direct way with aspects of the Secret Tradition. As to those which by imputation and otherwise belong to Alchemy, readers with antecedent knowledge might be prepared for the fact that the Hermetic subject reflected into Masonry would yield little in the way of result, because it is precisely that aspect of the Secret Tradition which throughout its history has been peculiarly liable to the distractions of pretenders, and there is further the difficulty arising from the two schools, one of which signifies under the best circumstances a part of the Tradition that may be called negligible. Of Ceremonial Magic and its derivations, few persons in their senses have expected anything, and it is in the fitting order of things that Grades dedicated thereto should be characterised by folly and imposture. It is only astonishing that such a claim as that of Pasqually's system should intervene in the series, and that even the Count Cagliostro should have produced a Rite which, although it is negligible in the last resource, is curious after its own kind. But I confess on my own part, and believe in so doing that I am reflecting the feeling of others who have followed me so far— I confess that I should have expected a better result from Grades which, by their titles at least, are supposed to have borrowed from Kabalism. The connection between the Craft and the substance of Jewish tradition is curiously intimate, as I have shewn in earlier sections, but the reflection into the High Degrees is less if possible than nothing. The real explanation, I infer, is that those who knew at the beginning, though they left their evidence on the root-matter of the mystery, had veiled it too closely for recognition on the part of later Brethren who had nothing to guide them but their own unaided judgment.

BOOK VII

Of the Mysteries on their Mystical Side, and of this Subject in its Relation to Masonry

a·N·N·E·S·

oH.

THE ARGUMENT

I. Of Rosicrucianism in its connection with Masonry

*Early documents concerning the plan of the Fraternity
—Their initial circulation in manuscript—Testimony
of Montanus — Of the notary Haselmeyer — The
tomb of C∴R∴C∴—Of two sections in the Fama
Fraternatatis—Futility of some modern opinions—
Question of the incorporated society in 1610—The
opposing views—One difficulty concerning them—
The case of J. V. Andreas—Authorship of the
Chemical Marriage—A decisive testimony—Authorship of the other memorials—Of imitative associations—Their traffic in imposture—Rosicrucianism and
Masonic High Grades—The year 1777—A Brotherhood of the Golden and Rosy Cross—The existence
of an unknown Ritual in several Grades—Sequence of
the Grades—Their content—Their place in the Secret
Tradition.*

II. Of Masonic Rosicrucian Developments

*Influence of the name Rosicrucian—The tale of Zanoni—
A Rosicrucian Order in England — Associations*

bearing the title in France—*Of German and American developments*—*The Societas Rosicruciana in Anglia* —*Points connected with its foundation*—*Its series of Grades*—*Its Rosicrucian elements*—*That there is no connection with the Secret Tradition.*

III. CONCERNING GRADES OF NEW RELIGION AND OF SWEDENBORGIAN MASONRY

The High Grades and Universal Religion—*The vision of the New Jerusalem*—*The modern Rite of Swedenborg*—*The question of its origin*—*A criticism of the scheme of Grades*—*The Grades as a reflection of the Craft system*—*An astronomical interpretation*—*The entrance of the Lodge*—*A mystic side of the subject* —*Spiritual nature of the Craft experience*—*The Swedenborgian Grade of Apprentice*—*The Lodge as the Garden of Eden*—*The Grade of Fellow-Craft*— *Some curious points of symbolism*—*The pledge in the Master Grade*—*The claim of the system*—*The earlier Rite of Swedenborg*—*Doubts and confusions regarding it*—*A summary of legends*—*Question as to the initiation of Swedenborg*—*Conflicting accounts of the Grades.*

IV. A HIDDEN RITE OF INTERPRETATION

High Grade accounts of Masonry—*Existence of a cryptic Rite*—*Particulars and reservations concerning it*— *Analogies with the Rite of Swedenborg*—*An approximate date of origin* — *Mysteries of ancient and primitive Masonry*—*A doctrine of the soul*—*Lifting of the Temple's veil*—*Of Martinism and its influence in the Rite*—*Primeval knowledge of man*—*The soul's genesis*—*Of perfection in Knowledge*—*The doctrine*

The Argument

*of the Fall—The Temple of Universal Mysteries—
The scheme of redemption — Perpetuation of the
primeval Knowledge—A veil placed thereon—Origin
of Pagan idolatry—Vicegerents of the Eternal Word
—Lapse of initiation itself—The election of Israel
—Plans of the Temple—Mysteries in Egypt—The
Allegorical design and work—Destruction of the First
Temple—Initiation and the Second Temple—The
Second Temple destroyed—Rejection of the Universal
Restorer—Mysteries of early Christianity—Perpetua-
tion of Secret Doctrine from the time of Moses—
Vicissitudes of Masonry—The Instituted Mysteries
as a consequence of the Fall—A little company of the
Elect—The narrow, open way—The veil of emblem
and hieroglyph—The veil of Masonry—The Doctrine
behind the veil—Further concerning the Temple of
Solomon—The occasional cause of the universe—The
scheme of secondary Agents—The struggle of the
Cosmos — The return into unity — Of man as a
metapyhsical centre—Mission of primeval man—The
death of the Fall—The Reconciler—Of three mystic
Temples—The scheme of interpretation judged—
Further concerning Martinism—Influence of the
Unknown Philosopher—Analogies of the interpretation with certain phases of High-Grade Masonry—
Merits and defects of the construction.*

V. REFLECTIONS FROM HIGH GRADE MASONRY TO MODERN OCCULT RESEARCH

*That these reflections are at once fortuitous and real—
Martinistic and Rosicrucian schools—Their claims
and their research—That none of them possess a
connecting link with the Secret Tradition—Overt*

The Secret Tradition in Freemasonry

and secret schools—*The Tradition in secret schools
—The occult and the mystic—The case of the occult
schools—Of psychic research—Old magic and modern
phenomena—Recurrence to High-Grade Masonry—
That occult and Hermetic Masonry represent a
spurious process of grafting—That the things grafted
are dead.*

VI. A Preliminary Excursus Concerning the Divine Quest

*Why this digression is necessary—A review of the Christian
centuries—Two kinds of inheritance—Christian Mysticism and the Secret Tradition—The cosmic mystery of
Christ—Dionysius and his Mystical Theology—Duns
Scotus—The Doctrine of Divine Immanence—The
Doctor Angelicus—St. Bernard and St. Bonaventura
—The Admirable Ruysbræck—The Cloud of Unknow-
ing—The Church and the world—Mysticism at the
Reformation period—The Secret Mystic Doctrine—
The Mystery of Contemplation—Traces of an exotic
practice—The attainment in Christ—The secret
ways of mystic life—Further concerning occult and
mystic schools — Further concerning occult and
Hermetic Masonry—The influence of Éliphas Lévi—
That this section is an introduction to the next.*

VII. Intimations of the Term of Research

*The soul in her awakening—A review of the High Grades
—The House of Christian Doctrine—The Word in
Christian symbolism—The Craft Word—Of Christian
elements in the Craft—The externalisation of Doctrine
—The formulæ of Tetragrammaton—The letter Shin*

The Argument

—The world behind the Secret Tradition in Christian Times—Epochs in the History of the Word—The secret Masonic transmission—Of three Paths—A time-immemorial doctrine and practice — Words of the dying Plotinus—Church sacramentalism—Divine Immanence and Divine Transcension—The silence of the Resurrection—The Cube and the Cross—Mysteries of the Divine in manifestation—Plotinus and the Path to the Centre—An intimation of the Templar Grade—Of Christian High-Grade elements and the Secret Tradition—Implicits of the Craft Grades— The root-fact of the Secret Doctrine—Further concerning the Craft Legend—The triad of the Stewardship —The hand of God in history and symbolism—The Law of Severity—The Presence of the Shekinah—The Law of Deliverance—Of the experience behind Secret Doctrine—An open path of return—The science of the Path—The Garden of Venus—The Mystery of generation—The Mystery of Re-Birth—Regeneration and Conversion—The secret doors of consciousness— The Palace at the Centre—The Divine Union.

VIII. Of a Rite within Masonry

An exotic enshrinement of Secret Doctrine—Of a Grade in Correspondence with the Masonic Grade of Apprentice—Of a Second Grade in correspondence with that of Fellow-Craft—Of one which stands alone—Of the Master-Grade in transcension—A Grade of completion—A personal testimony concerning the Rite—A word regarding its history—Its communication by way of the sacraments—Nature of its Masonic analogies—How it is a Key to the Craft.

The Secret Tradition in Freemasonry

IX. LAST WORDS ON THE MYSTERY OF BUILDING

The four measures of testimony—The ethic of life—The doctrine of religious duty—The transition into the Greater Mysteries—Of Masonry as a defence of doctrine—Of doctrine as a Key to the Sanctuary——The criticism of inward experience—The authority within—The Instituted Mysteries as signs of that authority—Of Finger-Posts on the Path of Knowledge—The true Mystery of Building—A summary of the whole quest—The House of Doctrine that is to come—Conclusion as regards this study—How the Great Quest goes on.

BOOK VII

Of the Mysteries on their Mystical Side, and of this Subject in its Relation to Masonry

I

OF ROSICRUCIANISM IN ITS CONNECTION WITH MASONRY

IT is a matter of common knowledge with every literate Freemason, that the Rosicrucian Fraternity was first heard of in Europe by the publication of certain documents in the second decade of the seventeenth century, or exactly in the year 1614–1615. There is some evidence that, whether in their extant or in an earlier form, they were circulating in manuscript for a few years previously. It seems prudent to set aside in the first place, because of its dubious character, the testimony of Montanus, who computed thirty years—that is to say, onward from the year 1592—during which he was misdirected by the Rosicrucians and their false processes, till they expelled him at the Hague in 1622. The same prudence dictates the disqualification as evidence of the date imputed to the second preface to the *God-illuminated Brotherhood of the Rose-Cross*, that work having appeared in 1616, but the year suffixed to the preface is 1597. As it rests solely on the evidence of Semler, I leave it also as an open question whether in 1603 it was said by any one that the appearance of a new star in *Serpentarius* was a sign of happy times approaching, or that *Serpentarius* and *Cygnus* shewed the way to the Holy Spirit—presumably to the House Mystic R∴ C∴ The new star is mentioned as a great portent in the *Confessio Fraternitatis, anno* 1616, but if it be the subject of reference earlier, in any symbolical connection, there is the question by whom and where. We get upon more solid ground in the year 1610 with the express statement of the notary Haselmeyer, that the *Fama Fraternitatis R∴ C∴* came at that time into his hands in the Tyrol, but was in "written form," and had not been seen in print. Publication took place—at the very earliest—only in 1614, but unquestionably in the early months, as a physician in the kingdom of Bohemia wrote on June 12th an application for admission to the Order. Adam Haselmeyer was notary public to the Archduke Maximilian and was afterwards a Knight of the Holy Cross. Finally, in the year 1613, a still earlier epistle addressed to the most reverend Fraternity was printed at Frankfurt, probably on the authority of manuscripts.

The question of date is very nearly inscrutable, if we attempt to carry it appreciably further back than the first published memorials ; it is in all respects comparable to the much more important possibility that these memorials were the work of an incorporated society prior to their public appearance. Leaving these issues, however, let us look at the subject for a moment under another aspect.

The second generation of Rosicrucian philosophers discovered, as it is said, the mystic tomb of their founder, and after having contemplated it for a time they again sealed it up ; but it is not on record that they found any cause to revisit it on a later occasion. On the surface we have therefore a mere fable and a story without an end. The discovery leads to nothing, nothing is taken from the tomb, and though it contains many wonders, it is not said that they were unfamiliar to the visitors at the shrine. The *Fama Fraternitatis*, in which the account is given, seems broken strangely into two sections. In the first of these we have the legend of a poor brother who has heard of the Eastern Wisdom, who in search thereof travels to a Land of the Morning and attains that which he needs. He desired subsequently that the western world, and especially the world of learning, should participate therein, but the learned world had then as now—to be frank, perhaps more than now—far other preoccupations, and thereto it was a laughing matter. He collected, however, certain zealous disciples—and hereof is the first section. In the second they discovered the dead body of the master, and it is this apparently unadorned fact which is the root-matter of Rosicrucianism in its later form, wherein that which is discovered is the Divine behind the universe—that is to say, it is the following of a certain path, at the end of which there is the testimony of God in the consciousness.

There are people at the present day who believe that the story of Christian Rosy Cross and his journey to a mythical city with a highly symbolical name in the blessed Araby is what children call a true story, that is to say, something which happened historically. Some of them even cherish a kind of hope that they may yet discover in Germany a relic which may pass in their amiable minds for the material remnant of the House of the Holy Spirit. The position intellectually is really no better than would be that of the person who should take the Craft Legend literally and expect on a day to discover some historical memorial of the Master Builder, or perhaps the mystic weapons which served at his destruction. Of course, at the back of the first curious enthusiasm there is the highly convincing opinion that early Rosicrucianism must have had a Founder, from which proposition the most skilful mind can find only one way of escape, which is by affirming (*a*) that the early memorials were not the work of an incorporated Secret Order, but were (*b*) a serious experiment on the mind of an age before which there had been set up many beacon lights of theosophy, alchemy and occultism, or (*c*) that it was what is called a *jeu d'esprit*, a mockery, a derisive but veiled hoax, immeasurably successful within the lines of its proper intention, which was to lay a trap for the fools of the period. The fools responded immediately far and wide.

The alleged circulation in manuscript of the memorials is in my opinion against this view, and so long as we do not accredit the original Rosicrucians with a marvellous degree of adeptship, there is nothing in probability to prevent us from supposing an early formation of alchemists and such like persons into some kind of order or brotherhood, if we can once place the fact that a nondescript Lutheran philosopher and theologian *à rebours*, who contributed a great deal in his day to the rag-fair of Protestant rubbish, has put on record in a biography of large proportions and preternatural seriousness the statement that he wrote one of the memorials in his boyhood precisely as one of the jests which have been proposed for our consideration in explanation of all the issues.

It may be just in this connection to mention as one distinction between the works of J. V. Andreas and the Rosicrucian memorial claimed as a production of his youth, that it is an exceedingly decorative, pageant-like and skilful romance which contrasts extraordinarily with the universal dullness of all his later works. This at first sight is a little opposed to the alleged authorship, but it remains to be stated, as an office of the clemency of criticism, that although Andreas did write an autobiography, was a Lutheran theologian and was native of some impossible and unknown place termed Wurtemberg in the records, he was assuredly a man of honour, and I find it difficult, firstly, not to accept his statement, but, secondly, not to construct it in its simple sense of expression. I mention the latter point because a few occultists who have dabbled in something which they are disposed to consider Rosicrucianism, have leaned to the idea that Andreas had a much more serious intention than he was disposed to admit. Personally I do not believe that he wrote the other memorials, and in this case we get back to the point that they may have been the product of an association which elected to publish under veils the fact of its existence without indicating any local habitation or offering a means of approach within its circle, though they invited the prepared to join it.

This presumptive opinion is the strongest that it is possible to express on the affirmative side, and everything is left open thereby, the statement itself included. If only it were possible to put back the date of Rosicrucianism to the last year or thereabouts of the sixteenth century, another face

SVFFICIT.

IOH. VALENTINVS
ANDREÆ.

N.
MDLX
XXVI
AVG
XVII

O.
MDC

J. V. ANDREAS

of things would be seen ; we should have done with any Andreas hypothesis and be at liberty to devise something more satisfactory to replace it. I have desired such evidence keenly, but there is no trace.

One thing is clear—that an association, or more than one, came into existence soon after the first memorials were published ; and the evidence of Montanus speaks volumes in respect of imposture, so far as a particular branch was concerned. In part through this, but in part through growing rumours and reports to the same effect, Rosicrucianism became a byword and a scorn alike in Germany and France. There were, however, later periods, when it looks as if some kind of cleansing had taken place. However, in that part of the eighteenth century which was comprised by the High Grade movement in Masonry, there is on the whole very little to encourage us in any good opinion of the brotherhood till the year 1777, when it was seriously at work on Alchemy. So far as records are concerned, I believe that the BROTHERHOOD OF THE GOLDEN AND ROSY CROSS, working a system of degrees which was outlined by Magister Pianco, and demanding the Masonic qualification, represents a noticeable Order after its own kind. Its Rituals are in their way curious, and in their way also important, connecting as they do with later developments on the symbolic value of which it is difficult to lay too much stress.

The identity concealed under the name of

Magister Pianco has been elucidated speculatively after more than one manner ; it has been said to conceal J. E. von Weisse and alternatively the Count Ecker und Eckhoffen, but I do not know that either attribution is colourable. Whosoever he was, the author of the work entitled *Der Rosenkreuzer in seiner Blösse* (*The Rosicrucian Unveiled*) is supposed to have been expelled from the Brotherhood prior to a reformation therein which took place in the year that I have mentioned, and his book has been treated as a revelation concerning it by way of rejoinder. This is, however, incorrect, as an almost indubitable inference from the text itself is that the writer was at the time in corporate union, though it is feasible that it may have led to his retirement. It is a frank criticism of the Order, and he asks those in authority for explanations of various points in regard to its teaching and working, though he claims that he is not actuated by any spirit of hostility. A reply appeared in due course, but in terms of personal invective and otherwise beside the purpose.

From Magister Pianco himself we can derive a good deal of information as to what, at his period, may be called the claims of the Fraternity. The book is exceedingly rare and its contents have never been made known in English, so that it will be useful to summarise it briefly. At some period of the far past, but when and where is not stated, there was a school of initiates, probably of the unorganised kind, and it had begun already to feel the need of specific incorporation with the object of combining the wisdom in Christ and the wisdom of the Magi. A sort of alliance was established, but of a confused and unsettled kind, as a consequence of which it passed through many changes and assumed many names. It was first called the Magical Alliance, and its members were termed Magical Brothers or Associates. This took place in 1115 and it lasted for two years in the state of flux which I have mentioned. The record concerning it passes over the period which intervened between the date just given and that of the Knights Templar, who were established, as we know, in 1118. It is affirmed that the cross-bearing chivalry became associated with the Magical Brothers and shared their secret knowledge. In this manner we are able to locate tentatively the supposed centre of initiation, which would be somewhere in Palestine, and we may recall at once the thesis of Baron Tschoudy concerning the Knights of the Morning. But, according to Magister Pianco, it was owing to the occult brotherhood that the Templars came into being, on the hypothesis that the need of a recruiting ground among men of worth was in such manner supplied. Why the drag-net could not have drawn those who were properly prepared direct into the ranks of the Alliance, and why if an outer circle were desirable it should adopt the guise of a military body, are problems which are left for solution according to our personal lights. The thesis is of course an example of the ineffable nonsense which was talked in the eighteenth century, and especially among High Grade Masons, concerning methods supposed to have been pursued for the custody and perpetuation of Secret Doctrine. However this may be, the experiment led to a decay in the Doctrine of the Magical Brothers, in proportion as the Temple system was itself consolidated. The secret knowledge also began to be lost when the Knightly Order was suppressed.

I do not know what purpose this myth can have served in the Rosicrucian mind, but the account proceeds to multiply confusion by saying that long prior to the year 1118 there was another association which held in succession from the last Stewards of the Mysteries under the obedience of the Old Law, and that it stood in the same rank as the Templars. Being comparatively unimportant and obscure, it escaped the proscription which fell upon these latter, but after their purgation by fire it made common cause with the Templar remnant and founded another fraternity, having the seals of permanence and a definite code of rules for its maintenance. The years went on ; like the Magical Alliance, it adopted various forms and names ; once it was the Brethren ; once it was called the *Noachites*, for I suppose that it had a claim upon pre-diluvian knowledge ; lastly but most important of all—

or at least for our purpose—it assumed the title
of Freemasons. This designation was particular
at first to a central Lodge at Berlin, and it became
universal within the circle of the sodality after
a certain time only. So also there was variation
in Grades, allegories and so forth, till the true
and fundamental system was promulgated by the
Head Lodge. In this manner the Craft Degrees
prevailed everywhere, as indeed under various
phases they had done from the beginning. There
had also been Higher Grades from time immemorial, such as the *Écossais of St. Andrew* and
the *Golden Thistle*, but they were confined to
archæologists of the subject and earnest students
of the secret knowledge. Brothers like these were
aware that the basis of the Fraternity was to be
sought in the old Mysteries, that the greater part
of its wisdom was drawn from thence, and they
pursued their researches in the hope of discovering the true nature of the Magical Alliance of
antiquity as well as to extend its field. For this
purpose they became incorporated separately,
firstly as the *Alliance of the Wise* and then as the
Golden Alliance, admitting into their ranks only
a chosen few among Master Masons, or Masters
of the Appearance of Light. This body was
inaugurated, as the deponent affirms, about the
year 1311, or just after the fall of the Magical
Brothers and the Knights Templar. The studies
were centralised (*a*) in 72 books containing
the archives of the Magi ; (*b*) in the Mosaic

books ; (c) in the Book of Wisdom ; and (d) the Apocalypse—to which other texts were added containing indications of the Ancient Wisdom. Out of all these the sodality constructed a new work of general and religious knowledge, meaning, I suppose, the cryptic Book M∴ of the *Confessio Fraternitatis R∴ C∴* When it was completed one further name was assumed, the custodians of the knowledge becoming Brothers of the Golden and Rosy Cross, under which designation they have remained since the year 1510.

The Rosicrucian Unveiled appeared in 1781, being that time at which the imputed author Eckhoffen is supposed to have been engaged in establishing the KNIGHTS OF LIGHT, around which so much curiosity, mystery and romance have gathered during the last twenty years, owing to suggestive allusions by writers who assume the accents of knowledge. According to German authorities who only lay claim to research, this institution was chivalrous and priestly, and in 1786 it was merged by its inventor in a later device of his own, the BRETHREN OF ST. JOHN THE EVANGELIST IN ASIA AND EUROPE. This also was Rosicrucian in character, and its last Grade was one of royal priesthood according to the Order of Melchizedek. An alternative title was ASIATIC BRETHREN.

Count Ecker und Eckhoffen is said to have denied the authorship of *The Rosicrucian Unveiled*,

Grade.	Membership.	Numbers.	Signs.
1. 9.	Magi.	7.	Urim, Thummim, and Semahamphoras.
2. 8.	Magistri.	77.	Cross of gold enamelled
3. 7.	Adepti Exempti.	777.	Cross of gold enamelled
4. 6.	Majores.	788.	Cross of gold enamelled.
5. 5.	Minores.	799.	Cross of silver enamelled
6. 4.	Philosophi.	822.	Cross of silver enamelled
7. 3.	Practici.	833.	Cross of silver enamelled
8. 2.	Theoretici.	844.	A crystal globus terrae.
9. 1.	Juniores.	909.	A ring with characters.
Forming the chief number in Kabalism.	*Membership is irrespective of religion.*	5856. *Number of the brotherhood, and a mystic date, being that of its predominance.*	*Recognition is by means these signs, together with the word, that hon may be given wh honour is due.*

The Brotherhood of the Golden and ℟

	Word.	Mystic Name.	Countries and Kingdoms where they are found.	Res
red.	An equilateral triangle.	Luxianus Renaldus de Perfectis.	Egypt, Persia, Venice, Madrid, London, Amsterdam, Cologne.	Hassan, Ispaha
	A compass	Pedemontanus de Rebus.	Scattered through the whole world.	Their President
ours.	Hitakel.	Janus de aure campis.	Also scattered through the whole world.	Their President but is absent secution.
ild.	Phrat.	Sphærefontus à Sales.	As the above, in different places of the world.	Their Governor but is driven unknown.
ilver.	Pison.	Hodos camelionis.	Residence completely indefinite.	Their Justiciar the Oder.
silver	Gihon.	Pharus illuminans.	These may indeed be called our Apostles, since two may seldom be found in one country; the whole world almost must be instructed.	Their Director
on	Wetharetz.	Monoceros de astris.	Almost everywhere, and work much with their brethren.	The General Tr
	Maim.	Porajus de Rejeceis.	As above, scattered and busied with learning.	They have m Chief is at Be
	Aesch.	Pereclinus de Faustis.	Are the most external lodges to be found in the world.	This President bruck.
of	These mysterious words serve for the enlightening of the mind, and are a special means of recognition, but the identity of the superior is concealed.	By the Kabalistic name the Magi recognise the good or bad qualities of each brother. It is subject to change.	Why they are scattered through the world is explained orally.	Presidents are of Lodges onl the times and arranged.

Places of Assembly.	Circles.	What knowledge belongs to each Grade.	Cost of Reception.
Smyrna in Asia, every 10 years.	1.	Nothing is concealed from these, and they are Masters of all, like Moses, Aaron, Hermes, Hiram.	99 Marks in gold.
Camra in Poland and Paris in France, every 9 years.	2.	These have complete knowledge of the three chief branches of science.	Little or much, as desired.
Basle, Augsburg, Nuremberg, every 8 years.	3.	These have the knowledge of the stone of the wise, the Kabalah and *Magia Naturalis*.	3 Marks in gold without dispensation.
Aix, Hamburg, Lisbon and Malta, every 7 years.	4.	They have the *Lapis mineralis*, tinged with red.	Much or little.
Königsberg, Stettin, Berlin and Dantzig, every 6 years.	5.	These know the philosophical sun, and perform miraculous cures.	Much or little.
Leipzic, Cracow, Breslau, Warsaw, Hermannstadt, every 5 years.	6.	They have the whole knowledge of physics, and the art of tingeing with wisdom.	3 Marks in gold without dispensation.
Not fixed, but summoned according to time, circumstances and opportunity, every 5 years.	7.	They know from practice how to create what is profitable, and understand the Cahot.	Much or little.
Same arrangement as the above, every 3 years.	8.	Understand the alchemical theories and natures.	Much or little.
As above, at convenience, every 2 years.	9.	Students and beginners.	3 gold marks. Dispensation up to a sixth at need.
Conventions are for the rectification of abuses and the taking of accounts.	*These 45 circles are the main foundation which no storm can destroy.*	*The sum of all natural and supernatural knowledge which it is possible for men to comprehend.*	*The fees are payable before reception, and are remitted at once to the authorities.*

[*To face page* 218, *vol. ii.*

s.

e, etc.   Sm)

Naples.   Can
                            F

e in Vienna,   Basl
count of per-   8

e in Prague,   Aix,
d his abode   e\

Frankfort on   Kor
                            D

den.   Lei[
                            I]

Zurich.   Nou
                            in
                            o[

ators;   their   San
Zoom.   e\

ode at Inns-   As :
                            y(

' by Masters   Con
this manner   ti
meetings are   a(

and its muddled thesis must remain therefore under its original cloud of pseudonym. Perhaps, like some other legends, no consistent account was intended, the design being simply to put forward under an obvious veil the identical origin of Rosicrucianism and Freemasonry in some kind of Secret Tradition dating from the far past. The veil itself is reminiscent of many Masonic reveries—of Baron Tschoudy, as I have said ; of the STRICT OBSERVANCE ; of Werner's *Sons of the Valley* ; and so onward.

The account which I have given concerning it is drawn from the pseudo-historical part, and does not deal with teaching or practice. The Rituals of the Fraternity, as framed in the course of the Reformation which took place in 1777, are, however, in my keeping, and offer proof positive concerning its proceedings under the new régime. The Grades of the revised Order were (1) *Juniores* or *Neophytes* ; (2) *Theorici* ; (3) *Practici* ; (4) *Philosophi* ; (5) *Adepti Minores* ; (6) *Adepti Majores* ; (7) *Adepti Philosophici*. Beyond these are the 8th and 9th Grades, the existence of which is indicated in secret documents but nothing transpires concerning them. The titles are shewn in the tabulation which I annex hereto, being a transcript from *The Rosicrucian Unveiled*.

The conditions of reception into the Order were (1) the Masonic qualification ; (2) by inference, the possession of a high Grade corresponding to that of Rose-Croix ; (3) the desire for knowledge, capacity to acquire the same and the virtue of obedience ; (4) readiness to take a solemn pledge and give a response to certain questions in writing. The questions were thirteen in number, and were designed to elicit from the Candidate an intimation concerning his preconceived opinion of the Order, his acquaintance with its purpose, his confidence in its leaders and his views concerning the transmutation of mètals. It was also intended to elicit whether he was already on the quest of the physical *Magnum Opus*, and whether he had passed previously through any secret schools. The Statutes of the Order provided that members should seek first the Kingdom of God instead of Mammon, and should be in search of wisdom rather than material wealth ; that nothing should be promised to a Postulant beyond that to which he might attain by the mercy of God, the instruction of his superiors and his own industry ; that the Great Mystery should not be shewn to any one, as it must be prepared by each for himself ; that the reports of operations should be transmitted to the Supreme Direction ; and apparently, for the clause is vague in its expression, that the ruling Superior of each circle, Temple or Lodge was to some extent in concealment and was not to be known as such by the Novices and lower members.

An introductory thesis regarding the origin of the Fraternity naturally involves its derivation from the secret traditional knowledge of the far past, but it is not otherwise in correspondence with the mythos of Magister Pianco. It dwells upon the wisdom of Adam, which as usual remained with him after his expulsion from Paradise, and was perpetuated from generation to generation without break or interruption to modern times. Its custodians were always apart from the multitude, and in the days of Moses they became more secret than ever. They were in Egypt and Arabia at that epoch, in Palestine during the reign of Solomon, and in Assyria during the Babylonian captivity. In the course of time the association spread over the whole globe, but, having suffered deterioration, the entire Fraternity was reformed in the sixth century of the Christian era by seven Wise Masters, who brought it into its present situation. For the purpose of further concealment, but also to act as a drag-net, the time came when the Superiors of the Order established the lower Degrees of Freemasonry. These also suffered from profanation, but the external Brotherhood is still the recruiting ground and the seminary for the Higher Grades.

The Fraternity is described as an immeasurable circle endowed with a dreadful power and incomprehensible beauty. This circle signifies eternity, the power is that of the Sons of Wisdom and the beauty refers to the virtue with which all Brethren should be endowed.

On the various Grades, as these are represented

by the Rituals, I do not propose to dwell otherwise than shortly ; they are highly technical in character, and they have also connections elsewhere of which it is unfitting that I should speak more fully. The Neophyte at the beginning of his reception was tested on the loyalty of his purpose and to prove further that he was seeking wisdom rather than gold. He is described by the officer corresponding to the Inner Guard of Masonry as an earthly body which keeps the spiritual man imprisoned, and in response to the question : " What do you ask at our hands in this man's favour ? "—the answer is : " I ask you to kill the body and purify the spirit." As there is no need to say, this is symbolically understood and the intention is (*a*) that the imperfect may become perfect ; (*b*) that in the union of the two parts the body may be justified by the spirit. The discourse attached to the Grade is concerned largely with the explanation of Masonic symbolism in a Hermetic sense.

The Second and Third Grades are exceedingly slight in their character ; in that of *Philosophus* the Candidate enters in the name of the Most High and communicates immediately in bread and wine, being told to remember that in the vegetable or middle kingdom there is nothing more noble than these gifts of heaven, whereby God Himself elected to make and confirm His holy covenant with mankind. There is then a rite of ablution, after which a brief obligation follows. The Candidate is finally anointed and the official secrets of the Grade are imparted in due form. The 5th Grade, being that of *Adeptus Minor*, was evidently an elaborate ceremonial, having three chambers reserved for the communication of its separate sections. There was that of the vestibule, the middle chamber and the innermost Temple. There is reason to believe that the documents on which I depend do not represent the Rituals in the plenary sense, but are rather shorthand notes which were amplified by the presiding Officer to some extent at his will, preserving, however, the general scheme of the landmarks. The Candidate was subjected to a searching examination, as one who was about to look into some part of the Eternal Mysteries. He was also enabled to discern that harmony and connection which subsists between all the Grades. It is at this point that the Ritual for the first time becomes expressly alchemical, though indicating, even in this practical part, a way of procedure which was rather of things spiritual than those of the physical world. By means of philosophical and theosophical contemplation, and so only, would the Candidate be enabled to know the essential powers of the elements and the Great Work of Nature in its nudity. The Triune Stone of the Philosophers would be to him a clear proof not only of the Divine Being but of the treasury of souls emanating from His endless love. The Candidate, at this point, was placed upon his knees ; he made a general confession and received absolution in the name of the Order.

The Obligation followed and the mysteries of the chief symbol belonging to the Grade were communicated in ceremonial form ; the Recipient was clothed in the vestments of the Rite ; and the Superior then committed to his care the secret process promulgated by the Headship at the last reformation of the Order. This process was metallurgical in character, and all which can be said concerning it is that it may have led up to a knowledge of the Philosophical Stone, but it was not the Stone itself, which is called the highest secret of Nature and was communicated only in the last Degree.

In the Grade of *Adeptus Major* another process was divulged, and it is said never to have been possessed, seen or worked, save among exalted members of the Rosicrucian Order. It is called an approved mastery set apart for the 6th Degree in view of its correctness, harmony and utility. The Grade of *Adeptus Philosophicus*, being the Portal of the Great Mystery, is mentioned but not described.

✠   ✠

CHRISTIAN ROSY CROSS

II

Of Masonic Rosicrucian Developments

The name Rosicrucian has been always something of a talisman on the romantic side of occult literature and history.   The set of ideas and feelings which came to be gathered about it was also talismanic in character and depending from the romantic side.   These elements worked in an inverse ratio to any knowledge of the subject, of which there was little or next to nothing at the period—at least in those places which I have more especially in my mind.   The vague reports of early essayists and writers of monographs caused the Rosicrucian image to dilate in a false atmosphere of dream, which, as it happens, was dream no less when the criticism, if it can be so called, was actuated by a hostile motive.   I am speaking rather of England, for any sentiment of the kind on the Continent belongs to a much later period. I suppose that the peculiar attraction culminated in that tale of Zanoni which has exercised so great an influence on persons with thin and somewhat tawdry occult or psychic dispositions ; the romance itself is thin and tawdry like these.

Prior to the period in question, some branch of Rosicrucianism was at work in Great Britain, but the circle was exceedingly restricted ; to-day it has known many developments, but now more especially out of these islands. In France there is *L'Ordre Kabalistique de la Rose-Croix*, which at the period of its founder, Stanislaus de Guaita, was simply an occult society borrowing a traditional name and making its proceedings a secret. Since his death we have heard very little concerning it, but certain publications of old texts have appeared under its imprint, and perhaps it may now class rather as a body of *literati*.

I suppose that in this connection I need not mention the Rosicrucian *salon* of the entertaining fantasiast Sâr Péladan. No one would expect a tradition as forming part of the programme belonging to this maker of pageants marshalled about his own personality, and few would know less what to do with it than he would know, supposing that an inheritance of this kind were unexpectedly placed in his hands. Dr. Papus said aptly concerning him : *Les sciences occultes ne s'inventent pas* ; but the point is that the occult associations do perform this task—or at least more often than not—and Rosicrucianism has been a case in point through nearly all its mixed generations.

L'Ordre Kabalistique and the *Salon de la Rose-*

Croix are, however, quite genuine in their way, having perhaps very little that is calculated to deceive any one and not having cultivated the art. There are things, on the other hand, in Germany about which I should like to speak less certainly on this or on any side of their subject, and there are others in America to which one can refer only in the terms of a prolonged counsel of caution. Certain books, which *per se* are too negligible for specific mention here, are products of almost unmixed fraud, trading on the ignorance of people who have no opportunity to check the statements. So is the time-old custom which began to prevail with Montanus perpetuated with its proper variations to the present day.

None of the institutions and none of the literary devices here referred to possess a Masonic complexion. It is different, however, with the *Societas Rosicruciana in Anglia*, which was instituted in 1866 and has always exacted the Craft qualification from its members. It has traces of an interesting history in respect of its origin, the claim being that a former Grand Secretary of English Freemasonry communicated to the Founder a tradition in ritual-form which he had partly discovered in certain Masonic archives and in part had received by initiation, after the usual manner, from older members of the Fraternity. The scheme of the Grades is based on that which was published in 1781 under the pseudonym of Magister Pianco and under the title of *Der*

Rosenkreuzer in seiner Blösse. The folding plate of this work, which contains the scheme in question, has been substantially reproduced in *The Royal Masonic Cyclopædia* by Kenneth Mackenzie, who thought it worth while to record that it had never been published previously and had been specially constructed for the compilation in question. The number and names of the Grades are identical with those of the BROTHERHOOD OF THE GOLDEN AND ROSY CROSS, as recited in the last section, but the correspondence practically ends at this point. The Rosicrucian elements are of a very simple kind, and it is not pretended that the Society is more than a sign-post indicating a path which may be travelled much further by those who can find the opportunity. There is of course no vestige of the Secret Tradition, as that term is understood in these pages, but as a memorial which—according to the testimony concerning it—has arisen in a curious way, it has a side of interest, while it has the advantage of being modest in respect of its titles, its possessions and its warrants.

III

CONCERNING GRADES OF NEW RELIGION AND
OF SWEDENBORGIAN MASONRY

SEVERAL of the High Grades have been written up to some rough-and-ready thesis on the comparative analogies of universal religion, and it has come about in this manner that there are some perplexing admixtures in the minor issues of Rites. In virtue of such analogies, it is thought doubly reasonable that a *Rose-Croix* Mason should have the benefit of interment in accordance with ceremonies which, by the hypothesis, are drawn from the Egyptian *Ritual of the Dead*. And there are other stupefying marvels. Fortunately, there has been one attempt only to graft a new religion on Masonry, and it came about, as we have seen briefly, because Abbé Pernety had confessed to the attraction of Swedenborg and his vision of the New Jerusalem.

There is no evidence that he carried the

design to any express term, and albeit we have ascertained something concerning the aspirations and beliefs which prevailed among the Brothers who were incorporated after some fashion at Avignon under a Masonic ægis, we know little and next to nothing of their ceremonial procedure or their Rituals.

I shall have to speak of Swedenborgian Masonry under two heads, and I will deal first of all with that which is nearer to us in time and place—I mean, the modern RITE OF SWEDENBORG. I understand that it has been promulgated actively across the Atlantic, and it has also its custodians here. It is difficult to say when or where this system originated, and the fact that it reached England from British possessions in Canada does not create any presumption regarding its source therein, which antecedently, and in all other respects, seems not less than unlikely. In its phraseology the system offers certain marks of continental parentage, but it is not French, as it is much too clumsy and cumbrous. It may of course be purely modern, or subsequent, that is to say, to the year 1860, and in such case it might well be the invention mainly of Kenneth Mackenzie, who masonically would then have had obscure German or Swedish preoccupations to account for the peculiar style. Alternatively, he may have adapted existing materials which came from abroad into his hands. Whether or not it proves on examination to be a pretentious failure, it is in a sense important because it is chronologically last in a triad of intention to read a specific meaning into the Craft Grades. The other interpretations are lucid and this is cryptic ; of the others one is noteworthy on philosophical grounds, and one, although slight, is good within the limits of morals : this, after the labour of elucidating, does not repay the pains. It is in three parts or grades : $1 = 4$, $2 = 5$, $3 = 6$. That is to say, it is grades 4 to 6 of a system depending from the Craft and presenting the three Craft Degrees in another sense. The recipient is therefore already a Master Mason, and he repeats his triple experience at great length, amidst new artifices of symbolism. As regards its canon of interpretation, I may say at once that the Rite places an astronomical construction on the whole mystery, and having regard to the situation of a Craft Lodge and the place of the officers therein, every Mason will understand that the task before the inventor was one almost of fatal facility. It is also one which, except in the hands of an adept, is liable to develop the confusions of solar mythology apart from all the graces and sanctities of the higher teaching which heaven and earth deliver to the soul of man in all the pageant of the universe. As an illustration of the kind of illumination which characterises the Rite, it is sufficient to say that a Brother in the Grades of Swedenborg is termed throughout a *Phremason*, recalling the best methods of Godfrey Higgins and the late Dr.

Kenealy. That is solar mythology as it is made, and in view of the device I shall confine my summary of the system to two points.

The Lodge has two entrances, respectively in the North and South, though we have seen from another High Grade that the North Entrance was walled up prior to the great event which took place according to the Craft Legend. The entrances and exits of the Candidate are made on the northern side of the Temple. I believe that, mystically speaking, this is the only correct arrangement, but the mystic reason is neither explicated nor implied in the RITE OF SWEDEN-BORG. I will explain therefore that the Masonic candidate has, *ex hypothesi,* come originally from the East; being the symbolic point of his location when he knew all things in God; but he undertook the outward journey until the sun set upon his soul; it was the exit from the higher Eden. He was plunged in material things, as the sun passes into the underworld. During all his uninitiated period he dwells in darkness, which is of course in himself, because it is light always in the Lodge of the Adepts. When he is received into Masonry, he enters the Temple —as I have said—at the North-West corner; he comes into the world of intellectual light—that world where the sun is always at the meridian, but he himself is not in possession of the light. It should be understood clearly, in spite of certain evasions and certain substitutions of lesser meanings, held to stand by analogy for the greater, that the Craft Mystery is on one side that of the enlightenment of the Candidate, who receives the experience of light symbolically in three stages, corresponding to birth in mortality, life on earth, and death in the body, together with an unfinished presage of that which follows thereon. But the symbolical ceremonies are not intended merely to reproduce in a pageant the past fact that he has been born, the fact present of his human life, or the prefigurement of his passage hence. The analogy is mystically exact, but it is a grave error to mistake the external correspondence for the inward mystery ; after the same manner, and in accordance with previous intimations, the course of the heavens foreshadows the soul's story, but it is a grave error to ignore the inward mystery and to take the external correspondence, great and macrocosmic as it is, for the sole concern of the true Instituted Mysteries, for the explanation of all mythology and the doctrine of all religion.

This notwithstanding, there are very curious occasional intimations in the system here under notice, and at the back of the compiler's mind I believe that, in a kind of undeveloped consciousness, he perceived dimly the spiritual nature of the Candidate's entire experience. It is very difficult, however, to educe a logical procedure from the confused sequence, and this fact seems to me especially stultifying in the specific case, for if the redrafting of the Craft does not serve for elucidation, but rather darkens counsel, then assuredly it serves for nothing.

In the Grade which is equivalent to that of *Entered Apprentice*, the Candidate is informed that he stands at the threshold of the Garden of Eden and the place of the Tree of Life. The proposal, however, is to build a Temple, in which an important part is assigned to him who is received. It is, I suppose, in connection with this that the Ritual is said to consist of six labours, terminating in the symbolic introduction of our race into its future dwelling-place, which is seemingly the Ur-home, the place of the River of Life and the Tree of Life. The corner-stone of the building is faith in God.

The 2nd Grade is singularly involved, for (*a*) the Candidate is said to be in Masonic darkness, and at the same time (*b*) in search of greater light, which is pure paradox. He is supposed to receive the light and to enter the Temple, which is called that of the Creator, presumably (*a*) the cosmic universe, (*b*) the Holy House of Doctrine, (*c*) the Temple of Divine Mystery. At a later stage the plans of the building are presented to the Candidate, and it is then described as (*a*) God's Temple in Nature, and (*b*) a symbol of the moral Temple that is within. The East is goodness rising into life ; the West is goodness setting into death ; the South is truth in light ; the North is truth in oblivion. Here is one of the suggestive points, but unfortunately sufficiently confused.

It is, almost obviously, the story of earthly life and the story of the soul ; but the two—although in parallel—should be distinguished more carefully. The Temple, finally, represents the Garden of God.

As regards the 3rd Grade I can say scarcely anything, because of its very curious, but withal bizarre, analogies with its marvellous prototype in the Craft. The Candidate is pledged to keep secret the Ineffable Name of God, and in this connection a certain communication is made to him—which comes to very little, as usual.

The RITE OF SWEDENBORG, as it is thus known among us, must be distinguished from what I may venture perhaps to term the historical Rite of the past, which—so far as I am aware—has been duly buried by the past and can scarcely be looking at this day for a glorious or for any resurrection. It has been entombed so effectually and obscured so wholly, that I feel a certain reluctance in admitting that it ever existed in the corporate sense, or otherwise than as a spiritual interest represented by two or three schools of thought in Masonry. The legend relates (*a*) that Emanuel Swedenborg was profoundly instructed in the Mysteries of Freemasonry ; (*b*) that he had traced Masonic doctrine to its source in Egypt, Persia, Palestine and Greece ; (*c*) that he was one of the most illustrious reformers of Masonic Rites. It is not stated, except on the negligible authority of Reghellini, that he established any system on his own part, and therefore by tacit consent the Abbé Pernety remains the first person who introduced the new religion into the Craft or its extensions. On the literal side of things there is no evidence and there is no reason whatsoever to suppose that the Swedish seer was so much even as initiated.

From Avignon and the Benedictine alchemist the legend proceeds to London and to that Benedict Chastanier with whom we have made acquaintance previously. In the year 1766 he is said on rather doubtful authority to have been Master of the Parisian Lodge *Socrate, de la Parfaite-Union.* There or in that vicinity, but otherwise in London itself and presumably for the French colony therein, he modified the RITE OF PERNETY and so established the ILLUMINÉS THÉOSOPHES, working seven Degrees, as here follow : (*a*) *Apprentice Theosophist*, (*b*) *Companion Theosophist*, (*c*) *Master Theosophist*, (*d*) *Illuminated Theosophist*, (*e*) *Blue Brother*, (*f*) *Red Brother*, and (*g*) *Sublime Écossais or the Heavenly Jerusalem.* The date of this foundation is dubious, though one that is impossible has been stated, and the fact itself is not certain. We may compare the content with that of the system which is referred by Reghellini to the seer himself. This is alleged to have comprised : (*a*) *Apprentice*, (*b*) *Companion*, (*c*) *Master*, (*d*) *Elect*, (*e*) *Companion Coën*, (*f*) *Master Coën*, (*g*) *Grand Architect and Knight Commander*, (*h*) *Kadosh.* It is obviously an amalgamation of LES ILLUMINÉS THÉOSOPHES with

EMMANUEL SWEDENBORG

the RITE OF ELECT COHENS, and it existed only in the imagination of the first witness concerning it.

The legend reverts to Paris, and affirms in concluding its thesis that a certain Marquis de Thomé, seeking to disengage the doctrines of Swedenborg from much foreign matter that had come to be incorporated Masonically therewith, established in 1783 the RITE OF SWEDENBORG properly so called. The testimony is that of Clavel, who gives also the nomenclature of the Grades, which is identical with those of Chastanier, less the Degree entitled *The Heavenly Jerusalem*. The system is said to have been still practised by certain Lodges of the North in the year 1838, but whether this is a reference to France or to northern Europe there is no means of ascertaining.

IV

A Hidden Rite of Interpretation

We have seen in the course of this work that
in certain High Grades there are instructions or
lectures which present some particular aspect of
Masonic history, some general judgment thereon,
or some hypothesis of origin which is intended to
be understood historically. These are entirely
distinct from the legends and histories attached to
individual Grades. Cases in point are found in a
few which are communicated or worked under the
obedience of the Scottish Rite. We have seen
also that in the modern so-called Rite of
Swedenborg the Craft Grades are re-expressed
with the design of presenting a philosophical view
of Masonry. As such, I consider that it is a
failure, but the experiment is not without interest.
Occasionally, in the discourse addressed to the
Candidate, other Degrees make—as one would say,
almost casually—a reference which on consideration may prove to be more suggestive than any

laboured thesis. From my own point of view, the genius of Masonry declares itself to a better purpose by means of its symbols and allegories than by any formal proclamation of its genesis ; but the experiments which have been tried naturally raise a question whether in the wide world of Rites and their content something more adequate can be found.

The answer is that there does actually remain for our final consideration in this department of research one cryptic Rite which on rare occasions is still communicated on the Continent of Europe, where it has been taken into utter concealment. It has antecedents in history which, apart from its content, are not without importance, and it was once incorporated in a collection of Grades which is otherwise well known to students ; of that collection it was then an exotic part, and it is exotic still—so much after its own kind that it will scarcely suffer comparison with anything now extant in the wide world of Degrees. It is far removed from all the decorations of pageant and the dramatic side of ceremonial. Those who are acquainted somewhat intimately with the rarities of Masonic Ritual are very likely to have heard its name, but they will have heard nothing else concerning it. I have met with it—but there are indeed two names—in certain encyclopædias, and, as indicated, it may be found in certain lists of systems. I do not offer the means of identification concerning it, because I have received it on condi-

tions which make absolute reserve essential. I
put on record this statement with a very full
realisation of that which is involved thereby, for
Masonry is a secret society in respect of its official
mysteries, but not in respect of its name, its
available history, or the titles and general purport
of its various Degrees. Indeed, the public sources
of information are much less reticent on specific
points of Ritual than I have thought it desirable to
be, having regard to the conditions on which
Masonic knowledge is received at first hand in
the Temples. It cannot, therefore, fail to create a
very curious impression in the minds of Masons
when they learn for the first time that a living
part of their symbolic science is veiled even for
themselves, in a place which at first sight would
seem most unlikely, and under circumstances which
make it attainable—when the right direction has
been found—only after long and patient waiting,
as a kind of crown of adeptship in the Brotherhood.
Those who are acquainted with its mystery by
the same lawful participation as that of my own
therein are bound equally with myself, but the
reticence which makes every indication of its
place, its title and period, together with its
historical environment, a high counsel of honour
does not, in a study like the present, forbid all
allusion to its philosophical side.

If the Rite has any analogy among the curious
things of the outside world of Masonry, it is inevitably with the so-called RITE OF SWEDENBORG,

but it is a comparison of things great with things small, and, even on this understanding, the analogy is not substantial. Speaking now of its purpose and term, it exists chiefly for the most profound interpretation and mystically enlightened comprehension of the Craft Grades, and, so far as it succeeds within its own measure and horizon, it is entitled to be regarded as the *ne plus ultra* of the Craft ; it does not reduce the High Grades ; it does not interfere with any of them ; it recognises and presupposes some ; but it arises entirely from the Craft, to the extent that I shall present it here. I could not speak certainly, if I wished even, regarding its place of origin, though there is a notion to which I lean. I have seen it mentioned loosely within the limits of several dates, and taking a mean between those, I should allocate it approximately to the year 1783, or if anything rather later. There are names which could be cited in connection with it which would astonish many brethren, especially in France, who have followed the quest of the High Grades prior to the Revolution in that country, more particularly on the mystical side.

The Rite claims to contain the mysteries of Ancient and Primitive Masonry, and it communicates in secret instructions a certain doctrine of the soul. It is therefore, above all, of our subject, and whether it proves in the result to be an expression of Divine Truth attained through that first-hand experience which is called manual by the mystical alchemists, or whether it is perhaps suggestive only, and perhaps only fantastic, the consanguinity of its purpose with the long exposition of my own seems not only to justify an adequate account of its content but in a sense even to demand it. There is an Orient from on high which in fine rises upon the soul ; it may not be in any sense the term of all research, but it is the indefectible portent thereof and the light wherein is accomplished the passage of the signs of faith into the signs of vision. If the secret Grade reflects anything of this morning light it deserves well at our hands ; it has at least the uplifted dignity ; and if we cannot earn our titles to the high thrones, we can dream by its aid of their holy state until something of their *grande manière* enters into our lonely hearts.

Herein the veil of the Temple is not rent but lifted, that there may be no impediments between the *auditorium* of the sanctuary and the light of the Holy Place. As I have intimated, there is no ceremonial, there is no symbolism, there is no dramatic part : all things have dissolved, and the meaning within the Craft is exhibited in the terms of a particular mystical philosophy, which is an adaptation and an extension in some respects of that which was in vogue at the period in certain centres. This philosophy—in one of its late aspects—was put forward anonymously in 1782, and there is no doubt that it made an instantaneous appeal to the spiritual aspirations out of which all that was good and true and serious in High Grade Masonry originated. It is said by an enemy—as we saw some time ago—to have become a kind of gospel, and the statement is substantially true. It was the antidote of the moment to all that had come out of the *Encyclopædia* and to the spirit which the *Encyclopædia* represented. The author was Saint-Martin, who had no hand in the Grades ; the book was *Des Erreurs et de la Vérité,* and its supplement—*Le Tableau Naturel.*

The interpretation begins at once from the root-matter of the subject, and although we shall see at the term of this summary that, in view of later and deeper knowledge of the mystic end, there is much which calls for re-expression, I shall reserve all criticism for the present and adhere to the simple texts, using only such additional lights as are available at those sources which are in approximate relation therewith. The first Grade opens therefore with a statement concerning the perfect primitive knowledge of spiritual man. It will be seen in this way that we are concerned not with the emergence of our race from the animal state through the dark region of original savagery, but with another form of development. The eighteenth century knew nothing of evolution as it is understood in the kingdom of this world, but it was familiar with the deep consideration of the great story of the soul, in its passage through the outward path and thereafter on its return to the centre. Evolution for this story is not outward but within. The soul came forth from God, and this is the story of its extragression, or evolution in the averse sense ; but the soul goes back to God, and this is the high story of its reparation, when it is reintegrated and belongs once more, by the assumption of consciousness, to that of which it was at the beginning. The history of what is called the prevarication—or more commonly the Fall—of man has never been told adequately even in admitted literature of the Secret Doctrine. It belongs to a withdrawn stage of the direct experience, and though I hope, with the blessing of God, to testify concerning it from the apocalyptic Patmos of the soul when I get to the end of my quest, the time is not yet, nor is a place found anywise in the Secret Tradition of Freemasonry. I render to the individual sanctuaries that which belongs to those sanctuaries, and I reserve for the Palace of the Holy One that which sustains all things.

The perfect spiritual knowledge follows from the hypothetical state which anteceded human experience on the external plane, and this state was one of essential consanguinity with divine, spiritual beings—when there was knowledge of all things in God. If we are to regard this as a rigorous expression of truth in the terms of experience, I suppose that it must refer to a condition in correspondence with the Briatic world of Kabalism, which is that of high, holy and glorious intelligences, from the Living Creatures

that are about the throne of God to the souls of
men as they came forth in a state of justice.   The
Secret Doctrine of Israel on this subject is an
involved development which is either at variance
with itself or has never been harmonised by the
scholiasts.   A much more manageable reflection
of eclectic tradition is found in the hierarchies of
Dionysius, but he is silent regarding the pre-
existence of the human soul.

However this may be—and speaking of course
ex hypothesi—that soul prevaricated.   A charge
was imposed upon it, between which and the
familiar symbolism of the Fall of Man there
seems to be scarcely a root of correspondence, or,
if there is, it is concealed so deeply that I should
not be warranted in seeking for it in this place.
It lies further back in the legend of the soul than
the calamity of Eden—we know not how far, God
help us, but between that immemorial epoch and
the unrealisable state which is predicated before
creation, before all that lies behind the imperfect
dreams of emanation, when there was neither soul,
nor spirit, nor angel, but the unmanifest Deity
dwelling in His limitless light.

Once more, the soul prevaricated, and the state
of its privation followed.   Man, who was to have
restored the universe—much after the same manner
as in the system of Martines de Pasqually—by
the salvage of that wreck which came about
when the Temple of Universal Mysteries was
riven by the event shadowed forth in the Fall

of the angels—this being, this Archetypal Man, was himself immersed in the wreckage, or, in other words, as a consequence of conceiving the desire of material fruits, he passed into the material. We shall see in another section, apart from these Grades, that the Secret Doctrine involves a mystery of sex—in which mystery is the Key of all things and also the point of contact with Edenic lore. This change of location would have meant that all his previous knowledge must have ceased to subsist in man, except for an intervention by Divine Providence which was part of the scheme of Redemption, and hence it is said in the Grade that there were means by which the primal knowledge was resuscitated and transmitted.

This is the legend that prevails everywhere, either on the surface of theosophical tradition or lying behind its veils. It is met with by hint or allusion in the most unlikely places. For example, it is that precious stone in the crown of Lucifer which was brought from the empyrean region after the rebellion of the angel and was enshrined on Mont Salvatch, where it was called the Holy Graal. It should be understood, therefore, that it is not of necessity a Kabalistic legend exclusively, though, I think, it was through this channel that it entered into the philosophical and perhaps, as we have just seen, even the romantic literature of Europe. It is very possible that the story of the stone is a reflection far off from the Jewish Academies of Southern France. The root-matter of the Kabalistic tradition we are acquainted with already ; that tradition was, according to its claim, the secret wisdom committed by Moses to certain elders and transmitted from these. The story takes another form in the Grades which we are considering ; as such it may be embedded somewhere in the *Zohar*, but is more probably Talmudic : I do not remember its source. The primeval knowledge, says the Grade, was handed down by Noah unveiled, but subsequently a veil was put upon it. There may be remembered in this connection the story of the so-called pillars of Seth on which was inscribed a memorial of the knowledge before the Flood. It is old in Jewish fable, and as it is certainly at the root of much occult symbolism concerning pillars, so it has perhaps some analogy with similar symbolism in Masonry. Moreover, that which is transmitted regarding Seth is in close analogy with the present legend of Noah ; both are variants of the supposed Adamite wisdom, and the two later names simply mark the line of succession. The veil which was subsequently put upon the knowledge transmitted by Noah is said, by the instruction of the Grade, to have been that of emblems, the inference being that it was Masonic, and it was out of this system of representation that initiating rites originated. There are other Mysteries which describe the Ark of the Deluge as carrying the typological elements of the old initiations, as if that which was saved from the primeval world was the wreckage of its symbolism, for according to this view the secret knowledge—which descended *ex hypothesi* from the first father—was as much veiled before the deluge as it was subsequently. If it were worth while to debate such a question, the condition of human affairs which brought about the judgment of that catastrophe does not consort with the idea of high knowledge unveiled.

In every case the witness with which we are concerned says that there was one science imbedded behind the palms, pomegranates and other vestures of primeval and early typology ; but the forms which it assumed were infinite. With time these forms suffered alteration, in which the idea of corruption inheres, and it was after this manner that idolatry arose. Through all the changes and growing abuses, the true initiation, however, remained, and that which it taught was the dual doctrine of immortality and the existence of God. This was the theoretical part, but there was also a part of practice, which included the means of participating in the action of powers charged with operating in this universe on behalf of man. The vicegerents of the Eternal Word may be that which is indicated here, to illustrate an additional sense of the scriptural utterance : He hath given His angels charge over thee. Be this as it may—for there is no clear statement in the text —another time came when the true initiation itself was contaminated by the opening of the averse and evil gates, and a part of it lapsed into the region of óccult phenomena, or into relations with secondary natures. This notwithstanding, the elect did not utterly depart from the earth. An ineffable power was decreed to preserve the true worship, and this, it is said, will yet restore the alliance between God and man—namely, the covenant of union.

It is in such manner that the particular election of Israel—which is indispensable to the Masonic scheme—is brought into the general providence of God's dealings with the world. In somewhat conventional language, the Grade says that Jewry was deputed to practise the acceptable worship, one reason being no doubt that this people belonged to the true legitimacy and were regarded as at the root of primeval initiation. The old notion that the Greater Mysteries were somehow enshrined in the world about the Delta of the Nile is not entirely overlooked, but it is said that the science of Moses was really super-Egyptian. As regards the building of the Temple and all that depends in symbolism therefrom, the mysterious plans were received by David; Solomon, by the instructions which they contained, conceived the edifice in his heart before it was born on earth ; and in due time he communicated so much of the design as he deemed requisite to the craftsmen, from which it would seem to follow that he who is known in Masonry as the architect *par excellence* had no hand in the production of the designs. It will save recurrence to an important point of detail if I say at once that this inference is quite opposite to Masonic tradition, and fatal to the proper interpretation of its peculiar symbolism, though there is no difficulty regarding the source of the conception, and, as might be expected, it is that of Kabalism.

Here, as elsewhere, however, the work in all its proportions was an allegorical work. After Solomon departed from wisdom, the initiates abandoned his court and went into other countries, where they spread the Mysteries of the Temple among different nations. Still the symbolic science was always found in Israel, and especially among the race of Judah—that is to say, external to the priestly caste. It follows herefrom that, by the hypothesis of the Grade, the Temple of Solomon was a House of Secret Doctrine, but this House and its later substitute remained when the doctrine itself had withdrawn either into other realms or amongst those who did not minister at the altar. The intention is not, however, to imply any common folly with reference to the craft of Priesthood, but rather to shew tacitly that the stewards of the outer Mysteries are not usually charged with the wardenship of the Mysteries within ; it is as if there were a priesthood within the priesthood, sometimes in the absence of all knowledge on the part of the external ecclesiastical polity. The analogy is found in Masonry, within which there are other secret and high orders, of which it has heard nothing—even at a distance.

The Mysteries on their Mystical Side

After the destruction of the First Temple, the system of initiation was re-established in Jerusalem by Zerubbabel, but the science again degenerated —though it was probably at best a mere shadow of its former self; the Second Temple was destroyed even to its foundations—which was not *ex hypothesi* the case with that of Solomon ; and the reason of this calamity was that the Universal Restorer and Master of all Science had been rejected of his people. What follows should be noted, as it is the whole thesis of transmission within the limits of a sentence. The Grade says that, this notwithstanding, the science continued to be cultivated by certain sages, who preserved in secret the initiatory system of the Temple. It was embodied apparently in the Mysteries of early Christianity ; but in any case this initiation, established, as it is said, by Moses—though it had obviously an antecedent history—and thereafter perfected by Solomon, is that which has come down to us under the name of Freemasonry. The hypothesis has been of universal mode and also utility ; we have met with it already under a slight adaptation as the particular claim of certain Grades of chivalry.

As such, Freemasonry represents figuratively that which Christianity imparts—I conclude— actually, directly and by experience in the Mystery of Faith. But Masonry became vulgarised ; its custodians took refuge in silence ; there was therefore no witness concerning its more hidden and deeper part, or concerning the sense of its allegories. The Grade, however, imparts what it calls the secret, namely, that the spirit of life must be sought elsewhere than in matter ; it is only by raising man above material works that temples can be built which shall be held worthy of God.

There is more in this intimation than may appear on the surface, though there it is of all truth, a little reduced by familiarity. I believe that behind it there was the notion concerning a real place of search and a mode of quest thereafter, because, in the most unexpected manner, the discourse leaps to a condemnation of physical Alchemy as proof positive concerning the folly of its pretended adepts. Not in this region, it is said, is the fruit proper to man ; such a labour cannot be united with the profession of the divine and spiritual sciences, where those who seek the spirit of life must turn the footsteps of the heart.

So ends the first Degree of this secret Masonic initiation, and it is affirmed at the close that the instructions were designed by the founders to introduce those who were received to the true object of the ancient grades of adeptship. I may. say at this point that the Rite is entirely anonymous, and is one of those systems which were referred to the hand of certain Unknown Superiors intervening in Masonry. The instructions particular to the Second Degree of the mastery are longer and proportionately more important than those of the first, but they are naturally a development of these, and may be said to proceed therefrom without break or intermission. I shall give them as before in a simple and summary fashion ; but it must be understood that there are certain omissions, as part of the interpretation deals with the official secrets of the Craft Grades and cannot therefore be printed.

The Instituted Mysteries are a consequence of the Fall of man, who was originally intended for the contemplation of unveiled truth. When he forfeited this prerogative the veils were woven, but according to the hypothesis of all the Mysteries there was a narrow way open by which man could go back upon his calamity and recover that which was his. This possibility explains the assumed existence in all times of a little company of the elect, among whom primitive truth was preserved, by whom also the veils were emblazoned and the system of initiation was established, to indicate and discover to prepared minds the only road which can lead man to his first condition and so restore the rights which so long have been lost to the world. Thus it comes about that the high destiny of our race and its degradation are the ground of all the Instituted Mysteries, and these are the quest thereof, terminated in certain cases by an attainment in the sense of symbolism.

The infinite alone can satisfy ; in its absence from his heart and his consciousness, man is no longer in his place. The science which was perpetuated by the ancient sages was of an order far superior to that of any natural sciences ; at once to know and neglect this mysterious and sacred knowledge would be a crime, supposing that it were possible, but it was and it remains hidden from those who would despise, even as from those who might abuse it. From the beginning of initiation it was presented under emblems and hieroglyphics, that it might not be exposed to disdain. I infer that the reference here is to the disdain of sense and the flesh. The incapacity of the ordinary man is by reason of the deep wells of his enchantment ; it is not the overt contumacy or opposition of the will, but its sheer inability till it is awakened.

Freemasonry, as already intimated, came from that initiation of which the scheme of Temple building is the symbolic vesture and evasion. It was divided into two classes, the first of which was preparatory and communicated the various allegories that make up the three Craft Degrees. The second was secret and unknown, and therein the meaning behind the allegories was imparted. At a later period an intermediate class was devised, and this may be described as a system of successive degrees, the intention of which was to enlighten and yet restrain or reserve. Here, as elsewhere, the interest of this interpretation is not its historical verisimilitude but its comparatively early attempt to read in.

The Mysteries on their Mystical Side

The centre of all symbolism is said to be the Temple of Solomon, which offered a real type of an universal and cosmic mystery ; it formed a catholic emblem, and the plans were of no human invention. As indicated in the previous Grade, they were given to David by a superior hand. The history of the universe was interwritten therein ; they represented, in fact, the great temple of the universe, and as with this macrocosmic temple, so also was it with the material edifice of Jerusalem. Both were conceived in the Divine Thought, but both were executed by secondary agents. Hence it follows that there was what is termed by the Grade an "occasional cause" of the universe, which cause was once known by man, as it should and may yet be known. There were actually several secondary causes charged with the decrees of the Creator. These agents lost for a time the perfect possession of unity—apparently by the necessity of their mission, though they enjoyed it through their love and obedience. It is presumably in this sense that, according to the cryptic language of the Grade, the universe was produced and is maintained by violence. This condition must endure until Divine Justice is accomplished and the guilty are reintegrated by the law of the Eternal Unity. Behind this mystery of the agents there is, however, a deeper mystery, and this also accounts more intelligibly for that law of violence already mentioned. In a veiled and moderated form, apart from all that is absolute, it is the old doctrine of dualism ; there are two causes opposed unceasingly ; one is in the bosom of the Creator and one in degradation, from which it must follow that there was a prior epoch when the second of these was in an original state of purity. As the two are diverse in virtue so are they also in power, and that which has fallen from the exalted and perfect mode is unable to penetrate the pure essence of spiritual beings. It has thus been cast out of the centre and is void of effect when it opposes that law by which it was once constituted. The opposition and the warfare endure, all notwithstanding, but the duration of the struggle is fixed and the cause of disorder will be enchained in fine. We may not find in the sequel that there is here any better explanation of the mysteries of sin and misery than was offered so long ago by the religion and philosophy of Zarathustra, but this system, while it reduces the tension of a clear and equal alternative, has the difficulty of additional complexities. It is said that the universe is foreign to the Eternal Unity— though it might be more properly called its illustration. So long as it remains, however, the universe is sanctified by the agents concerned in its maintenance. Among intelligent beings, man only exhibits the immediate action of the Eternal. He, as a particular unity, is in similitude with the unity that is Divine. All this is symbolised in the construction of the Temple of Jerusalem. The Grand Architect did not Himself build the universal Temple, nor did Solomon that of Jerusalem. Both were fashioned in six days or symbolic periods of time, and after this was a Sabbath, which—in the case of the microcosmic work—represented the dedication of the edifice. As the material Temple was destroyed, so ultimately will be that which it typifies, namely, the universal Temple.

In a sense we have dealt so far more especially with cosmic philosophy, but as the Sabbath was made for man, and as it was for him that the House of God was built and dedicated at Jerusalem, so also in so far as his consciousness can possess the universe it is for him that it has come into being ; for him its messages exist, to him do its forces communicate, and Masonry which is, *ex hypothesi*, a type or summary of the correspondences between God, man and the universe, with vital reference to man as the middle term of the triad ; Masonry, I say, would be wanting in life and efficacy if all its symbolism and all its meaning did not ultimately have its root in him—in his history, his antecedents and his destiny.

After what manner we do not know, for it is *a priori* to be expected that the things which issue in mystery should also commence therein, the mission of primeval man was to have directed those agents which were commissioned in the work of creation. His sin came about from a desire to make use of that power as if he were the author of his own action, whereas he was the mediator therein. As a result of this, he became flesh and died intellectually. Had he remained in his first estate, he would have been an efficient means for the reconciliation and return to the Eternal Unity of all adherents to the principle of evil. The reintegration is now delayed, though the external voices are crying, as they have done from the beginning—all willing rebellion notwithstanding —How long, O Lord, how long ? In his glorious condition, man had immediate communication with the Creator, and all the Instituted Mysteries embody a memorial of this time and state. The intellectual death which supervened upon his crime was the passage into passivity of his thinking and intellectual being. There was no operation of fatality herein, for it was man who exiled himself from the centre of purity and happiness. It came therefore to this, that he who was meant to be the universal agent of reconciliation stood now in need of a Reconciler, and there was one at the gate of misdeed from the first beginning thereof. It was immediately after the crime that the Repairer—Who is Christ—came to manifest his interior action upon the guilty in the Universal Temple.

The Temple of Solomon represented man's original and incorruptible body ; that of Zerubbabel his imperfect, physical body. The first was an oblong square, and it corresponded also to the four regions of the universe. We have in this manner a triplicity, and here are its further analogies : (*a*) The Universal Temple and its threefold division—terrestrial, celestial, super-celestial, *i.e.*, the firmament ; (*b*) the Temple of Solomon and thereof also the threefold division—Porch, Inner Temple and Sanctuary ; (*c*) the Body of Man, which in respect of his trunk is triadic in like manner—abdomen, breast and head. But further, the triad obtains in the mystical history of man, or of the immortal spirit in the external and manifested state. There is (*a*) his archetypal condition when he was clothed in a robe of glory, like that of the First Temple : but this was destroyed ; (*b*) his second estate, when he was clothed in the body of his humiliation and with the vestures of loss, typifying the Second Temple : but this was also destroyed ; (*c*) the state of his impenitence, when he rejects Christ, whether by a collective and national act, like that of the Jews when they crucified the Lord of Mediation, or by a personal rejection in the case of each one of us who sins mortally. This is the loss of the Sacred Word, which Masonry seeks to restore in its highest Grades, that he who was once sent from the Sanctuary to the Porch may return from the Porch to the Sanctuary.

The things which lie *perdu* are not calculated to exercise a considerable influence unless it be from beneath the surface and in secret, like themselves. Apart therefore from any question of its essential merits, it may seem that I have given almost an undue space to this curious construction of the Craft Grades in respect of their inward meaning. But I might even have carried it further, for it proceeds subsequently to the consideration of certain High Grades which arise in the particular system and, as I have said, *ex hypothesi*, from the Craft. Their supplementary matter is not essential to my purpose, and it could not be included here without betraying some part at least of the source, which it is my intention and my pledge to conceal. I have spared no pains to present the explanation adequately, but though I regard it as exceedingly remarkable and important in its own degree and for its own period, it is not adduced here as an exalted grade of interpretation which cannot be exceeded. It is so much the best of its kind that it is, as I have also said, almost without comparison, and it assuredly represents a tradition which has come down to us from the middle way of the eighteenth century, while it has memories or derivatives of things that are much older. It recalls the theosophical hypotheses which connect with the name of Saint-Martin, and its vague glimpses of a shrouded practical part do also recall the strange dream of occult workings which was cloaked under the name of Masonry by the Sieur de Pasqually. As it reflects something at the beginning from the *Traité de la Réintégration des Êtres,* so in the development it suggests that here

L. C. DE SAINT-MARTIN

is indeed the missing sequel of that memorable work ; but the whole is uplifted to a higher and more luminous plane. From the internal evidence, I tend to think that it issued from the school of Lyons and represented as such a mean in philosophy and literature between Pasqually and the great mystic who was his disciple.

There is no question indeed that, regarded as a philosophical rather than as a Masonic system, it is out of this reservoir that the Grades came. I speak of a single reservoir, because Saint-Martin took over the philosophical matter of his teacher, in the sense that he developed much out of it, but did not set anything aside which will seem appreciable to those who contrast *Des Erreurs et de la Vérité* or *Le Tableau Naturel* with the tract which is the work of Pasqually. The hand of neither mystic nor magus is to be traced in the Masonic Rituals, and I question whether they would either have subscribed fully to the instructions contained therein. Saint-Martin assuredly would have disassociated himself from any formal attempt to philosophise upon Masonry, regarded as a tradition descending almost intact from the far past, and from the important place which is thus assigned to Masonry in any catholic scheme of spiritual amelioration. There is no trace anywhere in his public or private writings to lend the least colour to such a notion, or to the concern that it would imply ; there is also the least possible suggestion of his dependence anywhere on tradition ; he might not have denied the tradition or even its perpetuation in some form, though probably amidst much contamination, but he would, I think, have held that it had long ceased to communicate anything vitally. This was his position in respect of the Church of his childhood, which above all represents tradition after its own kind. Apart from any personal claims, he comes before us in the light of an immediate recipient, or, in more commonly acceptable terms, of one who thought out for himself and did not derive from the past that which he has put into expression after a manner so largely new. The fact that he has a debt to Pasqually would scarcely in his understanding have been a debt to the past, for he always regarded his master as one in the enjoyment of immediate communications. Whatever claims that master made upon the past himself would have counted for little with his disciple.

And now as regards Pasqually, the catechisms attached to the Grades of his own Rite shew indubitably that the construction placed upon Masonry by this other Rite with which I am here dealing, would have commanded anything rather than his unreserved sympathy. He comes before us more especially as an Adept of occult science, and would have been the last to concur in the judgment passed on that science, as, for example, the strictures on physical Alchemy. Our Secret Grades are therefore the work of an unknown hand, which borrowed in part from the theurgic Mason and in part from sources like those of the mystic. The explanation of the latter point must be sought in the immense repute and consideration in which *Des Erreurs et de la Vérité* was held far and wide in all the Rites and under all the Masonic obediences of that period in France ; in a more restricted sense, but still indubitably, the same may be said for Germany. It is this—as we have seen —which accounts for the time-honoured, idle fiction which connects Saint-Martin with the reformation of a Masonic Rite. All the reputed authorities in France—and others in all places who reflect from these—have spoken of this reformation, the result of which no one has seen any more than they have seen the Rituals attributed to Ramsay. The truth is that Saint-Martin became, apart from all design of his own, a fashion, an influence, a school on the more spiritual side of High Grade Masonry ; his seal is in this manner on many Grades, but there is no Rite of Saint-Martin ; so also the seal of Ramsay is on all the Grades of Chivalry, but the RITE OF RAMSAY is a matter of romantic invention.

Those who read over my summary of the Secret Grades, if they happen to be versed in the claims and legends of other Masonic systems, will be reminded of several things. The departure of the initiates from Solomon when he fell away from the law of Israel is a hypothesis brought in to justify pretensions like those of Baron Tschoudy, as developed in *L'Étoile Flamboyante*, and all that is implied in Werner's strange story concerning the Sons of the Valley. I do not mean that the myth was invented to support either specific claim, but to justify the position of Christian High Grade Masonry it seems to have been held necessary, on all sides, to shew that a Secret Tradition resident in ancient Jewry was passed on to the time of Christ and was perpetuated thereafter, usually in Palestine, until the period of the Crusades, when it began to move westward. Our Grades do not particularise the place to which the initiates repaired, and they therefore leave open the chivalric connections of Masonry, though I think that this is practically implied in the later statement that so-called Masonic tradition was preserved by certain sages who carried on the initiatory system of the Temple. The reference is probably to Thebaid solitaries, the Essenes, or the so-called Knights of the Morning and of Palestine.

And now, moving towards the conclusion of this part, the instruction with which I have been dealing is infinitely better than the cumbrous, artificial and laboured pretence of that RITE OF SWEDENBORG with which—in respect of it—I have made a tentative and reserved comparison, which is also so unlike anything that is historically connected with the name of the Swedish seer. The moral explanation of Masonry is deficient enough, but the purely astronomical is the forbidding phantom of a wasted journey, as if we

had travelled through ages from the circum-
ference to the centre only to find thereat the cruel
derision of a vacant space. It is also so much
the worse, because it is the wresting into all
confusion of a high truth. The day which
speaks to the day, the night that shews knowledge
to the night, the stars which send tidings to one
another, and the Sons of God who utter their
joyful shouts, do assuredly discourse unto earth of
the great things of the soul and do shew forth
the soul's history. Our own legend is written
across the starry heavens, and this is the essential,
the vital, the religious side of astronomy ; it is
for this reason also that " the undevout astronomer
is mad " ; but those who, in the common adage,
put the cart before the horse, who say that the
mysteries, the mythologies and the faiths of the
whole world are only the symbolic presentation
of the path of stars, shall inherit the confusion
into which they lead others, and when they are
looking for honour shall be drawn like the Knight
Gawain in a chariot of derision rather than abide
in the holy and adventurous place of the Graal
Castle. The results of early prolonged research
and deep contemplation in vigil beneath the
heaven of stars and the heaven of sunshine, may
have passed into secret doctrine ; but that was a
doctrine of religion, a book of destiny, full of
living messages, and in the workings of the
celestial bodies man communed with his soul.

I should be sorry if my readers were to infer

265

that I put forward the interpretation of the Grades as an adequate construction of Masonry in its higher message to the mind, or as representing the Secret Tradition as it stood in the hidden Sanctuaries towards the end of the eighteenth century. It is not less far from the term in both respects than it is as a convincing or even a tolerable attempt to set forth on warrants that are unknown the almost unknowable mystery of the Fall of Man. The machinery which it employs notwithstanding, it leaves the root difficulty as Saint-Martin, Pasqually and other theosophers leave it—that is to say, in so much the worse position as it is enlarged upon so much the more. The conception concerning Adam and Eve in the Garden of Eden and in a state of virgin innocence, apart from all knowledge and experience, offers no difficulty to the episode of their temptation and their lapse ; man in a higher Eden, charged with universal powers, with duties also universal, and in enjoyment of the Divine Vision, offers us a picture with which it is impossible to connect the idea of temptation or desire for lesser things than those which he possessed in fulness. Still, amidst all its limitations and all its crudities, amidst its implied attempts to justify High Grade legends, which are taken in the wrong sense when they are taken in that of history, I shall always regard this curious Rite of Interpretation as the work of one of my precursors, and I say this the more certainly because the thesis of the present work was already developed when the Grades came into my hands. That which they put forward differs radically from my own construction save in one vital respect; both depend upon the doctrine that man came forth from the centre and that he returns thereto.

V

Reflections from High Grade Masonry to Modern Occult Research

THE subject-matter of this section will come so much as a surprise to its readers, within and without Masonry, that perhaps it may be prudent if I qualify it in some manner at the inception. My thesis is that what is called the occult movement at the present day, but rather on its philosophical, intellectual and literary side, has an unrealised debt to High Grade Masonry. The concerns and outcomes of Masonic research and quest have reflected into it ; the reflection has been real of its kind, but in a sense it has been also fortuitous. The source of illustration has been the occult and transcendental side of Masonry, or that in particular ; it has also been the more general set of feelings, aspirations, horizon and content ; all these have contributed, sometimes in a substantial way and sometimes in the constitution of an atmosphere. They are capable of enumeration broadly and in a few words. If we take the schools which for a period were incorporated in Masonry at the close of the eighteenth century, my view is that it was largely in virtue of the place which they thus held that they came to be factors when the occult interest rose up again in Europe. On the purely philosophical and to some extent the mystical side, there has been the influence of Martinism which came down through Masonic channels. On a side that was in part one of the practical kind, but in part also specu-lative, there was the influence of Rosicrucianism, and this again has been derived through another Masonic channel; there is also at least one Rosicrucian School in existence at the present day which is purely Masonic in its form. It is thus that there arises the question whether through Masonry there has been any perpetuation of the Secret Tradition into a few of the current schools, and whether they are transformations or renewals of Masonic, Semi–Masonic or other in-corporations existing prior to the beginning of the nineteenth century. We have already considered the question of modern Martinism, and have reached a decided negative in this respect. As re-gards the others, by the hypothesis of their respec-tive claims, they draw from the past, and therein is the authority which they have sought to establish. It proves, however, on examination to be almost exclusively an authority residing in certain litera-tures of the past, for most of them are products of the last thirty years. They are of Magic, of Alchemy, of Kabalism, of the phenomenal side of things in the world called transcendental, and of all the curious arts. Prior to the year 1850 their literary centre was, roughly speaking, in the Masonic writings of J. M. Ragon, from whom in a sense they passed over to Éliphas Lévi, who was the champion and interpreter of the whole circle which circumscribed these fluidic sciences. I do not intend to suggest that the personalities in either case were encyclopædic in respect of their representation, but they stand for a starting-point, and as throughout the history of the movement France has been always more especially concerned, we are in a position to see from what directions occultism was derived to France, and through France not only to England and America, but in a measure also to Germany.

The theurgic school founded by Martines de Pasqually under the ægis of Masonry was perpetuated by his survivors, such as the priest Fournié, the merchant Willermoz and the Comte d' Hauterive, not only through the French Revolution but well after the year 1800, even to the time when the sun of Napoleon set at Waterloo. We have seen that Pasqually's disciple Saint-Martin, far as he departed from the path pursued by his first teacher, carried something of his lights and reflections, and that his influence in no sense died when he himself departed this life in 1805. We have seen also that, his theurgic preoccupations notwithstanding, Martines de Pasqually moved in an atmosphere of mysticism and leaned towards the mystic term on the side of thought. It was this side of his master that Saint-Martin did not leave when he surrendered the external ways to follow the inward light. At the present day, apart from incorporated Martinism, he is still an important factor in the modern interest and movement.

Rosicrucian preoccupations in France, England and America, considered on their more public side, are inferentially and almost certainly the reflections of the Reformation which took place in that fraternity about 1777 within the Masonic circle. We can trace these influences, in England at least, by three independent classes of documentary evidence, which bring the subject practically to our own day. There are incorporated societies passing under the name both in France and America : but the latter may be set aside as embodying the common ingenuities of occult adventure ; and of the former, one of them has its foundation in simple, literary phantasia, while another is rather an association established for experimental research of a particular and curious kind, having little recourse to tradition and no claim thereon. These have been dealt with already.

In Alchemy I need only mention the Alchemical Society of France, a foundation of recent years and purely on the side of physics, without any intimation concerning the mystic aspects; its most approximate antecedents are Pernety and his Masonic industries; he is also, on the literary side, one of its chief authorities.

These intimations will already have determined sufficiently the question whether the modern schools existing on the surface of things have any root in the Secret Tradition, whether or not through Masonry as a channel. The predisposition, the concern, the perpetuation on the literary side, and on the side of fact in history, are reflections from the High Grades and the circle of activity of which these were the outcome in their day, but there is nothing more. It is substantial enough, however, in its own way to have called for this brief record.

There is, however, a further point which concerns the Secret Tradition in its general sense rather than as it is embodied in Masonry, and I must take out a certain licence to speak of it in the present place so as to complete my sketch of the modern schools regarded in the light of Masonry. The overt schools are one thing; we know their laws and bylaws; we know their conditions of membership; we know what they have done; we might almost say with Matthew Arnold that, as concerns the particular world in which they live and move and have their being, " their voices are in all men's ears." We are not all Martinists, nor Kabalists of the Rose-Cross, nor artists of the salons of Sâr Péladan; but we know or may learn everything that is of importance about them ; they have nothing to tell us but in respect of their own findings. There remain, however, by the hypothesis the really secret schools, the proceedings of which are not published, the names of which are unknown, of which some of us have heard the rumour, to some of which we can testify in part. We will suppose that they are difficult of entrance, that they exact pledges and so forth, like Masonry. Is there any reason to suppose that the derivations of these is through any form of Masonry ? With perhaps one exception, about which we shall hear later, the answer is again no ; but again there is a certain reflection, as of kinship in concern and research.

It is in the direction of these schools, and there only, that—if anywhere—we must look for the vestiges of Secret Tradition ; the intimations concerning them, as they existed originally, are found in the old books, and there are other ways by which we may become tolerably satisfied as to the fact of their existence, though if the question were whether any living occult writer—not as such a mystic—has been affiliated thereto, the answer would be almost certainly an unreserved negative again. The tradition which is so strangely divided in respect of the occult and the mystic in philosophy, experience, science— whatever it may be termed—is divided as utterly in respect of the schools, the Rites and all that is understood as the instituted side of their Mysteries. We are about to approach at the term of our debate the mystic side of tradition, and I seek to take out of the way the occult aspect because it intervenes as a hindrance. It will be understood that this aspect looms largely in the conventions that are most current in respect of the Secret Tradition ; it has offered proportionate opportunity to the makers of occult history which belongs to the order of imposition —sometimes in the conscious sense and sometimes otherwise. It is also the source of false evidence appealed to in American claims, with their derivatives and analogues.

The question arises whether, on the hypothesis of occult schools now persisting in concealment, there is evidence within their own lines that they have carried their subjects further than these have been taken by the inchoate mass of the past literatures. There is of course no evidence, but it might seem a little idle to dispute the unadorned possibility that an Hermetic Society perpetuated from generation to generation should not have attained a further point in its especial objects than is marked by the old books of two or three centuries ago, or by the independent gropings of unaffiliated students at this day. Whether they may have reached any goal of their research is a very different question : personally I neither know nor care, for I scarcely think that spirits by the throne of God could be more indifferent to the issues of occult research than I who—in my glass and darkly—have seen the true end of all adept-ship. To continue the detached speculation, another occult association engaged, solely or chiefly, in the reading of the stars, and in keeping the records of results, ought to have some strange archives and rectified calculations which would be the desire of the eyes of astrologers living under less happy auspices in this dawn of the twentieth century. In fine, a magical order, following the path of evocation, and other mysteries of iniquity usually grouped under the title of ceremonial work, must in long periods of time have opened worlds of hallucination, whirlpools of vertigo and slopes of the great abyss which none of our sanatoria and none of our amateur temples dedicated to formulæ of the most truly accursed arts have ever reached in a dream.

I do not say that such societies have existed in the unbroken sense which is posited for the arbitrary benefit of this argument ; I do not think that they have been corporate except in the most fluidic sense. I think that the gods of Julian the Apostate would have looked more substantial in comparison if the two cohorts could be assembled together. In any case, association of this kind is usually sporadic, and I do not believe that there is anything which can count further back than two hundred years in respect of consecutive working. Moreover, it is of all most likely that some have perpetuated without extending a traditional practice belonging to their especial concerns. I should be false to everything that I hold most sacred if I lent one moment's countenance to the old futile dream concerning the occult sanctuaries. The *vel sanctum invenit, vel sanctum facit* of Éliphas Lévi was never true, either as condition or consequence of adeptship in the practical path, and I should not understand holiness if I spoke otherwise than with derision of such asylums, taverns or temples under the elect, dedicated, divine name of sanctuaries. I do not believe that they have kept anything from the world of which it stands in need. I doubt, if their greatest secret were sold for thirty thalers, whether it would be worth the price ; there is not *per se* one word or syllable, one letter or mark of a letter, in the literature of occult arts, occult sciences, or occult philosophy which was ever put upon paper with the consciousness of God present in the soul. It is a place of the marriage of many cousins together, such as folly and imposture, stupidity and diabolism, idleness and evil-doing. But these bracketings do not exceed a commonplace in the high regions of debate, though to the innocent and beloved beings whose elementary psychic gifts, yearnings for the powers of the spirit, ambition for a new basis of belief in immortality and intimations of a demonstrative faith, have brought them to the threshold of occultism, or even within the precincts, they are likely to be novel as they are entirely certain to be unwelcome. It happens very often that the anxiety to meet with some one who can speak with authority on these subjects, who has the atmosphere of the dubious temple and the terminology of the oracles which pass in such quarters for the liturgy of the chancel of adeptship—all this, and all its circumambient nimbus, eats up the heart of such people, and a sudden disillusion might make them of any men most miserable. They are often so good and so trusting, that if I had nothing to indicate in respect of a more excellent way, I might shrink from the incivility of unveiling.

For their further consolation let me add that the limits of my criticism are, as they should assuredly be, drawn with sufficient rigidity that nothing is included which represents the honourable region of research. Within the charmed circle are the occult orders and all appertaining thereto, their artificial revivals in books, the preternatural seriousness belonging to the subject at large, the occasional imposture and the vain pretence. It is a strange combination, and round about it stands the curious and uninstructed world that goes after these things, while in another category—than which nothing can be more distinct—is the great, practical, exact science of the mystics, the schools of which are reducible in the last resource to a single school, existing for its better protection under veils of evasion that are not likely to be penetrated because they are certain to mislead research. Though in a certain sense there is no part of it which is not of the gods, the veilings are like the cinctures of a mummy which has not been unrolled.

As regards any official school of psychic research, I must confess that it is saved by the intention rather than by performance accomplished ; but there are notable exceptions, if it were possible to enumerate them in this place. I have no intention, however, to create distinctions which in a sense might be almost invidious, because they cannot be inclusive. Moreover, in directions which are least commendable, I have found something, and even much, to redeem or at least to reduce censure—obscure intimations, predispositions, a setting of the face towards Jerusalem, however far from the term may the obvious trend have seemed. It would be therefore cruelty and falsehood to say that the whole effort is always wasted.

·It must of course remain that the horizon of the occult sciences in the present rebirth of those sciences is exactly what it appears in the past ; that which it was in the beginning it now is, and that it shall ever be ; it is not possible that it should pass beyond its proper measures. If it were sought to say one word in favour of the schools which are embodied within the horizon, this could be only in reference to the old idleness —already mentioned—concerning demonstrative faith. The expression is of course grounded on a misconception of terms. The demonstration of faith is by the passage of its subject-matter into the grade of experience, through the following of the inward life—understood as that of sanctity. The certitude which then dawns in the soul is generically better, higher, deeper than anything that can be obtained in the outer ways. Hence Christ said : Blessed are those who have not seen and have believed,—appealing to the sacredness and the intimacy of the inward knowledge.

It is, however, so ingrained in human nature to desire the lesser certitudes, which reside in the sensible signs, that something must be granted to their ministry. The clairvoyance, the spirit vision, the putative travellings therein, even ceremonial invocations and other dangerous paths, are on the fringe of that proof palpable of immortality, a solution as to the problem of which is ever desired and for ever unattainable in the outer ways. Even I and others of my school must confess to such hauntings at the beginning of our quest, before we had come to know of that more excellent way to which all the memorials of mystic life bear witness. We can therefore understand very readily how they draw the untutored hearts, and we can be merciful to the mistaken aspirations : did such paths lead to the root of knowledge, then indeed *ludus puerorum*, an easy task, would have been put into our hands.

No one, of course, will question that there is a secondary and derivative satisfaction all along the line of occult research and all along its modern variants. In both, and in the latter especially, those whom the shipwreck of faith have cast upon the reefs and deserts of materialism have very often obtained a tentative and dubious consolation when face to face with certain facts which materialism cannot explain. But the psychic experiences which some forms of occultism do thus offer to those who pursue their paths, work in a vicious circle. Furthermore, if we contrast the claims of the old occult schools—by which I mean those that appear in the literature and not the glorified expositions that, in the absence of all evidence, have been put forward by some of their spokesmen—usually self-constituted—if we contrast these claims with the natural development of natural psychic faculties, apart from all initiations and practically apart from training, we shall find nothing in the magical records which offers a wider experience. The Rituals of Magic are coarse and stupid impostures overlaid upon the common ground of psychic experience, and they are the substitution of a laborious for a simple process. I want it to be understood that this statement is without qualification or reserve and, as I have sought to explain elsewhere with the utmost fulness, that the prevailing distinction between White and Black Magic is stultified at every turn on both sides of the texts which it is thus sought to separate.

As regards the superiority of the process on either side, the claim of Ceremonial Magic is that (*a*) the preparation of the Operator ; (*b*) the ceremonial workings; (*c*) the litanies, symbols, suffumigations; (*d*) the prayers, conjurations and compelling forces of Divine Names, do in the last resource produce a response in the world of spirits ; but, after we have separated the elements of tolerable consistency from the masses of monstrous absurdity, there remains—the condition of procedure excepted—nothing more than will rest over equally in spiritualism, when the mass of its impostures is set aside. The particular and distinctive condition on which I have just laid stress is that Magic is the work of the active and modern psychic phenomena are generically of the passive way.

When the head and crown of all practical occultism is disposed of in this manner, I infer that it will be idle to dwell upon the analogies, the differences, or the comparative superiorities of the modern modes of inducing clairvoyance and the old forms of divination, the intimated but dubious results in the past of ceremonial and magical procedure for the induction of skrying in the crystal and our present simple mode, which at the same time produces its particular secrets in suitable subjects with almost fatal facility.

VI

A Preliminary Excursus concerning the Divine Quest

It must be understood that the section which here follows is in one sense another digression, because on the surface it will seem to have no real connection with the Masonic subject; but on the assumption that emblematic Freemasonry enters into the Secret Tradition, and as that Tradition is mystic in the sense that I attach to the expression—is concerned, that is to say, with the integration of human in Divine consciousness —it is necessary that some sketch or summary of the mystic preoccupation in Christian times should go before an attempt to give expression to the term of research which is implied, though not followed, in Masonry. It is obvious that if the Brotherhood were at this day consciously dedicated to that term, many things would be intelligible that are now in the high clouds, and this book would have been written in a very different key. As it is, many precautions are needed to insure understanding.

There is a very true sense in which the glories of the Christian centuries are the glory of all the world which is about us at the present day, in which all that we are, and all wherein we live and move and have our being, is our high inheritance therefrom. We are in it and we are of it, and it is so much our very selves that in so far as it has entered into expression through twenty centuries its expression is our consciousness as it is realised ; while so far as it is implied, one may think, and not unreasonably, that the great world of its intimations is that world outside our consciousness into which consciousness may yet enter. We are in this manner the inheritors of a fulfilled but also of an " unfulfilled renown," and just as it has been said by some experts that Egypt seems to loom more grandly as one penetrates further back into the mystery of life in the Delta, so outside the actualities and realisations of the expounded secret in Christ there shines the greater splendour of the suggested secrets looming in the hidden fields. It is as if external and explicated Christianity were of the microcosmic order, specific, determined and limited like our human personality, while without it, yet not indeed without—beyond, but too intimate and immanent to be called beyond indeed—there were a greater analogical macro-cosmic part, united indissolubly in the heights with the cosmic altitudes of universal religion, and also with our own cosmic side—too vast, too infinite, too holy to be contained by anything which seems to contain its minima. It is the oversoul of religion ; it is that which subtends and extends over all formulæ of creed and dogma, all normal rules of life and sanctity of prescribed observance ; it is that which is outside the law but does not reduce the law ; it is the power behind the Church and the grace behind the Mass and the authority above the priesthood, intervening only to exalt, but to dispense or cancel never. It is the sense of the infinite behind the great mysteries, as that sense awakens in those who belong—at their best—to the infinite. I put on record so much concerning it—in opening this part of the conference — that I may not in the higher tribunals be sent down as one who goes about with unopened eyes when there are vistas prolonged for ever ; but my concern is in lesser realms.

There is also a very true sense in which the modern world, taken as it is, and all its things as they are, is the last resultant of the Christian centuries which lie behind us. But Christendom is then only like an Immediate Past Master in the great Lodge of humanity, with a long line of other Past Masters behind it, dating from the founders of the Lodge ; and however we may seek to affirm it with the grand accent and manner, the statement is only a commonplace, and I am not elected to take part therein.

If, however, our attention is fixed on the religion which is understood by Christianity and, under that aspect alone, if we consider our inheritance from its past, I suppose that there are many points from which it might be lawfully approached, because the variety of concerns is boundless. There is one of these which more especially and greatly and fully connects with that higher side of the mystery of Christendom about which I began by speaking ; there is no other which to myself is possible by comparison therewith, and for the reason just cited ; it is that which for me of necessity is therefore my point of starting ; and when I speak of our inheritance from the past, I refer, above all and only, to that which the Christian mystics of all the ages have bequeathed to our trust. In the great body of doctrine, formulæ, processes, experience—all things whatsoever—which may call to be included in surveying the Secret Tradition of Christian Times, that which I understand—that, indeed, which can be understood only by mysticism— forms a very small part on the surface, though it is the essence and permeation of whatsoever is best, whatsoever indeed is tolerable therein. I propose to consider it in this section apart from all its subsidiary and extrinsic connections, and I shall do so under two aspects—speaking first of that which is open, at the disposition of the wide world, and after of that which arises out of it, issues into secret ways and is lost—or rather goes before us—upon great seas. We cannot understand the Secret Tradition apart from its font or root, because this Tradition is either concerned with the Great Work or else with its adjuncts, its travesties and its wrestings.

I do not propose to discuss the implicits of Christian Mysticism in the holy gospels, or the question whether the roots of the whole subject are to be found therein. I think that the cosmic mystery of Christ was native to the great sanctuary —was conceived and born therein. I am entirely certain that the virginal conception was—so to speak—the first ceremonial act in that great mystery ; that the three Kings of the East beheld His star and came to adore Him, bringing their symbolical offerings ; that He questioned the doctors in the Temple, as one who would remake all things ; and that the other scenes of the drama were enacted literally and mystically, actually and essentially on the plane of the Divine Master's consciousness and by reflection on the plane of this world. But this is no place to present, as I should need, in its fulness the Secret Tradition in Universal Mysticism ; such a task belongs to the term of my research and not to the present intermediate grade. I must take rather the life mystic at one of its early stages of development, and we have a natural point of departure in the *Mystical Theology* of Dionysius. The inward life which is of Christ, and is in Christ, is found in this treatise—so minute and yet so pregnant—as an essence of undiscovered power and grace, but it is in a setting which is largely Neo-Platonic, and it is more especially this fact which enables us to see with some tolerable accuracy how it stood with the higher minds of that momentous period, *circa* 100 A.D. or later.

It is a thesis for the doctorate of the union with that and with Him which is exalted above all essence and above every notion of the mind; it is the counsel of the soul's precipitation into the mysterious brilliance of the Divine Obscurity, the path of which is a path of unknowing rather than a path of knowledge, while the term is an union on the highest side of our nature in proportion to the renunciation of knowledge. The casting out of the images of matter is therefore followed by an expulsion of the images of the mind, and the last image that is destroyed, or sent forth rather, like the emissary goat of Israel, is that of the personal self. The reward is an acquaintance, an experience, a familiarity, an inexpressible intimacy which cannot be grasped by understanding; in a word, it is a modal change in knowledge, because it is henceforth of the substance and intrinsic, not of the external and phenomenal, elements.

I think that Dionysius carried over a great deal of baggage and admixture from many hier- archies of philosophical reverie and systems of theosophical complexion. It is perhaps only here and there that we make contact with the life-giving font of experience ; and even the Theology itself is foreshortened in almost every direction towards which we should have liked it to be extended. There are, of course, certain respects in which it is definite enough, but the definite does not assist us ; it is rather like a shorthand note, a *précis*, or mere summary ; in a word—it is the heads of an instruction ; it either presupposes the experience of which it sets out to treat, or it leaves the attainment to the reader, as if referring him thereto for all that it passes unsaid. But the suggestion remains, and can scarcely, I think, be put away, that Dionysius saw many great things looming on the horizon of the logical under-standing in regions which he had not entered ; perhaps it would be too much to suppose that in the dawn of the Christian sun there should be the full light of its meridian. To my own mind the *Mystical Theology* is rather an illustration of the horizon and genius which are particular to the apostolic age, that had neither expelled the images of Jewry nor those of Plotinus and the successors ; which had also other shackles—chiefly in the middle way between the Oriental and the Greek ; they were curious and interesting enough ; they were full of the gradations of fantasy and allure-ments of that kind ; but they did not make directly for the end. I speak, however, under the reserves of all my proper imperfections, and these may stand to be illustrated for the purposes of some minds by such a leap as I now make to the ninth century and to that great and hardly formulated figure of Johannes Scotus Erigena—of whom many of us have heard so much and all know so little. He carried mighty harness and rode in great lists ; he set up his theses at all gates and against all comers. It is only their least part that can be said to concern us now, and indeed he connects with our subject more especially as a translator of Dionysius into the Latin tongue. He had his own lights on the hierarchies, and in some sense he may be said to have remade his original, so much was Dionysius extended by his own system, but we are not seeking assistance on the intermediaries between man and God. He had other illuminations on mystical theology, and this is why he is worth naming at the living moment who is great by so many titles. It is to him above all that we owe the conception of God as the principle of *essentia* and life within the universe. As it is usual, but on a very slight basis, to identify Dionysius with pantheism as a fruit of emanation, so—and on the basis of the conception here stated—Erigena Johannes, or Scotus, is held to have formulated —as we have seen—the doctrine of Divine Immanence in substitution thereof. The practical effect of his teaching is that in virtue of the descent of the Divine Influence through all hierarchic grades there is an ascent of the soul possible, even as in higher Kabalism the path outward from *Kether* to *Malkuth* involves a return journey.

It is in this manner, and by an allusion at need only, that I pass to the Doctor Angelicus, and there should be reason to hope that he who scheduled all things must have laid out under his own lights and motives—if not under all lights—all highest motives—that part of the science of sanctity which is called the science of the mystics. And, in truth, he who omitted nothing could not have set aside or ignored the thing most needful. But if I must speak my whole mind, I think that the Angel of the Schools knew all the body of spiritual desire rather than the soul of the mystics. He reminds one rather of Athanasius Kircher, the Jesuit, writing the *Iter Extaticum* than of Juan dell Croce when he reached in a plenary sense the summit of Mount Carmel. The great Latin *littérateur* of the seventeenth century made an adventurous journey through a like distance of the mind, and returned with a budget of marvels which marked a definite stage of reasonable speculation—for his period—concerning the interplanetary spaces and the moving lights. The Spanish saint desired to be counted among those who had walked with God ; he came in the heights to his own and his own received him, and he spoke of the great things as one who had unmistakeably passed through experience therein. It is only on the way upward that he delivered some things *pro bono publico*, a few of which do not signify. Saint Thomas also travelled, though it was in another sense, through a mental distance, but I question whether he directly entered the great mystery. In other words, while he marks a real stage in the development of the whole subject, while he had an ultimate rational understanding of the relation between God and man, that which in him was rational was also scholastic understanding, having the advantages and limitations thereof; he speaks of the wonderful depths and breathless heights as one who knew them scientifically, as one who had drawn them to scale, but scarcely as one who had travelled them; he contemplates them with an intent eye, but not as one who has realised in an intimate sense that their whole world is within.

I may scarcely call it a limitation in a mind so responsive rather to things on their universal side, but the characteristic at least seems always in evidence. It is there even when he is expounding after what manner we are to understand that the kingdom of heaven is within and that God is regnant there; when he is expounding that perfection which consists in the love of God above all things and in all things; when he is putting into formal expression some profound philosophy of prayer; when he is speaking of solitude as an instrument of contemplation and the environment for the life of recollection; when he is making great distinctions on the rule of meditative attention; when he is describing mortal sin as the total abstraction of the mind from God Who is our end ; or when he is discoursing with St. Bonaventure, his contemporary. It has all the apprehension, but of the realisation at the centre little.

It is about the time of St. Thomas, and for a considerable period after, that the literature, the priceless records, of the mystic life begin to be around us on every side. I know nothing of what —if indeed anything—was produced under the obedience of the Greek Rite during all the centuries that followed the division of East and West ; I could not say a word here concerning it, supposing that I knew intimately ; I can give no details even of the western evolution ; and if I mention a few names it is merely as a direction of research on the part of my own readers, who must follow it as they best can, if they do not know already. The names are familiar enough ; I have mentioned them continually enough in my other writings, and have summarised as occasion offered the specific phases of the subject which they represent after their proper manner. Those phases are different indeed ; I suppose that there is no contrast which can be called more distinct in its way than that which stands out in their respective writings between St. Bernard and St. Bonaventure—the one an apostle of the ascetic rule of life, the other a doctor in ecstasy. Behind and about them both there stood the schools of the past and of their period, in which they were unconsciously steeped, though Bonaventure has

ST. THOMAS AQUINAS

vestiges of Hermetic readings to which the other was a complete stranger. I should not say that they were learned in the great body of scholasticism, but each might pass as such in correspondence with a name that is much greater than either—I mean the Admirable Ruysbrœck, for whom schools and academies might have scarcely existed, seeing that he found all things in the inward study of the Scriptures, and lights unseen on sea or land by any external eye in the Mass-Book and Breviary. At this day he is like all the great masters whom God has sent for our salvation; he is little but a dead letter to the non-understanding mind, and in proportion as the mind which does understand, and see with its own eyes, under the medium of its own light, so does it draw the records into the degree of its proper consciousness, and they are born anew. When it is a high degree, there is a new heaven of knowledge created from the old elements. It is for this reason and in this sense that everything calls for re-expression in the great world of mystic thought; it is only on this assumption that it becomes ours.

I think that Ruysbrœck may be taken to stand for another epoch in Christian mysticism; he is so utterly of himself and he owes for this reason so little to the things that preceded him; at his greatest he is so great, that he is marked off naturally; he is also the spirit in conformity with what had come to be regarded as the legitimate witness of the faith ; thereafter, under many modes, followed that other spirit which began to try new ways and to make for itself vestments which, though not intentionally after a new pattern, were variations from the ceremonial canons. I am not suggesting a perfection in the one or a quality of defection in the other. For whatever the fact is worth, as the soul of the Church came to be more and more overlaid with the body of formalism, as doctrine in the course of its development lost more and more the sense of its own symbolism, as the soul of this world took up its dwelling in the House of God, the marriage between the life of the Church and the mystic life became more and more itself a convention and a veil. What has been called the anti-papal spirit which preceded the thing called Reformation by derision was in respect of the mystics neither direct nor conscious protest against anything but the loss of life in grace ; it was indeed scarcely conscious on any side and in any sense, but the things which by essence had ceased to belong to one another remained in outward conformity by the help of external links only, or more especially. If we take such a tract as the English *Cloud of Unknowing*, belonging to the fifteenth century, which in itself is a very high, noble and deep consideration of the soul, and how it is transmuted in the most inward fixity of thought, there is no question that on the surface it conforms to all that

seemed requisite in the councils of prudence for
the period ; yet is there nothing more essentially
independent of all official and external churches
and their institutes. There is not throughout its
length more than a single reference to the sacramental ministries or to the exalted offices which
obtain in the ways without. That which is called
the "statutes and ordinances of Holy Church" are
not indeed to be abrogated, yet are those who
have authority in the cure of souls placed side
by side with others that are secretly inspired by
the special motion of the Holy Ghost in perfect
charity. We see in this manner—but more
especially in an hundred ways, which are in proportion the more eloquent as they are also the
more tacit—that in essence the most secret school,
the anonymous and other doctors of the inward
life, were drawing by the path of slow and unrealised detachment down ways which long since
the Church, as an institution, had ceased to travel.
That school in truth was never the spirit that
denies, it was never that which denounces ; I
suppose that it saw in its heart, and the more that
it saw clearly the less did it feel the weight of the
welded bonds. They lay indeed so lightly that
the soul in the secret ways arose untrammelled,
free through the blue distance of unbounded being,
using perhaps, I should think, all old words in
a new sense, repeating perhaps more often the
name of Jesus as the redeeming office in those
who had known redemption fell away in their

flight towards God ; testifying to the Christ
nature as all distinctions of nature melted in the
unified light of God ; preserving in fine the forms
of doctrine when the grace within the forms
had broken up all the vessels. It is conceivable
enough that men like him who wrote *The Cloud
of Unknowing*, being steeped in wells of experience
beyond all fields of language, were unconscious
that the old measures had ceased to contain what
he was, even as he may have been also, perhaps,
unconscious that he spoke—in so far as he did
speak—the tongue of all anterior theosophy.

It was a testimony throughout to the experience which lies beyond doctrine, and the quality of
the veils which are parted could not for such souls
signify. If we pass through the night of reformation, we therefore find the same quality of testimony borne by St. John of the Cross, St. Teresa,
Jean d'Avila, how many, on the one side, and—
subject to their especial limitations—by Fenelon,
by Molinos, by Madame Guyon, on another. But
the first triad held fast by the old tradition and
the old forms in the ark of safe terminology ;
while the second, never dreaming that they had
done it, made all the intermediaries void, cancelled
the church and its offices, and leaped direct toward
the union.

I am exercising no power of judgment, nor
even creating any canon of distinction ; I am
seeking in a few words merely to open the
horizon, knowing that ultimately it must cover

not only the West but the East, and that some day, after yet other travels, I shall marry the East and West in the unity of their one mysticism. That which we have to realise for the purpose of the present concern is that something very near to our hands has testified through all the Christian centuries to a veridic and catholic root-fact discovered by all indifferently in the deep paths of contemplation. It matters to me nothing at the moment that all Platonism stood behind Diony-sius, or the East behind all Platonism ; it is of no consequence that Bonaventure drew from Hermetic books ; I do not seek to inquire what Molinos derived from Dionysius. The point is, that from the days of Apostolic Christianity the true men have, in the words of Saint-Martin, spoken the same language, for they have lived in the same country. They have all returned to tell us the same story. It is the story of the religion which has been always in the world and which St. Augustine identified with Christianity, though it anteceded Christian times. It is the story of the doctrine which is always secret, because it depends upon experience and is only realised therein. It is not represented by anything that is now under-stood as dogma, deriving as it does from a single thesis only—that God is and that He recompenses those who seek Him out. He recom-penses those who seek Him in the public ways of devotion and observance, for which reason the church is the ark of salvation to every wayfaring man. But beyond this gate and way there is the secret path which opens to the elect, and through which the elect go down along the endless vistas of the Divine, for ever realised and for ever transcending. "I bear the Divine within me to the Divine in the universe," is the categorical definition of the state of eternal beatitude.

It should be clear in this simple description that what I have termed, in virtue of a very high warrant, the secret mystic doctrine, may be said to have two parts—a theory and a practice. The theory is triple in its expression : (1) that God is ; (2) that He recompenses ; (3) those who seek Him out. The practice was the mode and way of the Quest, as to which there was complete unanimity : it was the secret of going inward and entering the abysses of contemplation, with a fixity of consecrated will in the act of its utter surrender. Expressed after another manner, the theory or doctrine was that of Unity, and the practice was that of the Union. Having spoken of the will as the sum total of personality, and of its surrender as an act extending more deeply than can be realised in any common action of conformity, it should, I think, be understood how and why it has been always symbolised by the notion of death—represented macrocosmically by the death of the Master-Builder. Those mysteries of the past and present which I have been accustomed to call instituted, because they were and are artificial and ceremonial memorials, projected on the external plane as testimonies and sometimes as drag-nets, are mysteries of symbolical death, of the death called mystical, and they stand for that experience which is a mystery after another and real manner—the mystery of release by the suspension of the sensitive life. The word release is, however, a keynote, and signifies that after the first act of blessed death in the Lord there was a second, which is connoted by the term resurrection, also symbolised in the pageant of many moving ceremonials ; but in the experience there is such a merging and interpenetration that of the one it can scarcely be said that it ends definitely, or of the other that it has a beginning realised in consciousness. Looking through my own glass darkly, it seems to me that in recovering subsequently under the reflected light of the logical understanding there is an impression of coincidence at an indeterminate point, and this is the point when individual consciousness begins to shine in the Union.

It should be understood that this state is not brought about by the practice of active contemplation, which is the last hindrance that the soul in its quest must set aside. It is the passive direction of "a certain naked intent unto God," having abstracted all qualities. As far as may be possible to the mind, the distinction between subject and object has itself passed away, because union is in the inward nature and suffers no distinction between the thinker and that which is thought, between desire and its term, or, in a word, between the soul and God. All images are therefore cast out, however exalted, and what follows by the hypothesis is realisation, possession, intimacy, oneness ; it is the consciousness of the wholeness of the Divine Nature within us and of us in the Divine Nature. But it will be seen that this description is inevitably the antithesis of the state, expounding it by its admitted opposites and establishing division where it is intended to declare union. The force of language cannot reach thereto, and its essence is therefore sacrificial. We can only say in our imperfection that the union is the union, that those who have attained it, in such fulness as is here and now possible, have partaken of the Blessed Life and of the reintegration which is the sum of all desire. They know that the traditional Fall of man has not cast him off utterly from the Crown and the End of the Kingdom ; that he can again belong to his own and his own to himself ; that a complete spiritual certitude is possible in this life ; and that there is one way in which every desire and longing and thirst and hunger and aspiration can be swallowed up in possession.

We can trace this exotic practice through all Christian times, and by so much as the state attained was the more transcending, by so much also is the testimony as to what was experienced the more wanting. It will seem at first sight that it was known in the churches only, but there are vestiges of other schools which it is certain were Christian also, but were not exactly of the churches, though they were assuredly not of the sects and had no stake in the heresies. I have defined the nature of the Secret Doctrine which inhered in the practice under the orthodox ægis, and in the adyta of the other ways there was, I think, the records of the great illumination per- petuated in symbolism, so that in a sense they were schools of inheritance. In the *Hidden Church of the Holy Graal* I have tried to shew that the most momentous evidences are in the books of Spiritual Alchemy, and the suggestion is that within the sacred sanctuaries of this school, wheresoever they may have been set up, there was more derived to the consciousness of the logical understanding, and hence to the veiled records, than was done in the purely personal and, so to speak, unaided methods of the Christian mystics, who worked in cells and hermitages. This is, however, an intimation only, and the evidence to offer regarding any superiority in attainment is one of particular inference.

There is further no evidence that it was ever and anywhere in the West other than an attain- ment in Christ, Who was held to have opened the door to the heights of sanctity, even as the door to those who are redeemed in the lower degrees. I am not concerned here with anything beyond the bare facts, but it calls for record in connection with my opening words. Some day, under the

Divine Providence, should this only continue to watch over me in the way of my dedications, I hope to determine the relation of the personal Christ to what, I suppose, has been called the cosmic Christ-conception.

I have now dealt sufficiently for my purpose with the mystic object and fruition as it comes before us in what is the open way of its memorials, in the annals of Christian sanctity. It stands apart from all questions of dogma ; it neither added nor reduced anything ; no doubt for all practical purposes it depended on its implicits and on its explicated part, but it desired and reached out into another region. To set aside once and for all any predispositions with which I may be credited personally, I must, as an act of sincerity, acknowledge that the communion and union were of the kind which suggests that the Son had already given up the Kingdom to the Father and that all distinction of Persons had been merged in the unity of God. As an old author tells us, the work is in itself "the high wisdom of the Godhead, gracious and descending into man's, knitting and uniting it to God Himself, in ghostly prudence of spirit."

I have spoken so far of the open ways chiefly, and as to those that were secret there are such testimonies as a rational rule of interpretation can and does derive from Spiritual Alchemy, of which sufficient has been said previously ; from Kabalism, but of this also I have spoken ; and, as it seems to me, more expressly and intelligibly than all—at least to the untrained mind—in that which is the latest of all—that reflection of the old Instituted Mysteries which appears on the surface of Masonry, and in the things that lie behind it—of one of which we have still to learn.

We can put aside, as we have seen, the testimony and claims which have been made by the modern schools, whether occult or thinly mystic ; they are the reflections of the past, but they are not the perpetuation of Secret Doctrine, even on its negligible side. They bear precisely the same relation to the Divine Tradition that is borne by Occult and Hermetic Masonry. The sense of them all lies between the covers of certain books written by him who is called " the modern magician "—I mean, Éliphas Lévi. Like him, they are " false in sentiment and fictitious in story." That which remains among us as a real testimony from the past is the true and real Symbolical Masonry and its successors, lawfully begotten, in the High Grades. It is in this manner that there arises the question as to the term of research in Masonry, when the latter is regarded under the light of this declaration. The answer to this question will shew that the present section is a proper introduction to the next.

VII

INTIMATIONS OF THE TERM OF RESEARCH

AMIDST our many preoccupations, and under our many inhibitions, the great things seem lost or interned deeply ; they are hidden indeed until the consciousness within us is awakened. The awakening comes about in many ways, and among these there is the quickening reflection of the great things in symbols. Hereof is the light of Masonry, which recalls us to the old experience—that experience which, from my standpoint, has been always in the world, which is implied in the official doctrines of the great religions but is attained by a direct process in the holy places where the Secret Tradition is reserved. We are now in the last stage of our journey, and what is perhaps the most arduous task of all remains for our performance, since it is time to say something more especially of this subject.

We have seen that the High Grades which

are referable to the Ancient Alliance and its symbolic period neither can nor, for the most part, pretend to complete that mystery, some preface of which is shadowed forth in the Craft Degrees. Those that are anterior to the time of the Craft Legend are either concerned with details or with the circumstances under which the secrets of Masonry, amidst many vicissitudes, are stated to have been preserved. Those which are subsequent to that period are either Grades of vengeance —as if the judgment indicated in the Craft were not itself sufficient—containing no symbolical meaning of importance, though they suggest the root-matter of an intention which afterwards became for a moment almost manifestly political ; or they are things of imputed completion which testify for the most part to their own vacancy. We have seen that in certain Secret Grades of interpretation a great symbolical importance is attached to the dedication of the First Temple, and we have seen also that the one Ritual which gives some account of this ceremony is negligible from all points of view. It is the first obvious lacuna in the Masonic subject and a great opportunity lost. I pass over here all that had been missed' previously in respect of the Holy Lodge ; but as there was something thus wanting at the beginning, so there is a deficiency afterwards in respect of the Second Temple, for the *Royal Arch* represents only a vestige of that design. I have expressed with sufficient fulness my views regarding the symbolical position of this Degree, which is at once so important and yet falls so short of several reasonable expectations. It is a kind of half-way house in symbolism, presupposing a house before and a greater house to come after. There follows the great cohort of the Christian Grades, and I have selected some among these for . more extended consideration as possessing within their own measure very high and persuasive claims. They are one and all, however, in the present position of the Latin Church, for they have lost the art of building ; I mean that all notion of the Third House of Doctrine passes out of their horizon, and that the Temple of Christ is never built in the Rituals, though there is here and there a reference to an erection in the heart. The thesis taken up by the Christian Grades which count for anything is that of the Lost Word, and its restoration is shewn in Christ. This restoration should have discovered the true building plans, which were also lost, and then the Mystic House could and should have been erected in one catholic and glorious Grade. In place of this we have Rites concerned with the guarding of the Sepulchre, Rites of the perpetuation of doctrine through Orders of Chivalry, and a hundred other mysteries which are interventions of new symbolism, leaving the original, canonical types and allegories unfinished.

Let us now consider briefly, but from another point of view, what it is that we really attain by the Christian restoration in respect of the Lost Word.   I will deal in the first place with certain rumours concerning our present Grades in Jewry, if I may so describe them.   For what his evidence is worth, Kenneth Mackenzie, who in his time came across many strange things, has affirmed that the Craft once contained the true Word, and I am not only sure that in his own mind he meant a word leading up to a synonym of Christ, but that he was thinking, and perhaps with more knowledge than ours, of other rumours which have affirmed that the original Craft Grades embodying Christian elements were once extant, and were afterwards held in concealment, as they may be to this day.

I desire, however, to make it plain that, whatever importance we may attach to these intimations, it is necessary to exercise care lest we should draw a fallacious inference therefrom. The deeper the meaning behind the Craft-symbolism, and the more our construction of it may lead us to see that mystic Christianity lay at the root thereof, the more certain I am that it was never intended in the allegory to suggest a manifestation of Christ out of due season in Israel. I believe, therefore, that any Christian elements which may once have existed in the Craft Grades were not of their essence and were probably in the same position as the numerous traces of the New Testament that are found in the High Grades belonging to the Ancient Alliance.

If we could suppose for a moment that in the Great Legend of the Craft we were dealing with an historical event, my thesis would be that the House of Doctrine which, according to that Legend, it was intended to build in Israel, would have been, under the most favourable circumstances, and if apart from any catastrophe, a house of many veilings. The externalisation signified by any manifest House of Doctrine must always intimate a veiling, but the one with which we are concerned was finished in the letter and not in the Spirit, because, by the hypothesis of the story, the true artist was removed. Among the few messages which count for value in two or three High Grades concerned with the period prior to the Craft Legend, there is a statement that the last secrets would have been communicated after the completion of the building, but the scheme fell through and the mystery was interned with the Master. This is, of course, an evasion, and one which sets forth by a contrast the scheme which obtains in the Craft, as shewn by the intervention of the memorable event, which scheme was to reserve during the whole period of the old covenant that which would be manifested by the new, while indicating that the Mystery of Christ was always imbedded in Jewish Secret Doctrine.

Let us now consider for a moment one manner in which it was so imbedded and the things that follow therefrom. If we take it at the best and highest, it remains that when *Tetragrammaton* is parted in the middle way by the holy letter *Shin*, we have the answer of Christian Masonry and Christianised Kabalism to the world-wide loss of Jewry, as echoed in *Talmud* and *Gemara* and *Midrash* through the ages and ages. And the Master-Builder rises as Christ, the Lord of Glory. Now these things, on the surface, are opportunities for the exercise of faith or for the recognition of analogies between tradition and doctrine. It must not be said that their appeal *per se* to the logical understanding is stronger on the surface than the analogous appeals which the Divine Science of Theology has made to us through the Christian centuries. We have passed, or some of us, through too many initiations to be overmuch persuaded by that wonderful orthographical coincidence of a word and a letter, though they speak eloquently to the imagination, which is ever expecting miracles at any corner of the streets of thought. We also, knowing that nothing so great as the *Grade Écossais of St. Andrew*, the *Grade of Rose-Croix* on its inward side, and the *Grade of Heredom of Kilwinning*, has been brought into Masonry, must confess that we are moved strongly by such a resurrection as I have intimated. But the great story of old is not rendered greater by the new mythical variant. The purpose which it serves is not therefore one of persuasion along the external lines, but it constitutes a very clear illustration of something which lies behind the

The Secret Tradition in Freemasonry

Secret Tradition in Christian Times. In other words, it is an intimation that for this tradition the Christ-idea was always in the world. But if we are dealing here only with doctrine perpetuated in the hidden holy places, it would remain an intellectual concern, having no further appeal. We have therefore to see whether behind that doctrine there lay also a secret mode of experience, and with this object we will follow the question of tradition a few moments further.

There are three mystical events which represent epochs in the traditional history of the Word made manifest : (1) When the two tables of stone were "written by the finger of God," or as it is said more expressly : "and the tables were the work of God, and the writing was the writing of God, graven upon the tables." But what befell them was that Moses "cast the tables out of his hands, and broke them beneath the mount." (2) When the Word was in the hands of three or less stewards, but on account of a memorable event was so definitely lost that its recovery in the terms of the symbolism seems to lie between the hands of chance, destiny, or the providence which is veiled by these, and, in place of the pure light, the soul of man walks in the dubious obscurity of a half-light only. (3) When "the Word was made flesh and dwelt among us"; when "we beheld His glory, the glory as of the only-begotten of the Father"; when "He came unto His own and His own received Him" not; when He said,

"It is finished"; when He "gave up the ghost"; and when, in fine, the Word was removed by ascent to the Father. Now the unity of these epochs is in the resultant term of each, and this is that the Word was withdrawn. It follows that Christendom, like all Israel and all Masonry, is in search of that Word. The thesis is that it is hidden in the Secret Doctrine.

Let us take yet another step forward : there is a holy tradition in Israel, and it relates—as we know—how the great mystery which lies behind the Law and the Prophets was preserved among certain elders, who were the *co-hæredes* of Moses, by whom also it was transmitted. There is further a tradition in Masonry that certain memorials, connected with the passing of the Master, were instituted as analogies of the things that were removed, while it is otherwise suggested that they did not die with him, but remained thereafter among the secrets of the King. There is, again, a pregnant statement bearing on the return of Christ to the Father, namely, that He being lifted up shall draw all things after Him. There is also another statement, which says that He goes to prepare a place for them that follow Him. And the additional evidences are many of the same thing. The first path is that of the Secret Doctrine, and this same is a Doctrine of Experience ; the second is a path of search and expectation, which is followed by studying the Mysteries of Nature and Science, these being properly understood as Hidden Nature and Hidden Grace ; but the same things do also appertain to the Secret Doctrine, and as Grace is termed Science, I understand that here also is a path of experience. But the third path is categorically and without evasion described as the Imitation of Christ, about which it is said : " Him that cometh unto me I will in no wise cast out." This, therefore, is, in fine, a path of experience, the conditions, modes and particulars of which appertain to the Secret Tradition in Christian Times. And the motto of this tradition is : " Come and see."

I put forward, therefore, my new thesis—that the records of these epochs are testimonies to a doctrine and practice which have been in the world from time immemorial, and have been shadowed forth in many ways, under many veils. There are also other epochs which constitute further testimonies to the same thing, because that thing is everywhere.

And now, speaking once on authority which is not of my making as one who holds certain keys belonging to the house of interpretation— speaking rather as one who has dwelt under the shadow of the Secret Tradition and reflects the authority thereof—I proceed to give expression for the first time in public to its root-matter, so far as the past is concerned which lies behind Masonry. Readers of my former books and of these pages will remember that I have quoted more than once those last words of Plotinus when he said that he would bear the Divine within him to the Divine in the universe. The point with which I am here concerned is that expression—the Divine in the universe. It is not my proposal to pronounce on Plotinus himself in respect of his intention ; but it is observable that, for reasons of his own, he did not speak of union at the centre, or of the infinite abysses of Deity which lie behind manifestation and all relations therewith. Once more, it was the Divine in the universe. We may fitly connect with this statement the old theological doctrine concerning the distinction of Scotus Erigena between the Divine immanence and the Divine transcendence. God is immanent in creation or Nature, and it is for this reason that the whole universe constitutes a great sacrament, of which man is receiving daily ; but he does not for the most part know that it is a sacrament, and for the most part he has not been taught—or at least has not learned—how to receive it worthily. He has failed therefore to attain, except intellectually, and then even rarely, the consciousness of God's immanence in Nature—much less His presence in the soul. On this understanding I suppose that it will be realised with all readiness how remote in respect of consciousness is God's transcendence. It might be concluded that it is an intellectual concept only, after the mode of hypothesis. And yet a little thought at first hand will tell us that in respect of ourselves there can be no dividing line, and that the limitation is in fact in ourselves, so that many arbitrary barriers and lines that divide are raised up to separate us from the untrodden grounds of the human soul. The Holy Catholic Church has indeed intervened for our assistance, and, whether designedly or not in respect of its own high distinction as above expressed, it has given us the instituted sacraments —as channels for the communication of the noumenal grace, the grace transcendent, the grace from the deep abysses, being things superadded to the grace which is immanent in Nature. Now, these things remain with their implications as symbols only till they are taken to the inmost heart, and it is assumed concerning them that they are great in the shadows of our consciousness as they would be great in its light ; but that light is not yet. Those who have trodden the higher paths of sanctity have left strange rumours behind them, so that in our dubious manner we seem to see from far away how it might be, could we only on our part confess to other measures than those of daily life. The great secrets would then be declared in the soul which are now only implied therein ; but the fact that they are implied is shewn by another comprehensive and consoling fact—that no secret of any sanctuary which has ever been announced in the world has come to the prepared of the world otherwise than as an old truth suddenly remembered. It will be the same with the truth which concerns us here and now, for we can possess all things by intellectual conception, though we may not as yet by realisation.

The immanence of the Divine in the universe, as the term itself implies, is the concealment of the Divine in the universe. God hides Himself from all search which we make after Him in Nature, because Nature is a veil, and it is of the essence of a veil to conceal. When, according to the exalted symbolism of revealed doctrine, the Word of God became flesh and *ex mysterii hypothesi* the *Deitatis abyssus* gave up that which otherwise it is said never to yield, namely, a form, the veil in some respects is indicated as the deepest of all, since it is said that the manifestation was in " a man of sorrows and acquainted with infirmity," in one who was apart from all " sightliness, that we should be desirous of him." It was only in the Word of the mouth and the glorious contagion of the life thereto belonging that the Divine Nature was declared for a brief period, in virtue of which It spake as never man spake. And in this connection it should be suggested that when Christ returned in the glory of the *corpus supernaturale*, in the body of the resurrection—that is to say, when the sacraments of the natural world were interpenetrated by the sacramentalism of another and more exalted order —even in the most symbolic and extra-literal of all the Gospel records the most truly Divine speech recorded of Him, is that *Pax vobiscum* which is the formula of the Grades of Peace in the world of the Supernal Triad, in that world which the Kabalists have classified as *Kether,* *Chokmah* and *Binah*—the world of transcension. It will be remembered that when the young man was re-stored to life, he arose and began to speak, but we are told nothing of his utterance ; and that Lazarus, who had been dead for three mystic days, must have carried a strange burden in his heart, but it has not been drawn into language. So also we learn that Christ was in communion with His disciples, but there is no book of the words there-of. If Dante had made his pilgrimage otherwise than in vision, we should not have had the *Divina Commedia.* The conclusion is that when the Word is manifested in the symbolism of speech, the force of the super-nature cannot go further in respect of parting the veils, and, *vice versa,* mani-festation in the arch-natural body interns the speech of the Word.

These things are signified in the Secret Tradition by the symbol of a cube, which repre-sents the universe of created things ; this cube encloses, *ex hypothesi,* the Divine Word which operated in the externalising universe. Now, the use of this term intimates that the work may be one of eternal going on, and that as there is no assignable limit in space so there is none in the analogies to our concept of time. It follows that God is immanent in creation, that He is concealed in the abyss of material things—a *latens Deitas* in Nature as there is a *latens Deitas* in the Eucharist.

Certain High Grade Masons will be reminded here that in one of the degrees of chivalry the *Verbum secretum* is shewn to the Candidate in a cube. When the *Verbum secretum* manifests as the *Verbum caro factum*, the cube opens out and presents the only other figure which is possible to its geometrical dimensions : that figure is a cross. Therefore it was necessary that the Word made flesh should be exalted on a cross, or crucified. When so uplifted, it is said, as we have seen otherwise, that the Word draws all things after it ; but whereto does it draw them ? The answer is given by St. Paul : into that place or state where their life is hid with Christ in God. We can put it differently by describing the third stage of the same symbol. When Christ said *Consummatum est* and gave up the ghost, His body was taken down from the Cross, which is said mystically to have closed up its limbs, reassuming the form of the cube, and the Divine manifestation dissolved back into the Divine immanence. It is said also that He descended into hell, and His resurrection thereafter was not to the world but to the Holy Assembly. Now, this statement—by implication—answers the question, shewing that in being drawn after and following Christ the soul of man is taken inward and bears its divine part, like Plotinus, to the Divine in the universe. Then the Word which was made flesh becomes the Word which has been made soul in the abyss of our humanity. And this is the marriage of the Lamb. The state of being hidden with Christ in God is the state of union with the Divine immanence. St. Paul also says : " I live, yet not I, but Christ liveth in me." That is to say, the microcosm has become after the manner of the macrocosm and, even as the cube of the symbolism, it embraces all things by a catholic figure and contains God who is within by the intimate immanence of a close indwelling. The institution of this analogy carries with it the identical intimation which I have already shadowed forth in respect of the external universe. The marriage-work of the Divine indwelling is one of eternal going on, and seeing, as I have said already, that there is no dividing-line between immanence and transcendence, it follows that the soul of Plotinus does in fine bear the Divine within it through the deep abysses to the centre. And then Christ gives up the kingdom of the soul to the Father of the soul, and God is all in all.

It follows also, and is taught in the Secret Tradition, that man is, in another sense, like a mystic cube wherein the Word is immanent, that there is a way by which it is awakened, so that the Word speaks through the body of the Chief Adept and the Christ-life is manifested.

The most explicit Masonic symbolism of all this mystery is in the Grade of *Knight Templar*, wherein the whole duty of the chivalry is to guard the cubic sepulchre, which itself is never opened or explored, but the crucifix stands upon it, the lights of the first wardens of the expounded mystery burn for ever above it, while the panoply of the spiritual chivalry is heaped on it and about. And because of the equivalents of the Name *Jod, He, Vau, He,* which is the character name of all the antecedent Grades, confessing to the veils of doctrine within the meaning of the First Cove- nant, and because the Postulant is· symbolically and actually initiated therein, he is shewn at some time of the ceremony that which is as if an emblem of the Mystic City descended four square out of heaven. And the City contains the equiva- lent of *Jod, He, Shin, Vau, He.* And the Masonic Name of God, so far as it can now be pronounced upon this earth, *in hac lachrymarum valle,* is com- pleted, for those who can hear it, in the name of Christ—יהוה and יהשוה—so that the Military and Religious Order is in its own way the *ne plus ultra* of all the Degrees. But this is the true mystery of the Divine life in man. Yet are there Masonic Knights, as we have seen otherwise, who will say that the Military and Religious Order is not a Grade of Masonry.

We are now in a position to appreciate the mode of correspondence which exists between the Christian elements in the High Grades and that which I have termed throughout the Secret Tradi- tion in Christian Times. It offers, as though in a few words, the simple summary thereof. There is no one who can say with authority whether the makers of these Grades were acquainted with that

319

Tradition at first hand. Personally I think that they were like some writers of Graal romances : they had heard a rumour at a distance ; but they may have brought over something direct from past Rosicrucianism and from the Catholic mysticism of the past. If not, they are like L. C. de Saint-Martin, who, years after the publication of *L'Homme de Désir*, discovered, in the increased light which he derived from Jacob Böhme, that he had written more wisely than he knew. In such case, it should be counted to them for righteousness, though they knew not fully what they said.

All this is bright and shining in the light of a certain simplicity, but that which lies behind the Craft Grades presents another side of the shield of symbolism, and on the surface is more involved. Fortunately there is nothing inextricable, and I will at once put the comparative position shortly as follows : The Christian High Grades are a symbolical testimony to the immanence of the Divine in the universe and the manifestation of that immanence from within to without in the mission to the universal world of Christ the Saviour. It is in this sense that He brought life and immortality to light. Such is the root-fact *ex hypothesi* of the Secret Doctrine. Once more, the Craft Grades present in a traditional story the particulars of a plan to manifest the Secret Doctrine in a Holy House of Knowledge, and the failure of that plan because of a conspiracy among the lesser initiates to lay hold of the secrets prematurely. It will be remembered that the Craft Legend nowhere exhibits any colourable reason why the attempt should have been made or what profit was likely to follow therefrom, and hence it is not a story which carries any aspect of verisimilitude on the surface. It is only by its interpretation on the present lines that we begin to see the reason and understand the meaning. One inference is that, just as in the Graal romances, the world was not worthy. It must not, however, be assumed that the Master was visited for an intention to betray the Mysteries, though such an interpretation has a plausible aspect. He died to reserve the Mysteries, but that which—in the legendary sense—he was concerned in erecting was a House of Initiation for their communication canonically and in order. When he died the plan of manifestation closed up, as if the cross were refolded into the cube. It should be noted, however, that the cross is not a symbol which is allocated to the Craft Grades, because it was not *ex hypothesi* in the Master Builder that the deep gave up a form. The Stewards of the Mysteries are represented as acting on their own responsibility, and if they were historical personages it might be said that they miscalculated the signs of the times, because of which the fatality supervened. In any case, rather than betray his trust the Master carried it in the story where the

Immanence becomes the Presence, being that place where God recompenses those who seek Him out therein. It is perhaps of faith in Masonry that King Solomon was initiated, and shared in the trust ; but there was another king who has been, so to speak, co-opted into the mystery for the constitution of a triad in the stewardship, and as he was not under the Law and the Covenant there is nothing of faith concerning him. I believe, however, that the whole pretext of the triple stewardship is definitely later than the original system of the Craft Degrees, and that the involved symbolism which was devised to uphold the *Royal Arch*—important as it is in the sequence, taken as a whole—has done more than anything to confuse the issues of the subject. I have therefore qualified my statement on the question of faith in respect of the positive side ; but it remains that in the Craft Degrees *per se* there is something which does indicate, directly and clearly, that the King of Israel shared in the attributed secrets of the Master Grade. My reference to this subject is, however, by way of parenthesis, as it is as an accident or a side-issue of the whole research.

It remains that in three successive ways the hand of God is represented as interposed amidst history and symbolism, to lead some representative part of humanity from the letter which is without to the spirit that is within ; and I return in this manner for a moment to the three mystical events registered earlier in this section. There was, firstly, the promulgation of the esoteric, original law, but those who had come out of Egypt brought with them the preoccupations of Egypt; secondly, there was the building of the House of Doctrine, but the initiates of the Lesser Mysteries rent the channel of communication and the source of knowledge was dried up; there was, finally, the pure light of every enlightenment by Him who came for the redemption of all initiation and the eduction of all Grades to their full perfection; but they crucified the Lord of Glory. The *beneplacitum termino carens* gave in the first instance the substituted Law of Severity as an available school of amelioration for the fallen people, and the symbolic Ark of the Covenant was built in the Lower Wisdom as a symbol of the Law of Lesser and Veiled Doctrine. In the second instance it gave the *Shekinah* to the Temple, at that time when the Ark was placed in the Sanctuary; but the Ark after all contained only the Law of Expediency and not the Law of Deliverance : it was also an implied portent of the bondage to come. In the third instance— but here I can speak only of that which I divine, because neither Secret Doctrine nor Instituted Mystery has dreamed of what might have followed had the Prince of Peace been set upon the throne of the world; I can say only that the same *beneplacitum* gave us the Churches of Christendom in place of the Kingdom of Heaven.

The Secret Tradition in Freemasonry

Having now taken the subject as far as my present warrants enable me, there is an express question with which I must deal in the next place, being itself of a twofold character : What is the root-teaching of the Secret Doctrine, and what was and is the experience which in several ways I have indicated as lying behind it ? On the surface it may seem indubitable for the ordinary earnest student that such a subject must remain essentially undemonstrable, for two evident reasons : (*a*) because those who are initiated and know cannot speak, while (*b*) those who may endeavour to speak cannot know. Now in regard to the first dilemma, the fact that initiation does not act as a complete closure—or, like the cauldron of Ceridwen, as a process which restores the mystically dead to spiritual life, but does not give tongue in that life—is shewn by the illustrative fact that it is possible to write books, like the present book, which deal in an intimate manner with manifest and sub-manifest Freemasonry, and yet maintain, with religious fidelity, every secret veil that has been drawn over those external details which alone can be held as secret. At no time has the term of research been hidden from any eye which is capable of discerning that term. The second dilemma is therefore by implication set aside, and more especially because a few persons who—like Éliphas Lévi—have claimed that they owe their initiation only to God, and their researches have proved after all to be really

affiliated with the Mysteries in one or another
form, though they have not received the highest
initiation, which forbids paltering with the truth
on the great subjects.

As the Secret Doctrine is catholic it is for
that reason inclusive, and because it is inclusive
it can be approached from many points of view
and presents many phases. My object, however,
is to deal with the root-matter, which is capable
of expression almost in a net statement, namely :
that the path of return is open. This will convey
to the reader according to the measure of his
apprehension, while to those who have no apprehension it will communicate—as it is designed
to impart—nothing. There is a point from which
the mystic cannot err, and that point is in the
centre ; there is a way of seeking the centre, and
those who follow it must come to the end of their
journey. The subject of research is called by
many names, and one of them, which serves the
purpose here, is the way to the blessed life. The
soul comes from afar; but its outward path was
one of separation. The complement thereof is
called the path of return.

I have followed the intimate science of this
path through the literature of Christian Times,
and have found its traces everywhere. The
question does not fully concern us now, as this
thesis is not historical ; yet it is not merely certain
that the Science did not begin with Christianity,
but that Christendom, though it derived it on the

one hand, and this fully, from its own implicits, did also draw or at least receive a concurrent communication from another fountain-source in Greek theosophy, the succession of which on its own part is complete without break. It is symbolised on both sides in a multitude of ways from the time of Pausanias onward. The root Greek allegory is found in the fable concerning the Garden of Venus, which is the most explicit pictorial statement concerning the Secret Doctrine that I have found in Greek literature. I have already dealt with the subject in one comprehensive essay, and I must not recross my ground. The meaning of this fable has never entered into the heart of any commentator ; but beyond the steps which I have measured previously in respect of it, there is one step further which I will attempt to expose in this place. The Garden of Venus was a certain paradise of delight, into which the soul came forth by the way of manifestation. There is no description of the issue, and there are indeed no details of any kind, but there always remained in the Garden a very narrow path of return, and this path signified the process of reversion on the work of material generation by which the natural body comes forth with the things that are implied within it. I do not think that there is any one following now the life of thought who can err in understanding if I say that all men come into this life as into the Garden of Venus, and that the mystic work is actually a going back on the path of entrance. It is, of course, an emblematic work, for there is no need to say that the exit is not physical, as if a man should return whence he came through the body of his mother. Now it is in this extra-literal sense that the mystery of generation is the root-mystery of Secret Doctrine, which reminds me that mythologists and experts in folklore have always mistaken the sign for the thing signified. It is true, for example, as we have seen, that the solar mythology once served as a veil to delineate those deeper things which underlie all mythology ; it is true, as another example, that the secret doctrinal knowledge with greater depths behind it was draped in the mysteries of generation ; in fine, it is also true that vegetation, growth and decay, seed time and harvest, that last fashion of folklore, concealed those same mysteries which are not of fashion, because they lie below the common wells of understanding, and are not of a season, because they are as old as manifested consciousness. It is none of my concern that these veils and signs and fables were doubtless offered to the profane as the central truths of the cultures, so that spiritual darkness was perpetuated for the people through the long horror of idolatrous ages. But we are almost without means for deciding whether that was not given them which they were fitted to understand only, while there was often a way of entrance left open for the few who could find it. Here is another sense of Pausanias regarding the Mystic Garden. Again, it is no task of mine to qualify the abuses of the old systems; it is sufficient that a knowledge of what is called the lineal path is a very old *scientia sapientiæ*. I do not think that, in any exclusive, invariable, or even general sense, it was preserved among the priesthood, though it usually wore this aspect, and in some cases existed within it. It passed over in Greece to philosophy, and it seems to have been sustained and extended therein when little remained but the forms in official sanctuaries. There came that saving and enlightening time when all the old external theogonies dissolved before the doctrine of Christ, and were fulfilled rather than destroyed therein. During the Christian centuries I believe that the way was always known to a peculiar people, who, with the whole sincerity of detachment, did not merely render to Cæsar the things that belonged to Cæsar, but all that they claimed in the outward ways to pope and patriarch and priest.

Well, the Secret Doctrine was a mystery of going back on physical generation and being reborn into another Garden, which was not that of Venus. In the sense of sentimental symbolism, this was a Garden of Spiritual Flowers, but in better terminology the correspondence between the two ideas is like that of the House of God as it was externally built by Solomon and

Solomon's Temple Spiritualised. The mystery is one of rebirth, and it is separable into two modes, the first being that of its formal expression by means of doctrine, and, at a greater distance, by means of type and fable ; but the second was the process by which the mystery itself was melted in experience and the epopt did actually return and enter what I have called—not that the phraseology satisfies me—that other and spiritual garden. He remembered whence he came and he found whither he was going ; he was regenerated in the consciousness of the soul, in that state which is apart from the bondage of mortality. There is an almost generic distinction between this process and that which passes in the modern and reformed world under the name of conversion, although the experience of conversion is good, true and real experience, after its own manner. The one is like the firstfruits of redemption, the other is redemption realised.

It will be seen that the root-matter of the Secret Doctrine rests in the pre-existence of man's spiritual part, which, so long as it is distinguished from the material and arbitrary systems of metempsychosis and other forms of reincarnation, is not of necessity foreign matter to official Christian theology. It should be understood further, that although the theosophies and mystical schools of the East and West have very strangely divided and sub-divided the spiritual part of man, all the distinctions and all the shades of distinction .

are referable to stages of consciousness. It is a question of opening successively the closed doors within us, and it is in this manner that we reach what is called in mysticism the Palace of the King, the Holy Palace at the Centre, wherein we cease from our travellings, having reached the term of all; and seeing that the Presence, which is Divine Immanence in Nature, is also a Presence in us, it is at this term that the Divine Immanence is in fine withdrawn into the Divine Transcendence, and the soul passes with the one that it may attain the other. This is Divine Union; it is also the exaltation of Christ on the Cross, that He may carry all things after Him.

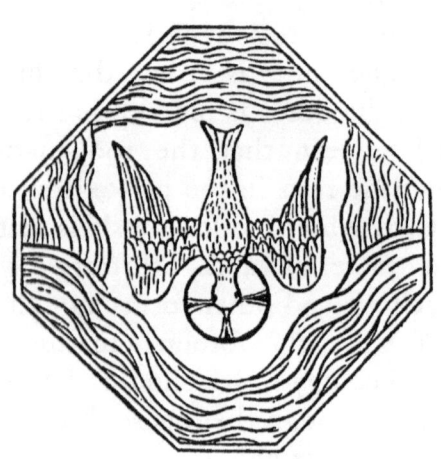

VIII

OF A RITE WITHIN MASONRY

HAVING spoken with all sincerity, to the full extent of my power, on that subject apart from which the present book would have no title to existence, nor could its existence seem possible, there is one branch of the instituted Mysteries of which something remains to be said, and because of its relation to the subject it has been reserved till this stage. The Secret Doctrine has within Masonry in one sense, and yet not exactly of or belonging thereto, another form of enshrinement which constitutes not only the most luminous veil of the Doctrine but contains an explanation in transcension of the Craft symbolism itself. It is a Secret Rite, and any allusions thereto must, for this reason, be very carefully worded ; it communicates a number of Degrees, arising one out of another in an ordered sequence and

forming thus an integral and inseparable whole.
For the purpose of the present allusion I
need, however, mention five grades only, as
follows :—

1. That which is in correspondence unaware
with the Masonic Grade of Neophyte : it
symbolises the birth of the soul in the consciousness of the intellectual understanding.

2. That which responds to the Grade of
Fellow-Craft, wherein the Mysteries of Spiritual
Nature and Concealed Knowledge open like an
immeasurable region—as they are indeed—outside
of time and space—before the soul on its return
journey and ascent.

3. That which stands by itself, apart from
all things in the Craft and with no real correspondence anywhere in the High Grades, though
it offers shadows of resemblance, as of great
things with small, to those of which something
has been said in their place—to the legend which
affirms that the Master was found, not dead but
sleeping ; to that also which intimates that he
lived for many years after his ordeal and sacrifice
in the further East. This is the mystery of Him
concerning whom it has been said, in many
regions of the universe, and in many religions of
the inmost heart, that *passus et sepultus est*. But
it is death in the grace of the Lord, and a mystery
of that sleep which comes by a gift to the beloved. It is the sleep of Christ in the new tomb
of a garden in Calvary. It is, moreover, a macro-

cosmic legend, and as such also it is that of Christ, as it is that of the Master Architect. But their story herein is told after another manner— not in identification with the Legend of the Craft, with the synoptics or the Fourth Gospel. This is the Grade in which the seeker finds the declared mystery of Divine Immanence and the first fruits of the resurrection are set forth on the warrants of the great testimonies of old. It is, as I have intimated, the mystery declared in the macrocosm, and though in the root-matter it deals with the same subject, it is not in correspondence with the dramatic part of the Craft Mystery of Masonry. There is, however, a very curious and profound correspondence with the historical side of the Craft Legend, which side in mystic chronology, if I can so describe it, precedes that mystery of speaking with which I am dealing in the present place. It is also the doctrine of man and his experience in passing from things without to the realisation of the Divine within.

4. That which conveys on the high mountain ridges, and as if in a language peculiar to those heights, the same message and tells the same story as the dramatic side of the Craft Legend tells and conveys on lower ranges of life and thought. It concerns that path through the darkness which is celebrated in so many Mysteries. It is a Rite of mystical death, as death is known to the Masters. It is a synoptic and

catholic Grade, which in terms of absolute philosophy gives explicitly and without veils the *raison d'être* of the previous Mystery, shewing the fundamental reality on which it is grounded, while it is equally an explanation of the Craft Legend in its historical aspect, and finally, as I have just indicated, it is the Craft dramatic mystery presented on the noumenal plane. There is nothing else required to understand emblematic Masonry to the very deeps of its meaning or to demonstrate why of necessity it is incomplete in the Craft Grades. Its ceremonial mystery is much too great for any legend to attach thereto ; it has abandoned all omens and signs outside the matter of the soul, and it unbinds the soul in symbolism from the yoke of the material world.

5. That which has no correspondence either in the Craft or the High Grades, but is the completion of all, as it is of all the crown and exaltation. In this, which is truly the *ne plus ultra*, outside the worlds that are supernal and the symbolic portal thereof, the Master who has overcome life and death, who has conquered the averse powers within him, as well as the kingdom of this world, who has passed through a greater mystical experience than that which was met with of old in the Cauldron of Ceridwen, is given the glad tidings which he shall speak henceforth and for ever in the Holy Assemblies. It is the Grade of the victorious epopt, the

Grade of the mystic city descending four-square out of heaven, or even of the Divine Word made manifest, clothed in the power and the life of a world to come.

I have searched in many realms of symbolism, and I have not only found that the great things are, as one might say, almost everywhere, but that they are imbedded in many places where no one would look to meet with them. As the result of all these researches and searchings, which I thus indicate by a mere phrase of allusion, I bear witness that in all the Instituted Mysteries there is nothing to compare with this great, secret system of complete initiation. The analysis which I have given should justify in the mind of my readers the initial suggestion concerning it, that it is actually the Key of Masonry, and as such it is the more valuable because, although it is in a sense at the present day within Masonry, unknown to the brotherhood at large, it could not be said accurately to have come out of Masonry at the beginning of its history, or to belong to it now in any incorporated sense. In respect of its history, this is singularly imbedded, but some of its roots go back to a period when the speculative science had not clearly risen into the light of day. I am not concerned in maintaining or assuming its antiquity, actual or comparative. In the mystic school which I represent otherwise, antiquity is respected assuredly, but it is not a test of value, and if one should arise among us who, out of his personal illumination, should produce a Minerva of symbolism, all armed and vested, we should be prepared on its own testimony to judge concerning it and to take it into our heart of hearts if it proved to be born of light. That which comes into its own is received among us. The new things unfortunately do not appear as a rule, if indeed ever, bearing the warrants which ensure recognition. But the system with which I am dealing is of a mixed nature in respect of its claim upon the past. I offer no means of identification concerning it, in part because I am not able, and in part because it is unnecessary in the present place. It is a matter of experience that those who are meant for reception are drawn at the proper time within the circle that leads thereto. As no great writer has remained in complete obscurity, so there are no elections which become void and go utterly astray ; but here it is necessary to understand the old distinction between the people who are called out of all tongues and nations, and those who in fine are chosen, these being comparatively few. There are, further, many disappointments in such exotics of life and thought ; and, even on the threshold of things which partake at their height of the absolute, disappointment sometimes awaits the seeker, from which it follows that some who are chosen for the preparatory part are not really pre-dedicated to that which lies beyond the first gates of reception.

The Mysteries on their Mystical Side

There is one point more, to close this part of the subject, and it follows a simple council of sincerity. Having spoken in such terms of this Rite within Masonry, it may fall out that some of my readers will err concerning its limits. I add, therefore, that, like all other systems with which this work has been concerned, it conveys the sacraments according to the order of the sacraments—that is to say, symbolically : as such it is the vestures of the Great Work ; were it otherwise—to adapt certain words of Saint-Martin —it would be the Great Work itself. Here, as elsewhere, it remains for the recipient of the mysteries so to translate them into his life that what is shadowed forth in types and emblems may pass into the certitude of experience. If anywhere in this world of ours there were one Rite or Grade which was warranted by God or man to convey the experiences, there would be no need to write of the Secret Tradition in Freemasonry ; there would be only to proclaim that Grade or Rite.

It is therefore within its own measures, and these only, that I speak of these peculiar claims and have briefly developed their relation to the Masonic subject, which is not the result of imitation, as if one had borrowed from the other, but of identity, variously developed, in the root-matter. In this connection, and that I may make the point clearer, it ought to be added that there is perhaps no Rite which seems upon the surface to have less of the

Masonic manner of presentation, except in respect of the universal and indispensable facts of opening and closing the Lodge, Chapter or Sanctuary. It is otherwise after its own kind and is comparable to nothing but itself. The identities are therefore of essence, and not of form, but even in respect of the essences they have undergone a strange transformation, as if they had been drawn into a celestial rather than an earthly language. Once only in the course of the system is there a claim made upon legend or the shadow of an historical aspect.

And so it comes about that there is a Rite within Masonry which is a key to the proper understanding both of the Craft and of those High Degrees which deserve, on their proper warrants, to be connected with the Craft and regarded as its development or completion. To shew that there is a sanctity in covenants like those which are taken in Masonry and some other of the Secret Orders, this key exists—as I have said—without any official cognisance on the part of the Masonic Fraternity, while the members of the more withdrawn sodality do not—for the most part—know that they hold the key of Masonry, though many doors have been opened within this Rite which lead to the sanctuary of the soul.

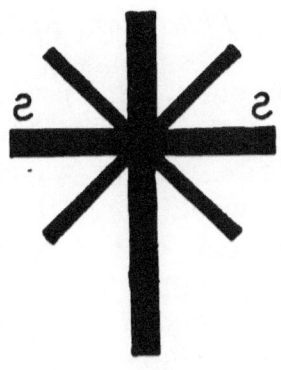

IX

Last Words on the Mystery of Building

HAVING heretofore, at such necessary length as the opportunity of the moment offered, displayed after what manner the treasures of hidden things are contained in Masonry, and—as that which remains over—having still the last things to express, it is desirable to pause for a moment and, apart now from outer ceremonial and defined symbolism, to try and realise how the Grades and the Rites give testimony on their own part within the measures of the literal word. There are, I suppose, three measures of testimony which may be considered without preface in their proper order, and moving as such from comparatively small beginnings to the greater end.

There is, firstly, the ethic of life, and this lies so obviously on the surface of the Rituals that the mind tends to grow weary of a recurring iteration, and may even take refuge in the rebellious mood, as I have done once or twice on my own part in the course of our quest. Let us therefore recognise now that the moral side of the Masonic concern is not only the gate and the way by which those must enter who would go up the Mountain of the Lord unto the House on the top of the Mountain, but is that also which has constituted through many generations the wide appeal and the great motive power of our Speculative Art. It is along this line that the speculative becomes the practical, and the emblematic is made operative in a high degree. My book has been written to indicate that it is not the sole appeal, nor is it the highest of all, but it is the preface and the one thing which is requisite and presupposed before any other can enter truly within our horizon and within the region of our attainment. I need not recite here the things that are included in the Masonic ethic of life ; they are familiar to all the Brethren and are matters of world-wide knowledge among persons who are outside the Craft and its dependencies. I need add only that for those who can go no further the moral side of Masonry, the doctrine of peace on earth—not merely to men of goodwill but to humanity at large—is a great and saving thing to take into the heart, and this alone would therefore justify the Brotherhood and constitute its clear title, supposing that there were nothing beyond. It is an art of building, within the limits of its proposition, the just and perfect man in Nature and Society.

But there is, secondly, the doctrine of religious

duty, as this is commonly understood ; it recognises that the Brotherhood of man depends from the Fatherhood of God, and that the duty of man to man presupposes another and more exalted duty, being that of man towards God. The Masonic sense of this subject has a wider aspect than is offered by the consideration of mortal life, and it belongs in a manner to an eternal standard, because—by the hypothesis—there are " immortal mansions " above in which we may have a place for ever. It will be seen that I am expressing this position in language which is not my own ; I am using that of Masonry ; but again these commonplaces of the great subject are important in their own way, because they are another side of that wide and universal appeal which Masonry has exercised for generations within the limits of the Brotherhood and has reflected to the world at large. It is a testimony of theism alone, conditioned by certain implications regarding Divine dealings under the Old Covenant of Israel, and there are many points of view from which it is deficient enough ; but in respect of its two doctrines concerning God and everlasting life, it is of the root-matter of faith. There is no doubt, as such, that it has led, and is still leading, many to an elementary recognition of Divine things who might scarcely attain it through the offices of church and creed. Hence also, effectually or not, it is the practice of another art of building—the building of a spiritual man : it is a work begun in order ; it may not do more than lay the foundations ; but these are ready—and established strongly—for a super-structure to be laid thereon. I am speaking rather of the Craft, for it would of course be the thesis on behalf of the High Grades that they do raise the spiritual edifice even to the capstone thereof, or, in other words, they have that by which man may be developed into the perfect stature of the Sons of God.

Morality and theistic religion : these corre-spond well enough for my purpose to the idea of Lesser Mysteries, and I know, also well, that in a proper understanding the Greater Mysteries are in Christ. But there is thirdly and lastly a transi-tion in the Craft itself which is at least an intima-tion concerning the bare existence of a *ne plus ultra* in the order of *Disciplina Arcanorum,* and out of it arises the deep consideration of mystical death and resurrection. Neither church, nor sect, nor creed, nor pageants of the Rosy Cross in their highest state of symbolism, nor the Grades above all Grades of the High Grade movement, can convey anything beyond, anything fuller or more vital, than is contained in the catholic understanding of this subject. It is the root of the Secret Tradition and leads to the term of its research. For those who know thereof, there is in Emblematic Freemasonry the hint of an art of building which is not of the stature of man in Nature or Society, but that of the self-knowing spirit, when it knows all things in God.

The explanation is that the state of mystical death is—in the simplest form of language—though not for such reason preferable—the setting aside once and for ever of the life of self ; and the union in the life of God is the state of mystical resurrection. There is no High Grade and there is no Craft Grade which does more than offer an allusive suggestion, a pageant, a symbol or an allegory on this subject ; but it is the suggestion, the symbol, the allegory, which give them their place in the true Mysteries. They are otherwise a defence, a proclamation of doctrine on the literal side—purely theistic or Christian as the case may be. It is for this reason that I have a word to say upon doctrine.

There may be some of us who have admitted to ourselves that the policy of the Vicar of Bray is not after all such a very improper policy towards official churches and religions, whether in East or West ; that, subject to the unwritten dictates of *la haute convenance,* none of their differences, and assuredly few of their warrants, are worth the price of a martyrdom ; that it was more especially in the early ages of our more particular Christian churches that men suffered the high passion for doctrine ; that it gave martyrs to the churches, but it gave also inquisitors ; that we in this present time are "like sunbeams lifted higher"—that is, above the concern

The Secret Tradition in Freemasonry

and its pleadings ; that men change their religions as in Masonry they pass from the Craft Grades to the High Degrees ; and that, for example, the transit from something called Protestantism to something else that was once called Popery is not unlike that from the Degree of Mark Mason to the 18th Degree of *Rose-Croix*.

But perhaps after all we shall find, if we choose to go far enough, that external doctrine is one of the keys which do open the Sanctuary, and, because of it, that many in the East and the West shall ascend with a deeper understanding to the Altar of God, as they did in those days of old when no man thought it necessary to renounce the signs that are without, because he was on the Quest of their inward and withdrawn meanings. It seems to me, therefore, that the current criticism of religion on its recognised ground, including a nondescript sometimes termed higher criticism, may be left to those who pursue it, bestowing such blessings as we can now bestow thereon. It is often the valuation by those who do not know of that which above all things is calling for direct knowledge—in other words, for the criticism of inward experience ; as such, it is no part of our concern.   I believe myself that dogma is passing through the kind of dissolution that goes before its resurrection in a new and transformed body of our desire after spiritual attainment.   Among other things, the spirit of so-called liberal Christianity seeks to set us free from nearly everything, including the yoke which once was sweet and the burden that was once light ; but it is like physical science *per se*, and cannot offer us the true charter of our liberty. If it could, we should be rather in the place of attainment than in the place of search.

In its proper understanding the authority within does not set aside any lawful authority without ; it is sometimes its spokesman. We are bred in the letter, but it befalls that at some period many of us depart therefrom : if we do not enter into the spirit, we drift towards open disbelief; if we do so enter, we may one day come back to the letter with a higher understanding thereof. Whether in the East or the West, like the fairy gifted poet, we may see that the same thing is everywhere, all Grades—Masonic and extra or super-Masonic—the expression in lower terms of that Grade which has never been drawn into language, and the aspiration towards that Lodge which has never been consecrated on earth ; all Christian churches the symbol of that Church of the plenary grace that is entered only from within ; all great religions the spokesmen after their own manner of that ancient, ever new truth and beauty, the subsistence of which has been declared to us from the beginning of things, and there is not one of the elect who has not heard the voice of it in the centre of his heart.

We have seen in various ways that the experience of religion is everywhere ; we know that it is heard sometimes even at the corners of our streets as the imperfect testimony of a clouded light rising in the consciousness of a Salvation-Army speaker or of an itinerant preacher. But herein, as in all other parts of our subject, as in all the scattered ways of thought and activity through which I have been seeking and in-gathering the vital threads and fibres by which they are connected with realities, I must bring back these memorials to the point which is at issue throughout. I must keep faithful to those gifts of evidence which I have received and to their light breaking over paths which I have travelled. As regards, therefore, all that which the outward ways of official religion intimate and keep alive in the heart concerning the religion which is within, let me say in conclusion that, expressed in symbolism, the mementoes, the shadows, the lights of a direct experience, by which I mean the religion that is within, are preserved in some of the old Instituted Mysteries as they are preserved in those other shrines and sanctuaries of which I have been speaking recently.

It may be a hard saying for the tyro, but I call it fortunate on my own part, that we only bring out from the Instituted Mysteries that which we have taken therein. We bring it out, however, as I have affirmed elsewhere, after another manner ; but as in the churches them-selves, so in these, we are only given the materials

of our spiritual building and we must build with
our own hands. The issue from the Garden of
Venus must be by our own act. The road is short
to the gate of direct experience, and short to the
church-door of that religion which is within ; but
it is not for this reason easy to open either.

Now, therefore, seeing that we have reached
the term of our research, we may pause and
enumerate some of those new things that have
been found in the course of our quest, because
the ground has not been familiar or travelled
often ; much of it, indeed, has lain in unfrequented
quarters.

I. Symbolical Masonry is a testimony to the
existence in the past of a knowledge which has
not found expression in words respecting its
practical part. It is therefore a closed, and not
an open, testimony.

II. Masonry is the hypothetical record of an
assumed intention to put that knowledge forward,
if not in the plenary sense, at least with fewer
veils : as such, it is an excursion in symbolism
for a specific concealed purpose, and it goes on to
shew that the intention was frustrated under circumstances of which we hear only in still deeper
language of evasion and parable. The intention
itself is more especially a mode of commemorating
the existence of the Secret Tradition.

III. The secret knowledge referred to was
concerned not with hypothesis but experience,
not with doctrine, though it had an essential

347

ground therein, seeing that theory must precede practice, but with practical science.

IV. As to the nature of the experience, we have conceived in part concerning it, and we have tried—not so much under reserves as tentatively —to reconstruct the hypothetical method.

V. It is almost certain that the reconstruction is, as such, substantially a failure, because parts are wanting of necessity, and it may well be that those parts are vital to the reader. The hindrance is in the limitations of expression.

VI. But I feel sufficiently convinced to affirm that the conception, as outlined, is not itself *ex hypothesi*. I am sure that it is very truth of truth divine.

VII. Craft Masonry is a memorial of these things, and so being it is good and precious. It has borne very helpful witness in my own case, and I doubt whether in its absence I should have reached my present grade of certitude.

VIII. At the same time I had the master-key from elsewhere, or I should never have opened the secret door and Closed Palace of the King.

IX. I had also a clear notion otherwise as to the nature of the Hidden Treasure, or I should not have recognised that Masonry was a witness to its existence.

X. That Treasure is not, however, offered to possession therein ; it is, as I have just intimated, the fact of its existence certified.

XI. The certitude offered by the greater

High Grades is also concerned only with a question of fact ; namely, that the plans for the House of Doctrine were restored in Christ ; but those plans are not fully communicated, and as to the Treasure of the House, there is no deeper indication given than is that of the Craft Grades concerning the Old Law.

XII. It should be noted that no Grade—Craft or High — imparting the sense of Masonic symbolism connected with the Ancient Alliance exhibits any mystery as taking place or abiding within the official Sanctuary : this is reserved for a far more secret Order.

XIII. So also there is no High Grade, communicating imputed secrets connected with the New and Eternal Covenant, which offers any suggestion of a Mystery or Rite as abiding or enacted within the official Christian Sanctuary.

XIV. These are facts of singular symbolic importance which have never been noticed by Masons.

XV. The Grades of Templar chivalry, with their consanguinities, developments and imitations, are concerned with or exhibit a vacant sepulchre in place of a living *Locus Sanctorum*.

XVI. There are other Grades which say that the Word is Christ, and that His is the Ineffable Name. From this it would seem to follow *ex hypothesi* that although there were mysteries— and especially of the instituted kind, under the ægis of the Old Law, there are none, or there is

349

nothing communicable, under the Law of Christ, Who is at once the sum of all mystery and all revelation.

XVII. But this is not a correct although it is a plausible inference. The true intimation is that the House of Doctrine has never been built in Christendom—that is to say, has been never externalised, though it is built daily in the heart, and after many manners, *per omnia sæcula sæculorum.*

XVIII. That is to say, the secret and sacred Mystery which Christ came to communicate has not yet been published, though fragments of its Divine Body are found in all languages. I believe in my heart that this strange implicit would be interpreted wrongly as an impeachment of the official and external churches ; the reference is rather to a wisdom in Christ which lies behind authorised doctrine, and is its fulfilment, not its antithesis.

XIX. It is again a testimony to the fact of a secret doctrine enshrining a secret experience—as in Israel, so also in Christendom.

It must be confessed that this study has not proved exotic only, but elaborate after its particular kind. It has demonstrated once and for all, by clause and by clause, the relations subsisting between the Craft and High Grades, and the next question which arises in this concluding part is naturally the position wherein the latter are left. I have justified the title of the Quest by delineat-

ing after what manner there is root-connection
between the Crafts and the High Grades in
respect of the Secret Tradition in Christian Times.
A parte ante et a parte post, that tradition is
identical, and has never told its story to those
who have ears otherwise than in one way. A
remarkable thing regarding High Grade Masonry
is that those Rites and Degrees which officially,
and by their express claim, connect with manifest
departments of the Tradition—I mean, records
such as Alchemy, Kabalism and Magic—are precisely those which offer the least light—which
are neither integral to Masonry nor germane to
the Tradition itself; while variants of *Rose-Croix*
Grades, Grades of St. Andrew, Grades of Chivalry
and so forth, which report nothing and have
heard nothing concerning occult science, contain
the exact developments of those reflections which
in Craft Masonry are the most faithful pictures of
the Tradition in certain phases. The Kabalistic
School in Masonry, which is only represented
thinly, which obtained no currency and exercised
no influence, represents a tradition that is interesting in its own manner, but is derived through
Latin channels and is governed by the Christian
preoccupation belonging thereto. The Hermetic
School, which offers curious features, is parted
into three heads. That which confesses to the
predispositions of Abbé Pernety shews no consciousness whatever on the spiritual side ; Baron
Tschoudy has strange implicits in some of his

Grades, but his involved hypothesis, owing something to Templar tradition, something to physical Alchemy, and something to the astral-theurgic or religio-magical school of Martines de Pasqually, is much too confused to convey any certain idea as to term and purpose; finally, the Grades of Alchemy gathered into the Rite of Memphis and that of Mizraim are little better than spurious, and it is wise to say so frankly, rather than to confuse the issues. No mystic at the present day, and no one who follows in right paths the Quest of the secret Tradition, will expect anything from Magic, but something by way of exception must be said for the Rite of Elect Cohens, which had exceedingly high concerns within the limits of theurgic motives. We have, however, to set aside these for the adequate reasons given in their particular sections, but it will be seen that in this manner the High Grades, regarded as containing Masonic messages, and therefore separable from a multitude of extraneous issues, are reducible into a measurable compass, and a much greater reduction remains possible.

A final ceremonial supplement of the Craft Grades has as yet never entered within the horizon of Masonry. That which is requisite is an answer to the implied question left open by the central legend without exceeding the limits of the Old Law, or alternatively there must be an answer which shall embrace all laws and all dispensations.

Instead of this we have had particular responsions, and in one case—being that of the *Royal Arch*— a replica, which increases the difficulty while making the claim to remove it. Christianity has given a momentous answer in Masonry ; it has added one letter to the Divine name in Israel— יהוה—and has produced יהשוה. That is the true answer for those who can receive it, among whom I ask to be included, for the sake of the Kingdom of Heaven ; but it is not absolute, and it does not carry conviction *per se* to all tongues and tribes and peoples and nations, while the secret doctrine is Catholic on all the planes of manifestation and of being. Moreover, if we admit that the one word is a restoration and completion of the other, it still covers only a part of the Masonic subject, and if we admit that it completes the Word we have seen that a plan of the Secret Doctrine is not conveyed therein.

This is so far clear, according to my present lights and subject to the faculty of expression. There remain otherwise a few matters on which the last word must be said at this stage, and I schedule them for greater facility as shall here follow :—

(1) I have affirmed that certain unknown initiates took over and transmuted the Trade Guild and thus created emblematic Freemasonry, or alternatively — if by possibility we could accept the hypothesis of Mr. R. F. Gould—they were already the custodians of a Secret Rite which

in some manner and measure corresponded in the root to Masonry on the symbolical side. Who were these unknown initiates? My answer is and can be only that they were inheritors at some far distance of the past instituted mysteries. They may not have been learned in the antiquities of Egypt, because at their period there was no scholarship on the subject; the whole of Greek literature may not have been in their hands by an intimate acquaintance therewith; but they knew that which lay behind the mystic doctrine of figurative death, and the resurrection by which that experience is made perfect in the consciousness of the adept.

(2) In respect of such death and renewal they knew that the mystic life must first be led by the Postulant. It corresponded for them to that which I have termed throughout the Christ-life in the spirit, the mystery of which life lies like a hidden jewel in the House of Christian Doctrine, but the Keepers of the House know not where it has been hidden. They know not, moreover, that the House of Doctrine is itself a House of Consciousness, or the pearl of great price might not have been far from their seeking.

(3) The result is that the Christian Churches, with all the glorious intimations and pageants of holy rite, are in the same position precisely as Craft Masonry itself and the High Degrees, for at this day they are warranted only to impart the great things of all in symbolism, not in experience.

(4) The unknown initiates, on their own part, symbolised this fact by a loss in the Sanctuary, the loss of a Great and Holy Word. They incorporated emblematic Freemasonry and set the brotherhood therein on the quest thereof; and because of the holiness of the House of official doctrine, they depicted at a certain stage a substituted recovery, taking care that, this notwithstanding, the quest went on.

(5) Now the end of this quest is formulated by the High Grades, and that which they should have communicated for the plenary establishment of their claims is the Divine Life manifested in the world and soul. That which they offered actually was a replica of Christian doctrine, another attainment in symbolism, not in experience.

(6) Within their own measures they were right, but the result was a further substitution. This is how in the essential aspects the Christian Grades fail; this is why the Craft, under its present limitations in respect of consciousness, cannot recognise its highest sequels, even though some of them do connect in the external sense with the Secret Tradition in Christian times. They do seek to build a more perfect House of Doctrine; it is a spiritual house in theory, but it has not become for the builders a House of Consciousness. Moreover, the plans restored in Christ have not been put into the hands of perfect Craftsmen, and the work is therefore unfinished.

(7) The unknown initiates belonged to the Secret Tradition on its Christian side, though they must have known that there are other names. This is my answer to one of the initial questions as to the Christian implicits in the Craft Grades. The whole secret of Masonry formulated in a single phrase is *Christus intrinsecus*, which phrase contains the essential distinction between official doctrine and the inward realisation of that truth which is Divine. In such realisation that which is Divine in man and the universe passes from concealment through experience in the consciousness, and the adept carries, like Plotinus, the Divine within him to the Divine in the universe, and to the centre also.

(8) This is the term of the Masonic pilgrimage, when those who have travelled so long from the East even to the West take at last the return journey, by way of that North which is not a quarter of the world external, and are reintegrated in an eternal East.

(9) Here lies the pearl of great price behind the Secret Tradition ; and it is the hidden knowledge concerning the Lord of all the Mysteries. The name of this Lord is Christ, but again there are other names. I think indeed that He has been called by all names which have ever represented for man that which has been conceived by man concerning the Divine in the universe, which is also the Divine within.

(10) As a last word respecting the return

journey and the rest at the East thereafter, it is this which the old masters sometimes spoke of as the Wisdom in Paradise. The legend of this is recurring ; it means that which is attained at the East, but this East is a centre, and every Mason should know that he cannot err therefrom. The purpose of Emblematic Freemasonry within the limits of the Craft was to provide a memorial of the quest ; the purpose of Christian Masonry was to show where the quest ends ; but it has rested too much in the letter of those words which are communicated in the official churches. Their indications are beautiful and moving ; the true secret is within some of the Grades for those who know how to find it ; but most of them do not know, and the Wardens cannot tell them. So it comes about, for these and the other reasons, that the Lodges, Preceptories and Chapters have never been empowered to take the perfect closing.

That which remains is the quest ; even at the best and the highest, the Grades and Degrees can communicate only in symbolism. The path which leads to the term must be travelled in the world ot experience by each for himself. It is possible to indicate the path, and this. I have sought to do, but no one can travel it with another.

And so the quest goes on. And the quest, as it may be, ends in attainment—we know not where and when : so long as we can conceive of our separate existence in any sphere and under any veils, I know that the quest goes on—an attainment continued henceforward. And ever shall the study of the ways which have been followed by those who have passed in front be a help on our own path. And in the extension of our comparative knowledge of all that has been done and attained in the past along these directions towards the term, there is the most wise, enlightened and informed of all researches. Hereof are our warrants in considering, as I have now done, the claims and antecedents, the motives and prospects of the Rites included by Masonry. The lesson which we have brought away is not less important and not less salutary because few delusions remain in respect of most ; it is well always to know the paths that do not lead to our end.

It is well, it is of all things beautiful and perfect, holy and high of all, to be conscious of the path which does in fine lead thither where we seek to go, namely, the goal which is in God. Taking nothing with us which does not belong to ourselves, leaving nothing behind us that is of our real selves, we shall find in the great attainment that the companions of our toil are with us. And the place is the Valley of Peace.

Here ends the Secret Tradition in Freemasonry

APPENDICES

360

I

A SUPPLEMENTARY LIST OF GRADES, INCORPORATED AND
DETACHED, INCLUDING BRIEF DESCRIPTIONS

THE classification which follows is a bare outline and
register, designed to indicate that, for those who care
to follow them, there are further memorials in Ritual
which correspond to the motives classified in the text of
these volumes. They may serve the purpose especially of
inquirers and collectors, though I fear that most of them
abide in regions of fatuity which I have forborne to
enter, or at least to travel for a distance, because it must
perhaps be confessed that here and there I have paused
for a season on the borders. Some unheard of curiosities
in outline, the account of which here is given, may carry
with them an implied recommendation to let that outline
stand for the whole.

The *Grade of Sublime Master* is referred to the
imaginary RITE OF MARTINISM and to the archives of
the SCOTTISH PHILOSOPHICAL RITE. It is possible therefore that an existing Ritual was taken over or adapted
by the RITE OF MEMPHIS, which allocates this title to
the sixth Grade of its system. It is the fifth of the
ANTIENT AND PRIMITIVE RITE. The procedure supposes two apartments, of which one is the throne-room
of King Solomon and the other that sacred place

containing the tomb of the Master ; the ceremony is one of his interment. Except in so far as the grief and confusion of the period may be said to lend it a certain shadow of motive, the procedure is irredeemable in its folly, and the procession which carries a sham bier from one chamber to another combines the ridiculous with irreverence. The Candidate who has shared in this business is, however, proclaimed to be the Son of God as a consequence of the soul's immortality, which—in some inscrutable manner—is regarded as the lesson of the Grade.

As it is difficult to meet with any *oder suavitatis* in unrolling the Masonic mummies of Memphis, I will turn in the next place to the EARLY GRAND RITE OF SCOTLAND, wherein most of the follies are not made worse by irreverence. I think, in this sense, that we can recite our *Pax* over the ashes of a Grade entitled *Master of the Blue.* ·King Solomon has built his Temple as well as it was possible in the literal art of Masonry, and the Queen of Sheba has come from the uttermost parts to test his knowledge or discretion. She carries two wreaths, one of them being composed of artificial and the other of natural lilies. Throwing them at the feet of the King, she invites him to distinguish between them, but the artificial flowers are so cunningly devised that he finds himself at a loss completely. It happens, however, that the incident takes place in a garden, and by overturning a hive the King solves the difficulty, for after a few moments the bees in their wisdom settle on the natural flowers. Such is one of the specimens put forth by the prolific manufactory for the production of High Grades ; and yet one forlorn obedience thinks that it is worth preserving. Shall I for once be over-subtle on my part and say that the Degree offers a canon of criticism—though of what is another matter? I reserve my speech.

The Grade of *Intimate Secretary* belongs to a very different obedience, being that of the ANCIENT AND ACCEPTED SCOTTISH RITE. It should be regarded in symbolic chronology as preliminary to the *Mark*. The ceremony depicts a meeting between Solomon and the King of Tyre with reference to the exchange of certain cities in Galilee for cedars of Lebanon. The lessons of long research are learned in a school of patience, and the gift of discerning symbolism bids many dry bones live, but I know of no patience which can suffer the application of this kind of episode to the purpose of Ritual and no words of power which can say to this kind of effigy : Arise and live.

I have not pretended to class these things in any consecutive order, but this is as much as I shall cite in the concerns of the First Temple. The EARLY GRAND RITE, which has taken out a peculiar warrant for confessing its own issues, has gathered into its *Mark* series a Grade entitled *Master of all Symbolic Lodges*, of which I have spoken otherwise ; but there is also a Grand Mastery of the same denomination, which is numbered sixty-one in the RITE OF MIZRAÏM, and has been falsely identified with the Noachite or Prussian chivalry of the SCOTTISH RITE. The President of the Lodge represents Cyrus Artaxerxes, and the Candidate is Zerubbabel. He reappears as the *Knight of the Sword*, rather than that of the Trowel, in MEMPHIS and the PRIMITIVE RITE, claiming audience as the first among his equals, a Mason of rank and a captive in Babylon. His object is to remedy, by an appeal to the King, the condition of his brethren, to secure their return to Jerusalem and the building of the Second Temple. The offices of dream have prepared the royal mind to comply ; he invests Zerubbabel with full power to carry out his plans and girds him with the sword that Nebuchadnezzar took from Jehoiachim, King of Jerusalem, when the latter was drawn into captivity. The discourse attached to the Grade certifies that the mission of the Knight of the Sword is to deliver his brethren from misery, for the chivalry is an institution based entirely upon charity and the abnegation of self.

The Secret Tradition in Freemasonry

There is also the *Knight of Jerusalem* under the same obedience, and in this the Prince of the People, having reached Jerusalem, has discovered out of all expectation that the Sanhedrim is in session thereat, under the presidency of Nehemiah, the locality being the ruins of the First Temple. Zerubbabel is deputed to undertake a journey to Babylon and represent to Darius (*a*) that the Samaritans have prevented the glorious work of re-building; (*b*) that the monarch in earlier days had promised to restore the holy vessels. The reception of the Candidate involves this task and, apparently on his supposed return to Jerusalem, he disentombs the altar, the vessel of incense and the Sacred Delta of Enoch, another emblem which had been lost to the Craft since the destruction of the Temple. It will be seen that this Grade is preparatory to *Prince of Jerusalem.* Its procedure is one of complete and ludicrous confusion, as exampled by the President representing Nehemiah and the Senior Warden Darius.

I am without other noticeable specimens in respect of the Second Temple at its initial period, and as I do not propose to dwell upon *Knight of the Orient,* in which the Craft is plunged in sorrow because Judas Maccabeus is slain and the Temple of Zerubbabel profaned, I shall pass to the Grades of Chivalry ; but as I have intimated that neither gold nor gems will be found in the heap of waste products, I shall take up a few points with a certain glitter of title as the accidents of reference may lead. It should be understood, however, that such nondescripts as *Knight of Choice, Knight of the Sublime Choice* and other imputed chivalries in the days of the Old Alliance, do not enter into our consideration. We may distinguish two broad classes in those that remain over, being (*a*) Grades which are without allocation in respect of historical time and (*b*) those which, ap-proximately or otherwise, may be held to connect with events in the New Testament. As an example of the first, there is *Knight of the Red Eagle,* and this is of

Appendices

Memphis. The Candidate, who may be probably relieved from responsibility as one who does not know what he says, makes a profession of faith in what appears to be the doctrine of emanation and renounces the profane world ; he descends metaphorically into the earth, as the abode of death ; thence he comes forth alive, to be purified by air, water and fire, after which he is held to be liberated from the bonds of prejudice and the stains of vice. The reward of his trials is a version of the legend concerning the Dionysian architects and the revelation that St. John of the Apocalypse was an initiate of the Kabiric Mysteries, which existed in Judea at the time of Christ. In respect of Freemasonry itself, this art seems to have travelled from Palestine, and from the Temple of Solomon, to Rome under Numa Pompilius ; it was in Britain during Roman domination, and it was amalgamated ultimately with the Hermetic Societies. So do the spurious Degrees manufacture not only their own history but that of the Craft at large.

A transition from the obedience of Memphis to that of Mizraïm will enable the curious enthusiast to pass at the same time from the first to the second class of the two chivalries which I have distinguished, and he may become a *Knight of Palestine*. He will learn something of priests vowed to the service of the Temple in the days of Esdras ; but the opening declares that the temple of Zerubbabel is destroyed, and he finds that he is at Jerusalem in the apartment of Godfrey de Bouillon. He may become also a *Knight of St. John*, which—in this connection—is to be distinguished from *Knight of St. John the Evangelist*. The ceremory takes place in the sanctuary of that chivalry, and the pledge is without an imprecation, without penalties, a simple covenant of honour. The secret words communicated are those of the Order in Palestine, because others are said to have been used by the Knights who remained in Europe. The Grade has no point of interest, except

The Secret Tradition in Freemasonry

the shadow of an Eucharistic Observance, which is celebrated at the end. Bread is eaten in token of love ; wine is drunk in ratification of the vows that have been taken and as a bond between the brethren, to sustain one another. There is no Masonic connection, imputed or otherwise. There is also the *Knight of the Christian Mark*, as to which it will be remembered in the *Apocalypse* that neither the earth nor the sea, neither trees nor vegetation, were to be hurt till the servants of God had been sealed in their foreheads. So is the chivalry of the Christian Mark supposed to have been sealed and so set apart from the world, but whether the approaching destruction of all mankind, apart from this little company of the elect, was apprehended in the mind of its founder, I have no power to say. The signing is so utterly symbolical that it seems to take place automatically by the fact of reception into the Council, and the Candidate represents one of the guard supplied by the Knights of St. John to Pope Alexander. I do not gather which of these pontiffs is indicated, but the Knights chosen were well known as zealous and devoted Masons. This is, I suppose, one of the Grades which would have been termed Jesuitical by Ragon, but I think better of the great society in respect of its subtlety. The implied intention of the ceremony is to enroll a spiritual chivalry. Beyond this Grade there is the *Holy and Illustrious Order of the Cross*, but—the talismanic title notwithstanding—I am compelled to say that it is nothing, and if there be anything which is less than nothing, it is also less. The brief ceremonial proceeds from opening to closing, conveying no lesson, no history, nor even a legend. The form in which I have seen it has no doubt been subjected to editing apart from understanding, and an earlier codex might supply some vestige of design which is now wanting. In the *Knight of Bethany*, a transparency shewn in the Temple recalls an important point in the *Grade of St. Andrew*. The ceremony embodies a visit to the Holy Sepulchre, apparently at the time of the Resurrection. Here there is, of course, a reflection from the *Knight of the Holy Sepulchre*, and it is said as to the Object of Quest that "He is not here but is risen." The Candidate is reminded that the Word can be discerned only by the eye of faith till the Angel of Great Council is beheld in the world above. The sequel hereto is *Knight of the White Cross*, in which the Ascension is commemorated.

Those who are in search of some further vestiges concerning Hermetic Masonry will not discover that which they are seeking in certain Grades of Memphis which I have omitted to mention previously—in frankness because they seem almost to bear away the palm for complete fatuity. I will simply enumerate them for such a hypothetical student's benefit. The *Knight of the First Property of Nature* learns that this property is the general and indeterminate state of matter, understood to be at first chaotic, but order is evolved by stages. This is the 34th item in the miraculous system, and there are six further Grades dealing with other properties—namely, Cohesion, Fluxion, Coagulation, Accumulation, Station or matter at rest, and in fine Division. An old and banal exorcism testifies that seven are they who know not the law of order, and seven are these against sense, but such inventions lack even the jingle of bells on the fool's cap.

The sense of equilibrating justice tempts me to add that these seven temples of unreason under the imputed shadow of Hermeticism may be contrasted with , similar constructions which the unsearchable wisdom of Mizraïm has raised under the shadow of Kabalism. They are : (1) *Knight of Banuka*, which is concerned with the Jewish Feast of Light ; (2) *Very Wise Israelite Prince*, which may be regarded as introductory to (3) *Sovereign Prince Talmudim*, in which the most profound sciences are cultivated but not communicated ; (4) *Sovereign Prince Zadkim*, wherein is an astronomical mystery, for the Pole-Star is located in the West; (5) *Grand Haram*, in which the guide of the ancient mariner has reached the South in the course of a reverse circumambulation ; (6) *Grand Prince Haram*, where the sun and moon appear simultaneously in the East ; (7) *Sovereign Prince Hasid*, and several others, much after the same manner and to the same purpose.

Outside the classification which I have adopted, there are things of the detached kind that are a little curious, though they have no symbolic importance, Masonic or otherwise. There is *Priest of Eleusis*, in which the Postulant enters the Temple, seeking for light amidst the Instituted Mysteries of old. By the hypothesis, therefore, he is in the shadowed light of Paganism ; but Eleusis has been rectified and reformed, and he is required to realise the value of a strong contrast. The ceremony is in two sections, in the first of which Eleusis imparts her secrets, but they are nothing, for this kind of Isis does not readily unveil, more especially in the presence of those who are about to renounce her. The Candidate is, however, received into her priesthood. In the second section he is laid upon the ground ; a veil is cast over him ; it is said that he is the death of error as an expounder of the old mysteries, but that he shall be re-born according to the life and grace imparted by the truth that is in Christ. He becomes in this manner the priest of a more holy Temple and is raised into the Divine Light. The lesson is much too obvious and the dramatic setting is a mere rudiment of art ; it might have been made effective in less unskilful hands, but there is at least a suggestive reflection from the Craft Grades. A constrast hereto is the grade called *Priest of the Sun*, in which that luminary is represented by the President, who is also Father Adam—for one of those inscrutable reasons which occur in the manufactured mysteries. Other offices of the ceremony represent the rest of the moving lights, according to primitive astronomy. They are more correctly the angels of the planets and are described ignorantly as Cherubim, though the attributed names are characteristic of other hierarchies. The Candidate, after due proving, is held worthy to receive the high angelic instruction, but all that he learns is by inference and may be not a little confusing, as Father Adam seems to have adopted Christianity. This is the kind of thing that we should call foolish in the mummeries of our children, but it is the work of grown men for communication to persons also of mature age, and there is no reason to suppose that it was received otherwise than with tolerance, perhaps even with reverence.

The priesthoods are many, as the chivalries also are many, and one of them is that of *White Mason*, which is sacerdotal in the palmary sense. The Grade is a path of progress from the land of darkness to that of light, in search of the City and Tabernacle which are set upon the high hill. To be sincere, it is a very spiritual ceremony. The doors which open to the Recipient are those of faith, hope, mercy, utterance, salvation, perseverance and life, corresponding to the opening of seven seals upon the secret book by the Lion of the Tribe of Judah—as the Christ Mystical is termed in the Ritual, rather than the Lamb slain from the foundation of the world. The object is to institute and warrant the builders of a spiritual temple.

There are also systems which are other than collections of Grades, and which must be regarded as classes apart. In respect of their currency and importance they did not seem to demand a place in the text. Though I did not describe, I have mentioned, however, the *Knights of Light*, the story of its origin and the importance which has been attributed to the Order by a few writers who have made it the subject of somewhat mysterious references. It was first heard of in 1780, and Masonic authorities, who are wrong—as is usual in their dealings with matters of this kind — tell us that it did not continue much longer than two years. It was (*a*) merged in the ASIATIC BRETHREN, as we have seen, or (*b*) dissolved altogether. I have no ground for accepting or denying a recent counter-statement that it survives to this day, but it was represented by a German periodical called *The Signet Star*, publication of which continued till 1812. The system comprised seven unveiled Degrees of Mystic Freemasonry, but as it only made known five we may infer that there was a Grade of Postulance, and one at the apex in more complete seclusion than the rest. A Ritual account is available in respect of (*a*) *Knight-Novice of the third year;* (*b*) *Knight-Novice of the fifth year;* (*c*) *Knight-Novice of the seventh year;* (*d*) *Levite;* and (*e*) *Priest.* There is also a Ritual for the installation of the head of a province. The member elected made profession of faith in God, covenanted to love his brethren more than himself, and was cross-marked on the head with oil from a golden cup, various exhortations being pronounced. The communications were of an alchemical nature. The *Novice of the third year* was taken into a dark room, meaning that the Matter of the Wise is environed by a black matter ; he was stripped of metallic substances, because the Matter of the Wise is not found where metals are ; his shoe was removed, to signify his personal renunciation ; and his eyes were bandaged, because the luminous substance is found only in a dark place. At one point of the proceedings a battery was made on the floor, and this signified (*a*) that the True Matter is brought from the volcano ; (*b*) that the Order was concerned with the physical mysteries wrought by fire, apparently (*c*) on animal, vegetable and mineral substances. The work of this Novice was theosophical, magical and chemical. The *Novice of the fifth year* was instructed concerning the union of the three principles, the mystic significance of the number seven and the Creative Elohim. To the *Novice of the seventh year* there was given a specific interpretation of the Master-Builder and his legend, but it would be difficult to present it intelligibly to a reader who is not a Mason. The Degree of *Levite* offers nothing which seems to call for citation, but in that of *Priest*, being a sacerdotalism according to the Order of fire, there was the ceremonial and religious kindling of that element. The Candidate was told that he approached a certain barrier which, because he was himself enlightened, he would be able to pass. He was informed subsequently that he had reached the end of the Secret Mysteries belonging to the Royal and Priestly Order, the same being of such a nature that they must be sought in the light only and can there alone be found. It will be seen that the receptions are suggestive along their particular lines, but that on the surface they convey nothing.

A word may be said in conclusion concerning three systems the perfect obscurity of which is balanced by the magnitude of the claim which they made on antiquity. Of their origin, their locality and their literal history I can report nothing. (1) CHALDEAN MASONRY was founded *ex hypothesi spuria* by the Magi and flourished more especially at their chief centre in Media. It was a mouthpiece of the Wisdom of Egypt, and the records affirm that in days approximate to our own it was governed by seven wardens, one of whom was a Grand Master appointed for life by an irrevocable decree. Three Grades were communicated in Three Temples dedicated to (*a*) Wisdom, (*b*) Strength and (*c*) Beauty, being a triad which is known otherwise to Masonry. In the first the Candidate was brought forth from chaos into the state of moral life ; in the second he was reintegrated in his original dignity, was reconciled to his Creator and received the communication of the occult sciences ; in the third he had a picture of the golden age to come, when humanity shall enter into the state of resurrection, which is that of life in perfection. A similar doctrine of rebirth and reintegra-

371

tion was taught by the so-called MASONRY OF ZOROASTER, another venerable institution in respect of imputed antiquity. It required high qualifications in its Candidates and imposed on them the severity of virtue appropriate to a new life. It gave instructions in physics, geometry and astronomy, which were regarded as the most useful branches of human knowledge. The Grades were those of *Believer*, *Elect* and *Magus*. It would seem that PYTHAGOREAN FREEMASONRY has been also perpetuated, as I have met with the nomenclature of its Grades and a schedule of its official secrets, being words and signs. The Candidate suffered purification by the four elements, and appears to have learned (*a*) that all human beings are children of their Creator and citizens of the world ; (*b*) that the past is dead and irrecoverable ; but (*c*) that now is the accepted time. It is uncertain whether these secrets were imparted at once to the Neophyte or distributed over the three Degrees.· It may be charitable to suppose that he fared better by the time that he became an Epopt.

II

NOTES ON THE RECURRENCE OF GRADES IN THE VARIOUS RITES

THE classification adopted by the ANCIENT AND ACCEPTED SCOTTISH RITE is here taken as the basis because it is an actual *terminus a quo*, with which all High Grade Masons are or should be acquainted. It is beyond the scope of my design, and it would be almost beyond possibility to make the tabulation complete in the exhaustive sense, but it is complete in a reasonable— that is to say, in the practical—way, because I think that it will serve its unassuming purpose, which is to give some notion regarding the migration of Grades and the ruling of the most important in all the chief systems.

Appendices

It is, I suppose, unnecessary to add that the Craft Grades are outside the horizon of such a catalogue as they are presupposed everywhere — being the condition from which there is no dispensation—in all Orders and Rites which depend, integrally or by ascription, from the root of Masonry.

A.—*Secret Master* : ANCIENT AND ACCEPTED SCOTTISH RITE, No. 4 ; COUNCIL OF EMPERORS OF THE EAST AND WEST, No. 4 ; RITE OF MIZRAÏM, No. 4 ; also, under the synonym of *Discreet* [sometimes *Secret*] *Master*, RITE OF MEMPHIS, No. 4 ; old RITE OF HEREDOM OR OF PERFECTION,— *i.e.* CHAPTER OF CLERMONT—No. 4. In the A.·. and A.·. S.·. R.·. it is the 1st Degree of Perfection, otherwise Ineffable Degrees.

B.— *Perfect Master* : ANCIENT AND ACCEPTED SCOTTISH RITE, No. 5 ; COUNCIL OF EMPERORS, No. 5 ; RITE OF PERFECTION, No. 5 ; SCOTTISH MOTHER LODGE OF MARSEILLES, No. 4 ; RITE OF MIZRAÏM, No. 5 ; RITE OF MEMPHIS, No. 5, called also *Master Architect* ; PRIMITIVE SCOTTISH RITE, No. 4 ; said also to have been the first of the High Grades in the SCOTTISH PHILOSOPHICAL RITE, but I do not find it under this name in my lists : the Rite in question was almost exclusively chivalric.

C.—*Intimate Secretary* : ANCIENT AND ACCEPTED, No. 6 ; EMPERORS, No. 6 ; MIZRAÏM, No. 6, called also *Master by Curiosity* ; MEMPHIS, No. 6, called also *Sublime Master* ; RITE OF PERFECTION, No. 7.   This Grade says that twenty cities were conveyed by Solomon to the Master for his building services.

D.—*Provost and Judge* : ANCIENT AND ACCEPTED, No. 7 ; EMPERORS, No. 8 ; RITE OF PERFECTION, No. 8 ; MIZRAÏM, No. 7 ; MEMPHIS, No. 7 ; PRIMITIVE SCOTTISH RITE, No. 5 ; called also *Irish Master*, and under this title it is said (1) that it was founded by Ramsay, which is entirely false, and (2) that it was the first of three Irish Degrees of the Mastery instituted as a Jacobite

373

veil, which, on the question of the symbolism, appears quite idle.

E.—*Superintendent of Buildings*, or *Master in Israel*: ANCIENT AND ACCEPTED, No. 8 ; EMPERORS, No. 7 ; RITE OF PERFECTION, No. 7 ; MIZRAÏM, No. 7 ; MEMPHIS, No. 8, under the name of *Knight of the Elect* ; it is further said to have been the 9th Degree in the collection of the Metropolitan Chapter of France, developed from the COUNCIL OF EMPERORS and from Pirlet's COUNCIL OF THE KNIGHTS OF THE EAST.

F.—*Master Elect of Nine* : ANCIENT AND ACCEPTED, No. 9 ; EMPERORS, No. 9 ; RITE OF PERFECTION, No. 9 ; PRIMITIVE SCOTTISH RITE, No. 6 ; Metropolitan Chapter of France, No. 6 ; Adonhiramite Masonry, No. 6 ; RITE OF THE ELECT OF TRUTH, No. 5 ; MIZRAÏM, No. 9 ; MEMPHIS, No. 9 ; it is said also to have been the first point of the 4th Degree in the old system of the Royal York Lodge of Berlin. This is how the High Grades travelled.

G.—*Illustrious Master Elect of Fifteen* : ANCIENT AND ACCEPTED, No. 10 ; EMPERORS, No. 10 ; RITE OF PERFECTION, No. 10 ; PRIMITIVE SCOTTISH RITE, No. 8 ; ADONHIRAMITE MASONRY, No. 7 ; RITE OF THE ELECT OF TRUTH, No. 6 ; Metropolitan Chapter of France, No. 11 ; MIZRAÏM, No. 11 ; MEMPHIS, No. 10. This Grade is said to have been the second point of a 4th Degree in the old Berlin system, while the French rite once had under the title of *Elect of Pérignan*—now *Elu* simply—a combination of the *Elect of Nine* and *Elect of Fifteen*. Pérignan is said to have been a name invented by the Stuarts, who in the opinion of certain Masonic writers seem to have divided with Jesuits the honour of many darksome inventions. The name appears in *Elect of the Unknown*, which is the 10th Grade in the system of MIZRAÏM, and therefore precedes that of the *Elect of Fifteen*. *Grand Elect of Fifteen* was once included in the collection of the French University.

H.—*Sublime Knight*, or *Chevalier Elect; Sublime*

Appendices

Knight Elect: ANCIENT AND ACCEPTED, No. 11; MEMPHIS, No. 11; Metropolitan Chapter of France, No. 15.

I.—*Grand Master Architect*: ANCIENT AND ACCEPTED, No. 12; EMPERORS, No. 12; as *Knight Grand Master Architect*, MEMPHIS, No. 12. The Grade of *Grand Architect* or *Scottish Fellow Craft*, which is the 8th of Adonhiramite Masonry, is distinct from this Grade. There are also seven Grades of *Grand Architect of Heredom* included in as many different systems, but it is impossible to speak of their variations as compared with one another or their correspondence with innumerable degrees having titles which differ slightly.

J.—*Royal Arch*, concerning which it is essential to remember that it is entirely distinct from that *Holy Order of the Royal Arch*, which is a development from the 3rd Craft Degree: ANCIENT AND ACCEPTED, No. 13; as *Knight Royal Arch*, EMPERORS, No. 13; PRIMITIVE SCOTTISH RITE, No. 15; RITE OF PERFECTION, No. 15; as *Grand Royal Arch*, MIZRAÏM, No. 31; MEMPHIS, No. 13; it seems also to have been the 72nd Grade in the collection of the University.

K.—*Grand Scottish Knight of the Holy Vault*, or *of James the Sixth*: ANCIENT AND ACCEPTED, No. 14; MIZRAÏM, No. 20; MEMPHIS, No. 14.

L.—*Knight of the East*, or *of the Sword*: ANCIENT AND ACCEPTED, No. 15; EMPERORS, No. 15; RITE OF PERFECTION, No. 15; PRIMITIVE SCOTTISH RITE, No. 17; RITE OF THE ELECT OF TRUTH, No. 11; Metropolitan Chapter of France, No. 52; Royal York of Berlin, No. 6; French Rite, No. 6; RITE OF THE PHILALETHES, No. 6; Adonhiramite Masonry, No. 11; MIZRAÏM, No. 41; MEMPHIS, No. 15.

M.—*Prince of Jerusalem*, or *Chief of Regular Lodges*: ANCIENT AND ACCEPTED, No. 16; EMPERORS, No. 16; RITE OF PERFECTION, No. 16; so-called RITE OF MARTINISM, No. 8; REFORMED SCOTTISH RITE OF BARON TSCHOUDY, No. 8; PRIMITIVE SCOTTISH RITE,

The Secret Tradition in Freemasonry

No. 18 ; MIZRAIM, No. 45 ; MEMPHIS (as *Knight Prince*), No. 16.

N.—*Knight of the East and West*: ANCIENT AND ACCEPTED, No. 17 ; EMPERORS, No. 17 ; RITE OF PERFECTION, No. 17 ; MEMPHIS, No. 17— that is, *Knight Prince of the East and West.*

O.—*Sovereign Prince Rose-Croix*: ANCIENT AND ACCEPTED, No. 18 ; EMPERORS, No. 18 ; RITE OF PERFECTION, No. 18 ; RITE OF PHILALETHES, No. 7 ; SCOTTISH PHILOSOPHICAL MOTHER LODGE, No. 8 ; ORDER OF THE ELECT OF TRUTH, No. 12 ; SCOTTISH REFORMED RITE, No. 12 ; SCOTTISH MOTHER LODGE OF MARSEILLES, No. 18 ; MIZRAÏM, No. 46 ; MEMPHIS, No. 18. The nomenclature varies in several of the above, in addition to which there are more important differences as follows : as *Rose-Croix,* or *Knight of the Black Eagle,* three sub-grades, PHILOSOPHICAL RITE, No. 6 ; as *Knight Rose-Croix*—Adonhiramite Masonry, No. 12 ; as *Knight Rose-Croix*—MIZRAÏM,' No. 37 ; as *Magnetic Rose-Croix, ibid.,* No. 38 ; as *Magnetic Rose-Croix,* or *Sacred Wand,* UNIVERSITY COLLECTION, No. 195 ; another variant from the same with the additional title of Adept, No. 199 ; as *Knight Sovereign Prince Rose-Croix*—Royal York Chapter of Berlin, No. 7 ; as *Knight Rose-Croix of Kilwinning and Heredom*—MIZRAÏM, No. 46 ; as *Jacobite Rose-Croix*—Primordial Chapter of Arras, alleged sole Grade, but the question is doubtful : called also *Scottish Jacobite.* There were many others, but the above will exhaust ordinary interest.

P.—*Grand Pontiff,* or *Sublime Scottish Mason* : ANCIENT AND ACCEPTED, No. 18 ; with the additional title of *Grand Master ad vitam,* EMPERORS, No. 19 ; with the additional title of *Sublime Écossais of the Heavenly Jerusalem,* RITE OF PERFECTION, No. 19 ; the RITE OF MEMPHIS has several additional Pontiff Grades, but they represent putative Egyptian rather than *Écossais* Masonry.

Q.—*Venerable Grand Master ad vitam*—that is to say, of all Lodges ; called also *Sovereign Prince of*

Appendices

Masonry : Ancient and Accepted, No. 20 ; Emperors, No. 20 ; with the fore title of *Knight Grand Master of the Temple of Wisdom*, Memphis, No. 20 ; as *Venerable of Lodges*, Primitive Scottish Rite, No. 19. There was also *Perfect Venerable* in the collection of Viamy, and a *Venerable Grand Elect* in the so-called Persian Rite.

R.—*Noachite, or Prussian Chevalier* : Ancient and Accepted, No. 21 ; Emperors, No. 20 ; Mizraïm, No. 35 ; Memphis, No. 22 ; Adonhiramite Masonry, No. 13 ; Primitive Scottish Rite of Namur, No. 16 ; as *Sovereign Noachite*, Grade of the University, No. 120. There are others, but these will suffice.

S.—*Prince of Libanus*, called also *Royal Hatchet* or *Axe* : Ancient and Accepted, No. 22 ; Emperors, No. 22 ; probably as *Grand Axe*, Mizraïm, No. 22 ; Memphis, No. 23.

T.—*Chief of the Tabernacle* : Ancient and Accepted, No. 23 ; compare *Knight of the Tabernacle*, Mizraïm, No. 24 ; and the collection of F. Fustier.

U.—*Prince of the Tabernacle* : Ancient and Accepted, No. 24 ; as *Knight of the Red Eagle*, Memphis, No. 25.

V.—*Knight of the Brazen Serpent* : Ancient and Accepted, No. 25 ; as *Knight of the Serpent*, Antient and Primitive Rite, No. 15 ; Memphis, No. 26.

W.—*Prince of Mercy* : Ancient and Accepted, No. 26 ; seemingly without place in other systems.

X.—*Sovereign Commander of the Temple* : Ancient and Accepted, No. 27 ; Mizraïm, No. 44. It is said to have been the ninth Grade in the Order of Christ— but this is an invention—and was included in the collection of Lepage.

Y.—*Knight of the Sun* : Ancient and Accepted, No. 28 ; Scottish Philosophical Rite, No. 4 ; Philosophical Scottish Mother Lodge, No. 18. It is also called *Prince Adept*. There seem to have been variants as follows : *Knight of John* or of *the Sun*, Memphis, No. 29 ; *Solar Knight*, collection of Peuvret,

No. 76, and SCOTTISH MOTHER LODGE OF MARSEILLES, No. 18 ; *Knight of the Kabalistic Sun,* or *Adept,* collection of Pyron ; *Prince Adept* or *Cherubim (sic) Sublime Elect of Truth,* No. 1 ; MIZRAIM, No. 51.

Z.—*Grand Scottish Chevalier of St. Andrew of Scotland* : ANCIENT AND ACCEPTED, No. 29 ; called also *Patriarch of the Crusades* and *Grand Master of Light ;* PRIMITIVE SCOTTISH RITE, No. 25. The Grand *Écossais* Grades are too numerous, and their connections too uncertain, for enumeration.

A.A.—*Knight Kadosh* : ANCIENT AND ACCEPTED, No. 30 ; as *Grand Kadosh,* MEMPHIS, No. 31 ; alleged RITE OF SWEDENBORG, No. 8 ; PRIMITIVE SCOTTISH RITE, No. 28 ; REFORMED RITE OF TSCHOUDY, No. 10 ; so called RITE OF MARTINISM, No. 10 ; and many others.

B.B.—*Grand Inspector Inquisitor Commander* : ANCIENT AND ACCEPTED, No. 31 ; MIZRAÏM, No. 66 ; see also *Grand Inspector,* SCOTTISH PHILOSOPHICAL RITE, No 11.

C.C.—*Prince of the Royal Secret* : ANCIENT AND ACCEPTED, No. 32 ; as *Prince of the Royal Mystery,* MEMPHIS, No. 33.

D.D.—*Sovereign Grand Inspector-General* : ANCIENT AND ACCEPTED, No. 33 ; as *Sovereign Grand Inspector of the Order,* MEMPHIS, No. 84.

It should be understood that I offer no guarantee (*a*) as to the correspondence in Ritual of things passing under the same or similar titles, or (*b*) as to the accuracy of Grade lists ascribed to the lesser systems.

Appendices

III

P. x. Par, 6.—The Secret Tradition is the immemorial knowledge concerning man's way of return whence he came by a method of the inward life. The experiment is so old in the East that its first form therein may be taken for a *terminus a quo* as to the fact in history.

P. xi, Par. 11.—The principle or practice of communicating signs and passwords through all Degrees and the introduction in many of a word which is not a password carry on the idea of a verbal formula through systems which, although Masonic by the hypothesis, are not otherwise connected with the legend of a lost and recovered word.

P. xi, Par. 12.—That loss and restoration are essential to the idea of Masonry. The middle term is absence, out of which quest arises. When one of the triad is wanting, whether implicitly or explicitly, the Grade is not Masonic.

P. xv, Par. 28.—The delayed manifestation is a symbolism within a symbolism.

P. xvii, Par. 36.—Those who are called to the convocation are those who have conceived in their hearts the desire of the Secret Doctrine and would dwell in the House thereof.

P. 2.—It is not a point of any importance for my own purpose, but in view of what is said in the text it may be just to add that in the opinion of Mr. R. F. Gould (*a*) Mother Kilwinning did once possess more ancient records than are included now in its archives, and (*b*) that they were destroyed by fire or otherwise, in respect of certain items, while some were removed or carelessly dispersed.　Mr. Gould's view reflects that of Masonic authorities in Scotland.

P. 3.—The talisman was made, consecrated and exhibited by Ramsay, to whom we owe all the romance of Kilwinning.　Every further effort of research magnifies the importance of his dream—not of course in respect of its value, but in that of its influence on the development of the High Grades.

P. 8.—With reference to the three divergent cases which are not to be explained by a descent from the operative Craft, it is not my intention to suggest that the Grade of *Kadosh*, which is the 30th Degree in the system of the Scottish Rite, enters at any point into the Secret Tradition, as this is understood in these pages.　If in any of its forms it had been in correspondence with the title, such a question might have arisen, but there is nothing in the extant codices to connect it with sanctity and priesthood.　The true historical *Kadosh* was a Grade of vengeance—as we have seen ; when a philosophical aspect was substituted for that of assassination or vindication, it became a Grade of puerile and prosaic discourses.

P. 16.—The Regius MS. belongs to the thirteenth century, and has been edited by Mr. J. O. Halliwell. It contains (*a*) some account of the origin of architecture, otherwise Masonry, under the auspices of the great clerk Euclyde, who was a native of Egypt ; (*b*) the introduction of the art into England during the reign of Athelstan ; (*c*) its reformation by an assembly convened at this King's instance ; (*d*) the Articles of its Association in rude rhymed verse ; (*e*) points of procedure and conduct ; (*f*) a schedule of religious, moral and social duties ; and (*g*) the legend of the Four Crowned Masters.

P. 31.—Concerning the counsels of morality, that which is understood in Freemasonry by ethical qualifications is a title and not a title.　Apart from these no person can advance a single pace in the investigation of those Divine Mysteries which are of Nature, of Science and of something that is above either. But their simple possession does not mean even a rudimentary disposition towards the higher research and much less the possession of the other qualities that are necessary thereto.

P. 38.—The Veiled Masters chose the Temple of Solomon for their symbolism because it was of the tradition of Israel, had been utilised by its theosophical literature, and was sufficiently remote in time to be convenient otherwise for their purpose.

P. 41.—With reference to the seeming equivocation, the sacred text says (Ex. xxxi. 18) : "And he gave unto Moses, when he had made an end of communing with him upon Mount Sinai, two tables of testimony, tables of stone, written with the finger of God." The inference is that the tables were shaped for the purpose by the hand of Elohim. . . . But after the idolatry and in respect of the substituted Law, the text says (Ex. xxxiv. 1 *et seq.*) : " Hew thee two tables of stone like unto the first : and I will write upon these tables the words that were on the first tables, which thou brakest. . . . And he "—that is to say, Moses—" hewed two tables of stone like unto the first. . . . And he "— that is to say, Moses (v. 28)—not Elohim as promised —" wrote upon the tables the words of the covenant, the ten commandments," whereas the content of the first tables is not specified in Ex. xxxi. 18. On the other hand, Deut. x. 4, says that Jehovah wrote on the second tables. The Zoharic tradition on the whole subject is, I think, significant. The tables broken by Moses were those of tne Biblical Law and the Law of Tradition (Fol. 28*b*). It is said also (Fol. 26*b*) that the first tables emanated from the Tree of Life, while the second or substituted tables were from the side of the Tree of Good and Evil. Thence came the Law, as it was known afterwards in Israel. The first Law was on the side of life, the second on that of death, consisting of negative precepts and commandments. It is said also that, after the idolatry, Moses clothed the people in the vestments of the literal Law.

P. 44.—Mackey, the American Masonic writer, though he had few intimations concerning the term of his subject, says that the search for the Word in all Masonry is the search after truth—Divine Truth— knowledge of God, and he then adds plainly that this knowledge was concealed in old Kabalistic doctrine under the symbol of the Ineffable Name.

P. 48.—The nature of the significance which inhered in the barbarous words to which the Chaldean Oracles refer is explained by Iamblichus. They were drawn from the languages of Egypt and Assyria, had passed into corruption and were sacred more especially by tradition, but also because they had ceased to be intelligible.

P. 51.—The Talmud reports, on the authority of the old doctors, that the Ineffable Name was commemorated ten times on the Day of Expiation—thrice in the first confession, thrice in the second, thrice at the dismissal of the scape-goat, and finally *in sortibus*, referring to the *oblatio pro peccato Domino*. The voice of the priest was heard even in Jericho. Speaking generally, it must be admitted that there is some difficulty in reconciling the points of the hypothesis, which dwells now upon a lost pronunciation and the vital nature of the Hebrew vowels, but again upon the sacredness and separate import of the consonants. However, the confusion, such as it is, seems to be the result of a medley of text and commentary, some of the latter being late and not of real authority.

P. 60.—See the section entitled " Masonry and Moral Science " in *The Hidden Church of the Holy Graal*, pp. 584–587.

P. 70.—It follows from the Zoharic view of the Fall of Man that the idolatry and wantonness of Israel at the foot of Mount Sinai are part of a scheme of symbolism, though it is not excogitated in the text.

Appendices

P. 71.—It is sixty and more years since Adolphe Franck connected the Kabalistic doctrine concerning the *Shekinah* with the philosophical and theological doctrine of the Divine Immanence in creation. This is one side of the consanguinity, as of things spiritual, between the Cohabiting or Indwelling Glory and Messiah, the Prince of Daniel, who is also the Prince of Peace. It is also one of the exotic aspects of the relation between the Craft and Christian Masonry. But it is so exotic that I have not proposed to dwell upon it, except by occasional allusion, in this work.

P. 74.—With reference to the Four Worlds of Kabalism, it should perhaps be explained that they are (*a*) *Atziluth*, the world of Deity ; (*b*) *Briah*, the archetypal world ; (*c*) *Yetzirah*, the world of formation ; and (*d*) *Assiah*, which is the manifest world. I have made these brief descriptions as simple as possible, but the system which they summarise is exceedingly involved. *Atziluth* is really the Deity approximating towards a certain manifest state in concealment, by a path which suggests emanation : behind it is the uttermost Divine transcendence, called *Ain Soph Aour*. In a sense *Atziluth* is also the archetypal world. *Briah* itself is sometimes called the world of creation, but remote as such from the manifest ; it is also archangelic and intelligible. *Yetzirah* is the world of the angels, and in one aspect it is the moral world. *Assiah* is the sphere of the elements and the domain of Nature. The permutations of the hypothesis might be extended much further.

P. 142.—I have said that no true Grade depicts a Lodge in Paradise, and this reads like a judgment beforehand on that called *Knight of the Sun*, but my readers will be enabled to decide when this peculiar chivalry is considered at its proper point in the text. An old French writer tells us that certain enthusiasts are persuaded that the first Lodge was held in the Earthly Paradise when God appeared therein to Adam and Eve. Other chivalries or Degrees may incorporate the opinion, but I have not felt it needful to pursue the subject.

P. 156.—It is impossible even to speculate on the date at which the Grade of *Marked Master* originated, but the episode of the North Gate may signify that the traditional story concerning the memorable event differed in some minor respects from its present state. I can imagine one in which the symbolism might perhaps be more complete, but the question must be left at this point.

P. 157.—Other legends tell us that the Stone of Jacob was used at the foundation of the world, that it existed before the creation, and that the Temple was built upon it. According to the *Zohar*, it was the House of Jehovah, or rather the seat of judgment. It was the fundamental Stone. A Chaldaic paraphrase of Exodus xxviii. 30, affirms that the Great and Holy Name was graven upon it.

P. 177.—My affirmation that three victims would have been too many for the secret intention implies that this was political, and that the one victim signified the King of France. On the other hand, the murdered person in the Templar *Kadosh, i.e.* Jacques de Molay, represented the people, liberty, human right, etc. Perhaps I should add that M. Henri d'Alméras, a modern writer, concludes that French Freemasonry during the eighteenth century was Catholic and loyal, because evidence is wanting in respect of the opposite view. It was not indeed so revolutionary as supposed by some who have seen the conspiracy preparing everywhere, but except in a few Grades it was not catholic at all—I mean, in the Roman sense.

P. 220.—As the Areopagite and his writings are the subject of occasional reference throughout the text, I should like to note, though it is really outside my subject, that the weight of recent critical opinion, especially among German scholars, tends to reverse the views held previously and to place Dionysius in the first century, in which case he was probably, as his writings claim, a colleague of St. Paul and St. John. The change of opinion in this direction is summarised in the various notes and appendices to Parker's recent edition of the works. My attention has been called to the fact by my friend Mr. W. L. Wilmshurst, who has devoted considerable attention to the subject.

P. 231.—It will be seen later on in the text that the Rituals of the STRICT OBSERVANCE in the only available form are probably defective and do not fully represent the ceremonies as worked in the Chapters.

P. 238.—I ought perhaps to explain at this point that the Hebrew words given in the text are the consonants of Jehovah and Jeheshua, that is to say, Jesus.

P. 251.—Against this allocation of the *Rose-Croix* Grade to the year 1754 there must be set the opinion of Findel, who, I believe, followed Kloss, that it was not in reality invented till 1763.

P. 259.—I believe at the same time that Frère des Étangs was actuated by an excellent spirit and made use of all his lights. The large volume of his collected works is still suggestive reading, but he happened to mistake the Gate of the Sanctuary for the Holy Place itself. His reconstruction of the Master Grade is little better than a travesty ; it is as if one should say that Christ only slept in the tomb where He was laid by Joseph of Arimathea. The mystic death which precedes the mystic resurrection must be real like that which follows it. So also the discourses of Des Étangs are luminous vapour, and his attempted refutation of Barruel leaves a sense of complete void.

P. 301.—It is said that Faustus Socinus made frequent reference in his writings to the building of a new temple when he sought to put forward the principles of his reformed theology. He also exhorted his disciples to arm themselves with hammers, aprons and other things belonging to the building craft, when engaged in the foundation of a new religious belief.

P. 316.—The Chapter of Clermont is said also to have been propagated by Rosa in Holland, Denmark and Sweden. It has been termed the Rosaic Rite and has led to a confused notion that it was a phase or variant of the Rosicrucian system, for which there is no warrant in fact.

P. 319.—The chief propagator of the Jesuit hypothesis was Ragon, and his works may be consulted *passim* for the nullity of his method. He tells us (1) that all Grades fabricated by the Society in question were designed to turn Masonry into a school of catholicism ; (2) that the *Masonry Dissected* of Samuel Pritchard has traces of their influence ; (3) that in a certain *Écossais* Degree the word Jesuit should be substituted for the name of Jehovah, and then, presumably, the whole scheme is plain ; (4) that Ramsay was one of the convenient tools ; and so forth. The process is of similar simplicity throughout, and the value is, I think, transparent.

P. 333.—See the succession of High Grades ennumerated on p. 217. They are four in number, or seven with those of the Craft.

VOLUME THE SECOND

P. 11.—It has not, I suppose, been observed that the intervention of Elias Ashmole, of the Hermetic Schools otherwise, or Schools of Kabalism, presupposes that the first result was the creation of the Third Craft Degree in a form similar to the present in respect of the root-matter. There are a few students who attribute great antiquity to this legend ; personally I believe that it is old in the essence only, that it was not pre-existent in the operative craft, and is the chief evidence of intervention of what kind soever. It signifies the presence of the Secret Tradition, the existence of which was utterly unlikely in the Building Guild.

Appendices

P. 12.—Mr. Gould's view concerning the Regius MS. has an importance which is quite independent of any value attaching to his construction of the document, for the simple reason that it signifies the unrest of the informed Masonic mind respecting the theory heretofore accepted as explaining the development of the speculative and symbolic element out of the Operative Craft. It is a minor question whether the particular MS. offers a way of escape from an opinion which has been so far held adequate but which is rapidly becoming untenable.

P. 26.—I refer in particular to the essay prefixed to my recent edition of Thomas Vaughan's *Lumen de Lumine*.

P. 27.—It may be worth while to mention that Saint-Martin was not the earliest nor the first translator of Jacob Böhme into the French language. He was preceded in 1787 by le Sieur Jean Macle, who published *Le Miroir Temporel de l'Éternité*, which recalls by its title the first answer to *Forty Questions concerning the Soul*, but appears by its description to be a translation of *De Signatura Rerum*. I have not seen it.

P. 45.—The alleged connection of the Brethren of Avignon with political conspiracy is probably a reflection from Barruel, who in his usual style says that they were like the German Weishaupt but more atrocious.

P. 49.—It must be said, I suppose, that the two English pilgrims who journeyed to Avignon were not at the time, nor did they become thereafter, disciples of Swedenborg. They were believers in the prophetic mission of Richard Brothers, and expected to derive further elucidations and warrants concerning him by their visit to the French city and to the society at work therein. Some of my readers may remember the rhyme of Robert Southey concerning a visitation of Lucifer—

> He walked into London leisurely ;
> The streets were dirty and dim ;
> But there he saw Brothers the prophet,
> And Brothers the prophet saw him.

The Secret Tradition in Freemasonry

It is not necessary to speak of the prophet's mission or of the things that he foretold ; they were of the usual type concerning the Second Advent and the wrath to come.

P. 57.—The reference to the Craft Grades presupposes, according to Tschoudy, the existence of the Third Degree *ab origine symboli.*

P. 70.—Jean Joachim Estrengel is also said to have published the Statutes of the Unknown Philosophers, but I have not been able to identify their original form. A version is given by Pierre Zaccone, but the preamble is that of Ragon, while the rules are those of Tschoudy.

P. 75.—Ragon had even the audacity, for I cannot characterise it differently, to specify nine Grades in the ORDER OF CHRIST as follows : (1) *Knight of the Triple Cross,* conferred only on Excellent and Perfect Princes *Rose-Croix;* (2) *Knight of the Black and White Eagle,* or *Grand Elect Knight Kadosh;* (3) *Knight Adept* or *Cherubim;* (4) *Sublime Elect of Truth;* (5) *Grand Elect Knight of the Black Eagle;* (6) *Sovereign Grand Commander;* (7) *Knight Kaes;* (8) *Deputy Grand Inspector-General,* or *Prince of the Royal Secret;* (9) *Sovereign Commander of the Temple.* It is well known that the ORDER OF CHRIST is vested in the crown of Portugal and has no Masonic connection.

P. 108.—The intimations of the *Archives* make the pulses beat by their memories from far away of great and undeclared things concerning the Secret Tradition. The loss or non-existence of its later sections is a very grave loss to the larger aspects of the whole Hermetic subject.

P. 170.—The reference is to my *Life and Doctrine of Louis Claude de Saint-Martin, the Unknown Philosopher,* and more especially to p. 48, but the work may be consulted throughout.

P. 184.—He emerges also in some dreams of the foolish as a preacher of political illuminism and his system as a precursor in France of the plan which passed for a moment into the actuality of a secret organisation under Adam Weishaupt. But the ORDER OF ILLUMINATI was German and the dates do not work in harmony. See *La Franc-Maçonnerie dans sa véritable signification*, translated from the German of Eckert by Abbé Gyr, vol. ii. p. 81.

P. 187.—There is, however, a very full record of one intimate friendship, namely, between Saint-Martin and Kirchberger, Baron de Liebestorf, though they were acquainted only by correspondence. It is not met with too easily in either form, but that record is available both in French and English, in the latter case under the title of *Theosophic Correspondence*, translated by E. B. Penny. It is a priceless memorial of aspiration towards the inward life and experience therein, but I speak of it here to introduce a single reference, which is of interest more especially from the Masonic standpoint. It is an account by Krichberger of what occurred at the consecration of the Lyons Lodge of EGYPTIAN MASONRY. "The labours lasted three days, and the prayers fifty-four hours ; there were twenty-seven in the meeting. While the members were praying to the Eternal to manifest His approbation by a visible sign, and the Master was in the middle of his ceremonies, the Repairer appeared, and blessed the members assembled. He came down on a blue cloud, which served for vehicle to this apparition ; gradually he ascended again on this cloud, which, from the moment of its descent from heaven to earth, acquired a splendour so dazzling that a young girl, C., who was present, could not bear its light. The two great prophets and the law-giver of Israel also gave signs of their benevolence and approval." It should be understood that this is not the report of an eye-witness, and our acquaintance with the RITE OF EGYPTIAN MASONRY will enable us to conclude out of hand that the manifestation was not to the assembly at large, but to the young girl, who was a lucid of the Rite. It is noted otherwise by Kirchberger that Cagliostro, the Grand Copht, was not present at the proceedings, and I may add that in his presence the seering processes invariably failed to establish communication with Moses, which was one of his especial wishes. The prophets referred to were Enoch and Elias, the reputed founders of the Rite. Saint-Martin, to whom all such experiences, whether in cups, crystals or by the mode of form-appearances, were utterly indifferent, knew also by hearsay concerning "those adventures in Lyons," as he terms them almost derisively. He established no distinction respecting the kind of experience, as I have sought to do, but said in his detached way : "I do not hesitate to class them with the most suspicious order of things, notwithstanding that the good souls who were present may have received some happy transports, fruits of their piety and true desires ; God continually brings good out of evil." He adds that the manifestations which took place in his own school of Pasqually were much less tainted.

P. 193.—The Apocalypse naturally entered into the reveries of more perfervid Christian amateurs of Kabalism. We hear—though the authority is not too certain—of a *Kabalistic Society of Brethren of the Apocalypse*, founded in Germany, about 1690, by some one named Gabrino, who termed himself Prince of the Septenary.

P. 213.—It is unnecessary at this day to consider in any serious sense the old and idle dream put forward by Buhle and adapted by Thomas de Quincey concerning the metamorphosis of early Rosicrucianism into speculative Freemasonry. Even at the period of its appearance, there was nothing colourable in the thesis, and if it can have been ever said that it found favour in the past, it has been long since abandoned by all whose opinion on any matter of research can be held to count for anything. The connection between Freemasonry and Rosicrucianism is the root of both in the Secret Tradition, but they did not arise from one another any more than the romance-literature of the Holy Graal arose out of the Latin literature of Alchemy or *vice versa.* The story was that a branch of the Rosicrucian Fraternity had become established in England under circumstances which do not appear, but it was somehow, in addition to its own dedications, an attempt to give corporate expression to the idea of Francis Bacon's New Atlantis. Its alleged symbols were the Sun, the Moon, the Square, the Compasses, the Circle, the Five-pointed Star. This last was said to represent (*a*) Mercury, but probably under a philosophical aspect ; (*b*) *Archaios* : (*c*) the celestial fire ; (*d*) the Holy Spirit ; and (*e*) a healing balm poured through all Nature by the Eternal. The same symbols are said to be found in the *Mythologia Christiana* of J. V. Andreas, together with something corresponding to the plan of the Masonic carpet. A French writer who took over this phantasy went so far as to add that every implement and symbol now in use among Masons was borrowed from the Rosy Cross.

P. 237.—It will be scarcely necessary to point out that the visionary system of Swedenborg, some arbitrary attributions notwithstanding, owed nothing to traditions from the past. It is perhaps in the same position respecting a theosophical construction of the universe that spiritualism is in respect of religion. It is the common motive and reasonable spirit of this world transmuted and invested with an unchangeable office in eternity, as also with the conventional dignities thereto belonging. In a sense it may reflect from far away the Hermetic doctrine of analogy, but it is that doctrine in distraction. It is a vague recognition of this fact which made the sorriest of all religions and, as it seems to me, one of the least spiritual, a kind of fashion for the moment when the eighteenth century drew towards the tempest of its close. This was among those who had followed for a certain distance, as we have seen, the thorny path of physical Alchemy. On any other ground I do not know why it appealed to the ex-Benedictine Pernety, and it is he more especially who connects with it in Masonry. I may add that according to Barruel

Swedenborgian Masonry was confounded by some French people with the Illuminism of Weishaupt, and it is even pretended that by means of this confusion the latter was introduced into France by Mirabeau.

P. 326.—The reference is to my *Studies in Mysticism* and to the essay entitled *The Garden of Venus*.

IV

The Latin Church and Freemasonry

If the Christian religion, understood in its most plenary sense, can be regarded for a moment as constituting a single Church, then it may be said to exist for the communication of the Mystery of Faith to those who are capable of salvation by the entrance within this one fold of the one shepherd. As such, it has a ritual procedure, its signs, its symbols, its modes of communication; it has many Lodges of adepts and they are ruled by many masters. It has therefore in these respects—as in others which we have seen—a certain analogy with Emblematic Freemasonry. The comparison could be carried much further, for the Church in its sacramental system is emblematic, even as the Craft, and as the one Church is divided into many branches, not all of which acknowledge one another, so there is a great variety of Masonic obediences, some of which deny one another. Both institutions claim to impart Mysteries which are not otherwise attainable, and for me at least as a mystic there lies behind both an untrodden ground of grace and truth, of experimental knowledge and of reality behind knowledge. They are ministers of the Mysteries in part therefore only, and each is especially concerned on the surface with counsels of external conduct. It is no wonder that the Church, for the most part, resembles a glorified Lodge of Masonry, teaching the institutes of morality rather than the Great Mysteries of the Kingdom of Heaven, and experiencing so much difficulty in securing a common observance of the decalogue that she is almost perforce forgiven for finding contentment therein, without much recollection of all the untrvelled regions of the soul beyond those narrow measures. The gate is in this manner taken for the goal. It is no wonder also that, working on similar materials, the Masonic process is similar to the Church process, that the Craft is on the surface so largely an ethical system, and that its recognised or admissible extensions most frequently do little more than lift the sunbeams of morality a few points higher.

I have established here a broad bond of unity in purpose and in the method of attaining purpose. The Churches and Masonry are working in their several manners for the same ends : one might think that these sisters could dwell together in sisterhood. But the Churches denounce one another, when they do not exclude one another, and notwithstanding their necessary insistence on the natural virtues, of which Masonry is an independent exponent, there are some of them which denounce Masonry. The explanation perhaps is (*a*) that the supernatural motive tends unconsciously to disqualify the natural motive *per se*, and (*b*) that in some cases there is an inherent feeling of distrust for any alternative mystery.

One issue which arises in the general sense, and descends thence into every department of the particular, is that the Latin Church, for reasons of which some are obscure and some moderately transparent, has agreed to regard Freemasonry, and the secret societies that are connected by imputation therewith, as the culminating type, representative and summary of those forces which are at work in the world against the work of the Church in the world. The evidence which would be adduced, and is indeed adduced continually in support of this thesis, is (*a*) that the French Revolution was a product of the secret societies, and of Masonry chiefly ; (*b*) that the combination of those forces out of which came United Italy, with the subversion of the temporal power, had Masonry as their point of convergence ; (*c*) that the unhappy position of the Church in France has been created by Masonry ; and (*d*) that in so far as the other Latin races are disaffected towards Rome, and are tending towards naturalism in place of religion—this also is a Masonic tendency. Now, supposing that such a view could adduce in its support that historical evidence—abundant, sufficient, or even tolerably presumptive — which we, who are Masons, have been looking for our enemies to furnish, we should be left simply in the position of the Latin Church when that is confronted by competitive exponents of the truth of God. As this truth, from the standpoint of that Church, is unaffected by the pretensions of rival orthodoxies, pure apostolic Christianities and sects generally, so the Mason, who knows well enough what is the true purpose or rather the transparent term, what are the explicits and implicits of the mystery which initiation has reposed in his heart, will know also that Masonry would emerge unaffected, supposing that Grand Lodges, Grand Orients and Supreme Councils passed into corporate apostasy. If in certain countries and at certain distracted periods we find that the apparatus of the Lodges has been made to serve the purpose of plot and faction, Masonry as an institution is not more responsible for the abuse than is the Catholic Church as a whole for the poisoned eucharists of a Borgia pontiff.

It has been said very often that English Masonry is not to be judged by Masonry of the continental species ; that communion with the Grand Orient of France has been severed by the Grand Lodge of England ; and that Craft Masonry in the Latin countries generally has ceased almost to be Masonic at heart. But this is only a branch of the whole case : what is true of Great

Britain is true in one form or another of the United States, Canada, Australia and, among continental Kingdoms, of Sweden, Norway, Denmark, Germany and Holland. The Latin countries remain over—with a few others about which we know little masonically, seeing that they are in the South of Europe—and Russia also remains. Of these last nothing can be said with certainty, but in the Latin countries the position of Masonry is, in the part or the main, a work of the Church which condemns it.

There is no charge too banal, no *soi-disant* confession too preposterous in matter or manner, to be held adequate by the Catholic Church when its purport is to expose Freemasonry. The evidence for this is to be found, among things that are recent—or this at least comparatively—in the Masonic impostures of the late Leo Taxil, to whom more than one section of the Church lent a willing ear, whom it abandoned only when his final unmasking had become a foregone conclusion. I do not wish to go over an old ground carrying too full a search-light, but it seems desirable to say that Pope Leo x. granted an audience to Leo Taxil, and that the Cardinal-Vicar Parocchi felicitated him for exposing the imputed turpitude of imaginary androgyne lodges. Of two other squalid impostors, Adolphe Ricoux stood for an unimpeachable witness with Monsignor Meurin, Archbishop of Port Louis, while Margiotta had the papal benediction and a sheaf of episcopal plaudits. I do not doubt that even at this day, within the fold of the Latin Church, many persons are and will remain convinced—priests and prelates included—that Masonry is dedicated, as all these conspirators affirmed, to the practice of Black Magic and to the celebration of sacrilegious masses. Independently of this, and speaking now of the Latin Church in its official acts, it must be added that, from the *Humanum genus* encyclical to the finding of the Trent Congress, and whatsoever has followed thereafter, a long confusion of issues and identification of a part with the whole has characterised all the pronouncements.

Craft Freemasonry in its intellectual centres represents and mirrors of necessity the flux of modern opinion upon all speculative subjects, outside belief in a personal God and the other life of humanity—which are the fundamental part of its doctrine. Beyond this sphere it has no accredited opinions in matters of religion, while so far as the High Grades are concerned, those are few and unimportant which do not exact from their Candidates a profession of the Christian faith. We are therefore in a position to adjudicate upon the qualifications of the Trent Congress, which decided that the religious teachings of Freemasonry were those of Nature-worship, and that the public beliefs of Freemasons were those of Monism, Idealistic Pantheism, Materialism and Positivism, the connecting link between all being the identification of the universe with God. Doubtless Craft Freemasonry, even in England, includes in its ranks the shades of philosophical thought which correspond to these findings, but indubitably the same might be said of almost any large assembly, public or private, in any part of the world ; and hereof is the folly of the judgment. Freemasonry also numbers spiritualists, theosophists and representatives innumerable of the higher schools of mysticism. If it does not include convinced Catholics—and as regards intellectual certitude, apart from formal practice, it does include them assuredly—it is because the obedience of the one through the intolerance of the other makes the dual obedience impossible, though in itself it is natural and reasonable within its own lines.

It follows, as one inference from all preceding considerations, that certain High-Grade Orders do carry a second sense in their symbolism, and so also do the great Craft Grades, as we have seen in the fullest sense through our long research. But it is neither of Natural Religion, Idealistic Pantheism, Monism, nor much less of Materialism or Positivism. It is of that Great Experiment which is at the heart of all true religion, being the way of the soul's reintegration in God. I believe personally that the sacramentalism of the Christian scheme holds up the most perfect glass of reflection to the mystery of salvation, and that in this sense the Church contains the catholic scheme of the Mysteries ; but I know, after ·another manner, which is yet the same manner at heart, that there are Mysteries which are not of this fold, and that it is given unto man to find the hidden jewel of redemption in more than one Holy Place. I say therefore, with the Welsh bards, that I despise no precious, concealed Mysteries, wherever they subsist, and above all I have no part in those Wardens of the Gates who deny in their particular enthusiasm that things which are equal to the same are equal to one another, since these Wardens are blind.

I have mentioned the anti-Masonic Congress which was once held at Trent, and the deliberations at the city of Great Council are memorable after their own manner as distinguishing the position from which the Roman Church has not deviated for something more than a century. The Report of the Congress was issued in due course and is worth a word of reference for the reason which I have just indicated. Now the grey age of the Latin Church is not only within its own limits an astute and experienced age ; it is also one of honour and sanctity, and in a land where there remains little real prejudice and practically no Protestantism, Freemasons will be perfectly well aware that, however false her conclusions in specific cases, and however misguided her policy as dictated by those conclusions, she is acting in accordance with her lights and is saved in respect of sincerity. The Report of the Congress does little more than ‑italicise the salient points of the *Humanum Genus* Encyclical. In answer to that Encyclical, the Grand Lodge of England protested that Freemasonry in this country had no opinions, political or religious, and if this is not precisely a correct statement it marked a definite attitude which is practically of universal knowledge. In politics it has of course the grace of perfect loyalty to the established order, and in religion Freemasonry is based on certain doctrines which are at the root of belief. Beyond this, in their official capacity, Grand Lodges cannot go, because their consciousness reaches no further. That the ANCIENT AND ACCEPTED SCOTTISH RITE was at one period, and in the place which is its head and centre, making a bid for recognition under wider warrants, is shewn by the writings of the late Albert Pike, Grand Commander of the Southern Jurisdiction in the United States. Concerning the political aspect, I shall cite certain passages from his official reply to the *Humanum Genus* pronouncements, while as regards the religious views which he held personally, and designed to impress on Masons under the obedience of his Rite, very full information can be derived from the lectures attached by him to each of the thirty-three degrees included by the scheme of that Rite.

The reply to the Encyclical of Pope Leo was, I believe, publicly available at the time of its appearance, but it is not well known in this country, at least at the present day. The summary of the political position is briefly this, that Freemasonry has at no time conspired against any polity entitled to its obedience or to the esteem of men generally. " Wherever now there is a Constitutional Government which respects the rights of men and of the people and the public opinion of the world, it is the loyal supporter of that government. It has never taken pay from armed despotism, or abetted persecution. It has fostered no Borgias ; no stranglers or starvers to death of other Popes, like Boniface VII. ; no poisoners like Alexander VI. and Paul III. It has no roll of beatified Inquisitors ; and it has never in any country been the enemy of the people, the suppressor of scientific

truth, the stifler of the God-given right of free inquiry as
to the great problems, intellectual and spiritual, presented
by the universe, the extorter of confessions by the rack,
the burner of women and of the exhumed bodies of the
dead. . . . Its patron saints have always been St. John
the Baptist and St. John the Evangelist, and not Pedro
Arbues D'Epila, principal inquisitor of Zaragoza, who,
slain in 1485, was beatified by Alexander VII. in 1664."
The inferences from these statements are quite clear
and simple, and I do not pretend to regard them as
especially satisfactory either as a defence of Masonry or
as a charge against the Church of Rome. They are in
fact a declaration that governments, both political and
religious, may abdicate their right to rule, and that a time
may come when men, whether Masons or not, neither
can nor should continue to countenance, support or
tolerate such institutions. Personally I should not have
adopted this line of protestation, for the Church on its
part might regard it as an open door through which its
own accusations could obtain too easy entrance. The
right of superseding corrupt governments is unquestionably an imprescriptible part of human liberty, but one
does not with policy put forward the claim when attempting to prove that a particular body or fraternity has not
intervened overtly for the revision of specific constitutions
and the downfall of particular tyrannies. Furthermore,
the Catholic Church claims to be a Divine Institution,
over which there is no jurisdiction within the sphere of
human liberty, and it is not therefore likely to concur
in the validity of the line of argument. The two stand-
points cannot be reconciled, for they represent the
struggle of Divine Right in this or that of its two
aspects against the right of free government and of free
intellectual inquiry. On the one side, it is not more
the struggle of the Catholic Church than it is of political
autocracy; on the other, it is not more the opposing
effort of Freemasonry than it is of any enslaved people
demanding a constitution, or yearning and even plotting

for the downfall of some tyrannical dynasty. In continuation of his defence, Albert Pike affirmed that Freemasonry does not more condemn the excesses of the Papacy " than it does those of Henry VIII. of England, the murder of Sir Thomas More and that of Servetus, and those of the Quakers put to death in New England ; than the cruel torturing and slaying of Covenanters and Nonconformists, the ferocities of Claverhouse and Kirk, and the pitiless slaughtering of Catholic priests by the revolutionary fury of France. It well knows and cheerfully acknowledges the services which some of the Roman Pontiffs and a multitude of its clergy have in the past centuries rendered to humanity. It has always done ample justice to their pure lives, their good deeds, their self-denial, their devotedness, their unostentacious heroism. . . . It has always done full justice to the memories of the faithful and devoted missionaries of the Order of Jesus and others, who bore the Cross into every barbarous land under the sun, to make known to savages the truths and errors taught by the Roman Church, and the simple arts of civilization. It has never been the insensate and unreasoning reviler of that Church." In particular, " there has never been any opposition on the part of Freemasonry to Catholicism as a religion " in America. The private instructions of the Grand Commander did not differ from his more public utterances. " It is not the mission of Masonry," he observed elsewhere, " to engage in plots and conspiracies against the civil government. It is not the fanatical propagandist of any creed or theory ; nor does it proclaim itself the enemy of kings. It is the apostle of liberty, equality and fraternity ; but it is no more the high priest of republicanism than of constitutional monarchy." Here again there is perhaps nothing more than the commonplaces and truisms of a particular pleading which involves the suggestion that in political or other intervention, if any, Freemasonry has been actuated by honest and laudable motives. If in certain countries, and at certain distracted periods, we find that the apparatus of the Lodges has been made to serve the purpose of plot and faction, my contention would be that the Order as an institution is not more responsible for the abuse than is the Catholic Church as a whole for some crimes which have been perpetrated under its name. These things are matters of aberration, and I should regard it as far more wise to admit that, like other institutions in all ages and nations, Freemasonry has from time to time, indeed at too many times and in places too many, been diverted from her true ends. All that can be said notwithstanding, there is evidence enough and to spare that some of the Lodges and Chapters were put to the purpose of those subsurface conspiracies which led to the French Revolution, and it would be difficult to deny, even at the present day, the unofficial political complexion of several Masonic bodies in several countries of Europe. I do not see that there is anything to be lost by an admission of this kind ; in so far as it is political at any given centre, the institution has so far ceased to be Masonic ; in so far as it is at issue with official religion anywhere, so far also it has renounced its character and mission.

I am brought in this way to touch for a few moments on another aspect of Albert Pike and his writings. I suppose that he was the most important and influential member of the Craft who ever arose in America : it is to him that the ANCIENT AND ACCEPTED SCOTTISH RITE owes the eminent position which it occupies in the great body of High Grades ; it was he also who brought its rituals into their present American form, though I am by no means certain whether the form in question is to be counted among his best titles of honour. He had very definite tendencies on matters that make for religion, and though he is not quite in accord with himself as to the connection between religion and Freemasonry, if we take a mean between his contradictory statements, we shall find not only that he regarded the Craft, with its adjuncts, under a religious aspect, but that his lectures attached to the thirty-three Grades of Scottish Masonry are equivalent to a definite attempt at presenting a side of the Masonic subject which is militantly religious in its own way. In so far as his views are developed from the immutable dogmas of Freemasonry, they possess an inferential authority and there can be no doubt as to the influence that they exercised. I need not say that he concurred in the action taken by Great Britain and the United States with regard to the *Grand Orient* of France, when this body, without denying the existence of a God, ceased to make belief in a Supreme Being an essential condition of initiation. The *Grand Orient*, as it must be admitted, was in a position of peculiar difficulty ; to demand from its candidates an act of faith which was notoriously in opposition to all that was likely to be held by the considerable majority could only reduce the condition to a mere mockery : the course which was taken was therefore *per se* reasonable, but at the moment of so taking it the *Grand Orient* ceased to be Masonic.

From the standpoint of Albert Pike, the personality of the Divine Nature was also an essential dogma and, speaking historically, there can be no doubt that this was the original mind of Masonry, though there can be also no doubt that it has been at all times and everywhere evaded. It is sufficient to point to this dogma as a refutation of the impeachment advanced by the Latin Church in respect of Pantheism. At the same time the majority of Masons, supposing their best intentions, will occasionally talk Pantheism, by an intellectual confusion, when discussing the connection between God and the Universe ; but so also will as large a proportion of persons outside Masonry. Perhaps on examination they would not prove appreciably clearer on the subject of the soul's immortality. Beyond these immovable dogmas, neither Albert Pike nor another Mason can say anything of binding force under the simple obedience of the Craft, either in books or lectures, and this was especially pointed out by the American Grand Commander in the preface to his *Morals and Dogma*, when he observed that "everyone is entirely free to reject and dissent from whatsoever herein may seem to him to be untrue or unsound."

Though assuredly illustrious as a Mason, and one, as I have indicated, to whom the present prestige of the SCOTTISH RITE must be referred largely, I have quoted more than enough to shew that Albert Pike had his intellectual limitations, and though he began life as a writer of verse with initial signs of vocation, his literary methods are not less than intolerable. To state when introducing a work of almost encyclopædic proportions, that about half of it is borrowed matter by no means renders it superfluous to separate text from citation ; but in analysing *Morals and Dogma* one is everywhere beset by this difficulty. I cannot trace all its sources, nor does he offer the least assistance, but the volume swarms with citations from Éliphas Lévi translated without any acknowledgment, beyond that already mentioned, and also without marks of quotation. The work as a whole has the merits and defects which characterise such wholesale ingarnerings ; it is of course imperfectly digested, and the reader must expect discrepancies, even over matters of importance. The most conspicuous perhaps concerns the religious aspect of Masonry which I have mentioned in general terms. The disclaimer in this respect issued by the Grand Lodge of England found little acceptance with the SCOTTISH RITE in America. Among the influential members of that Rite, at and about the time of the Papal Encyclical, it appears to have been thought that "as a system of philosophy, Masonry must of necessity have a religious mission and a doctrinal propaganda," but not of a "sectarian kind," because it deals with those "fundamental principles upon which all faiths are founded." So far as the immovable dogmas are concerned, and their assumption throughout the Rituals

of the Craft Degrees, this is indubitable on the surface
and the statement proceeds no further ; so far as the
Christian Grades are concerned, it appears insufficiently
expressed ; and in respect of the Great Mystery of
Religion which lies behind the whole subject, it is the
wording of one into whom the consciousness of that
Mystery has not entered. I hasten to add that the
expression is not that of the Grand Commander, but I
hold it from a private source which was of an authority
near to his own and was possibly more consistent. In
Albert Pike's lecture attached to the Grade of *Illustrious Elect of the Fifteen,* it is laid down that Masonry is
not a religion, and that " he who makes of it a religious
belief, falsifies and denaturalizes it." This notwithstanding, in a later lecture, belonging to the Grade of
Grand Master Architect, it is said that " the religious
faith taught by Masonry is indispensable to the attainment of the great ends of life." It follows that the
writer did not choose his words very carefully, and not
only forgot what he said but was in confusion as to his
own opinions.

It is worth while, however, to extricate from such
formal matters of expression the teaching which he
offered to his Rite and which is probably at this day
less or more accepted by English-speaking High Grade
Masons who are under the same obedience. Here
then are the " religious aspects " which Albert Pike
attributes to Masonry. " If we could cut off from any
soul all the principles taught by Masonry, the faith in
a God, in immortality, in virtue, in essential rectitude,
that soul would sink into sin, misery, darkness and
ruin. If we could cut off all sense of these truths, the
man would sink at once to the grade of the animal."
It is possible that natural religion may cry to be
delivered from defenders of this calibre, but under all
its limitations it is the necessity of that religion at least
which it is sought to bring home by the argument. As
to revelation itself, a special construction is placed upon

the admitted Christian aspects which must tend to its rejection in the sense attached to the term by orthodox Christian Churches. "Believe that there is a God; that He is our Father; that He has a paternal interest in our welfare and improvement; that He has given us powers by means of which we may escape from sin and ruin; that He has destined us to a future life of endless progress towards perfection and a knowledge of Himself—believe this, as every Mason should, and you can live calmly, endure patiently, labour resolutely, deny yourself cheerfully, hope steadfastly, and be conquerors in the great struggle of life. Take away any of these principles, and what remains for us? Say that there is no God, or no way opened for hope and reformation and triumph, no heaven to come, no rest for the weary, no home in the bosom of God for the afflicted and disconsolate soul; or that God is but an ugly blind *Chance* that stabs in the dark; or a *somewhat* that is, when attempted to be defined, a *no-what*, emotionless, passionless, the *Supreme Apathy* to which all things, good and evil, are alike indifferent; or a jealous God Who revengefully visits the sins of the fathers on the children, and when the fathers have eaten sour grapes, sets the children's teeth on edge; an arbitrary *Supreme Will*, that has made it right to be virtuous and wrong to lie and steal because *It pleased* to *make* it so rather than otherwise, retaining the power to reverse the law; or a fickle, vacillating, inconstant Deity, or a cruel, bloodthirsty, savage Hebrew or Puritanical One, and we are but the sport of chance and the victims of despair." I do not know who, under the ægis of American Masonry, is qualified to deliver us from the mortal crassness of this species of debate. We know the strength and weakness of natural religion; we know also the full force of the objections raised on the subject of the only formal revelation about which there is any serious question at the present day; but this inchoate syllabus of moral emotion protesting

405

against the aspects of revelation which are in apparent antagonism with the fatherhood of God and with the apparent rights inherent in the everlasting sonship of humanity, is of the stuff that makes atheists rather than converts them. The Latin Church has little and less than nothing to fear from animadversions of this kind, and the Masonic interest has as little and as much to hope.

Now, it would seem out of all expectation, after such prolegomena, that the work of Pike is not only an apology for natural religion, so conceived and thus impossibly expressed, but is an attempt to present an account of the Secret Tradition, so far as it is understood by the writer. Albert Pike was a disciple of Éliphas Lévi, the French occultist, and Éliphas Lévi was the first writer in modern times who attempted to place a new construction on that part of esoteric philosophy which had come within his horizon. It was largely a negligible part and it was not a right construction ; the disciple, moreover, was merely a literal reflection, giving nothing on his own side ; but the fact remains that the Supreme Council of the Thirty-Third Degree for the Southern Jurisdiction of the United States published " by its authority," under the title of *Morals and Dogma*, what is really a translation in part and a commentary at large, having a special application to Masonry, of and upon the works of Éliphas Lévi, from whom all its inspiration is drawn and to whom all its curious material must be ultimately referred. Its " natural religion " is modified by the pseudo-transcendentalism of Lévi, and its Masonry is transfigured in the light of the latter's views concerning the old sanctuaries of initiation.

The lecture which is allocated to the 32nd Degree of the Rite, or *Sublime Prince of the Royal Secret*, is a presentation of the so-called " magical doctrine," the Secret Doctrine, the mystery of all Holy Houses, participation in which was the end of every initiation.

That doctrine, for Pike and for Lévi, lay behind the testimony of all peoples in all periods to the existence of revelation, but albeit it constituted for the disciple that Royal Secret imparted to the recipient of the Grade first mentioned, it was only the elementary doctrine of equilibrium, the Kabalistic " Mystery of the Balance."

Lest it should seem therefore that I am dealing with one who was my precursor, 1 will summarise this doctrine as it is presented by Pike, premising only that the words are those of the Grand Commander but the conceptions are for the most part those of his master. I have here adapted the words. (*a*) From equilibrium in the Deity—or between Infinite Divine Wisdom and Infinite Divine Power—there result the stability of the universe, the unchangeableness of the Divine Law, and the principles of Truth, Justice and Right, which form part thereof. (*b*) From equilibrium between Infinite Divine Justice and Infinite Divine Mercy there result Infinite Divine Equity and Moral Harmony or Beauty in the universe. (*c*) "By it the endurance of created and imperfect natures in the presence of a Perfect Deity is made possible ; and for Him also, as for us, to love is better than to hate, and forgiveness is easier than revenge or hatred." I put this verbatim, because Éliphas Lévi was usually more plausible and less in need of our charity as regards his modes of expression : the reader should understand that Abert Pike is at this time not offering translation—or its equivalent—but commenting under his own lights. (*d*) From the equilibrium between Necessity and Liberty, between the action of Divine Omnipotence and the Free Will of man, it follows that "sins and base notions," "ungenerous thoughts and words," are "crimes and wrongs justly punished by the law of cause and consequence." (*e*) From equilibrium between Good and Evil, Light and Darkness, it follows—the logic is Pike's—that all is the work of Infinite Wisdom and Infinite Love ; that there is no rebellious demon of evil, or principle of darkness co-existent and in eternal controversy with God, or the principle of Light and Good. (*f*) By the knowledge of equilibrium, and with the help of faith, we can ·see that the existence of evil, sin, suffering and sorrow is consistent with God's Infinite Goodness, as well as with His Infinite Wisdom. (*g*) By the equilibrium between authority and individual activity there arises free government, · and this is the conciliation of liberty with obedience to law, equality with subjection to authority, fraternity with subordination to those who are wisest and best. (*h*) By equilibrium between the spiritual and divine, the material and human in man, we learn to reverence ourselves as immortal souls, to have respect and charity for others, who are partakers like us of the Divine Nature and are struggling like us towards the light. This, says Albert Pike, is the True Word of a Master Mason, the true Royal Secret ; it is that also which makes possible, and shall at last make real, "the Holy Empire of true Masonic Brotherhood."

On my own part, I may add that equilibrium thus expounded is, like all ethics and all morality, the gate which stands between two pillars well enough known to Masons and giving entrance to the palace that is within, to the treasury of the Secret Tradition, but it is not the palace itself and its doctrine is not the Tradition. This notwithstanding, it is good and it is consoling to know that within the measure of his lights the face of Albert Pike was set towards Jerusalem —even if it was not exactly and in the full mystical sense the eternal city and the Zion of the blessed.

If those, in conclusion, who hold under the obedience of the Scottish Rite the Grades which are conferred thereby will take our English Rituals as they stand and will compare them with those in use under the ægis of the Southern Jurisdiction, they will meet with an extraordinary distinction in respect of development, apart from subject at its root. That distinction is the intervention of occult philosophy, and the mask worn by the philosphy in question is that of Éliphas Lévi. In so far as the symbols allocated to particular Grades are diverse from our symbols here, they are referable to the same source.

V

SOME BIBLIOGRAPHICAL MATTERS

IN a work which is so largely and perhaps almost exclusively one of interpretation, it will be understood that it does not depend in any real or express manner from antecedent authorities. It depends from the Secret Tradition, a part of which only has passed into writing. It has so passed not in particular texts which can be cited as dealing comprehensively therewith, but in the form of cryptic literatures to which it is possible that I should refer only in a general way. In the work itself I have mentioned those of Kabalism, Alchemy and the mystic writers of the West. On the historical side there are, however, certain sources which may be consulted by students who desire to carry further the research here initiated. I propose therefore to provide in the present section some part of the materials which will be most ready to their hand, and for additional clearness it will be advisable to schedule them with reference to the seven books into which my work has been divided. It should be understood that what follows is neither exhaustive nor even representative ; it is rather accidental and sporadic, offering here and there a casual light on the path that we have sought to travel. There are also few or no real and final authorities on the subject, but there are results innumerable of partial, defective and experimental inquiry.

Book I. *The Craft and the High Grades.*—Those who desire to enter into further detail respecting the antecedents of the Masonic subject in Kabalism should consult in the first place and above all the French translation of the *Sepher Ha Zohar* which is now in course of publication at Paris. The Latin writers, through whom Kabalistic literature has been known previously, outside the Hebrew and Chaldaic texts, have been already mentioned. The *Kabbala Denudata* of Baron Knorr von Rosenroth has been and still remains the most comprehensive of all, and does not offer any real difficulties to those who are familiar with the scholastic Latin of the seventeenth century. It is not, however, a critical work, and the confused intermixture of Zoharic citations with the expansions of late commentators has long misled research. Among later writers, outside those who used Latin, the study of Adolphe Franck entitled *La Kabbale* has long been the chief authority in France, though it has been attacked by scholarship for the imperfections of its Chaldaic renderings. Molitor's *Philosophy of Tradition* is serviceable for reference, and is to be had in a French translation as well as in the German original. The so-called Christian Kabalah is available in a French translation of one of the Rosenroth texts : *Adumbratio Kabbalæ Christianæ*, Paris, 1899. It is an extended dialogue between a Kabalist and a Christian philosopher.

For Masonic history on its external side I have cited the *Concise History of Freemasonry* by Mr. R. F. Gould, to which may be added the German history by Findel, made more accessible some years ago by an English version. No other general works are worth enumeration, in the English language at least. French writers must be taken at their individual value, including those who have been regarded as conspicuous authorities, for example : (*a*) C. A. Thory : *Acta Latomorum*, 2 vols., 1815 ; (*b*) Clavel : *Histoire pittoresque de la Franc-maçonnerie*—see in particular the third and extended edition of 1844 ; (*c*) J. M. Ragon : *Orthodoxie Maçonnique*, 1851 ; *Manuel de l'Initié*, 1853 ; *Cours Philosophique et Interpretatif des Initiations Anciénnes et Modernes*, 1842.

Appendices

These are the chief works, but among the great crowd there are certain others which seem to demand enumeration, including : (*a*) J. P. Levesque : *Principales Sectes Maçonniques*, a general historical sketch, 1821 ; (*b*) Reghelleni Da Schio : *La Maçonnerie considerée comme la resultat des religions Egyptiennes, Juives et Chretiennes*, 2 vols., 1833 ; (*c*) Pierre Zaccone : *Histoire des Sociétés Secrètes*, 4 vols., 1847–9 ; (*d*) E. E. Eckert : *La Francmaçonnerie dans sa véritable signification*—the German original, translated by Abbé Gyr, 2 vols., 1854 ; (*e*) C. A. Teïssier : *Manuel Général de la Maçonnerie*, 1856 ; (*f*) A. G. Jouast : *Histoire de la Francmaçonnerie*, about 1865.

It should be understood that the above works may be termed general in their character, and are historical rather than symbolical or interpretative, though there is no dividing line. The symbolism of Craft Masonry is dwelt with incidentally or otherwise, in the following works : (*a*) E. F. Bazot : *Manuel de la Francmaçonnerie*, 1819 ; (*b*) Dupontets : *Cours pratique de la Francmaçonnerie*, 1841 ; (*c*) J. Casimir Boubée : *Études historiques et philosophiques sur la Francmaçonnerie*, 1854. The following English works may also be consulted : (*a*) *The True Masonic Chart*, by J. L. Cross, 1820, and (*b*) *The Handbook of Freemasonry*, by C. H. Stapleton, 1857. Authoritative Rituals of the Craft Grades were published by J. M. Ragon according to French working, which is very different from that of England. The separate pamphlets were entitled : (*a*) *Rituel de l'Apprenti Maçon* ; (*b*) *Rituel du Compagnon* ; (*c*) *Rituel du Grade de Maître*. Extensions of certain references in the present work will be found as follows : (*a*) vol. i. p. 107. *The Journey from East to West* : see Éliphas Lévi, *Histoire de la Magie*, pp. 399 *et seq*. But the writer did not understand that there is a reverse journey which must be undertaken from West to East ; (*b*) the great Legend of the Craft, according to one of the recensions, will be found in the same volume, with an explanation of the symbolism which is particular to this writer and

411

shews a certain light, though it is not the true light of all ; (*c*) vol. i. p. 108. *The Loss in the Sanctuary* : there are casual references throughout Masonic literature, and I mention the fact because those who care to go further will find innumerable texts in French, German and Spanish which speak with much greater frankness than I have felt it possible to do ; there are intimations and side-lights even in official and purely monitorial productions like Mackey's *Manual of the Lodge*.

Book II.—It must be understood here, and elsewhere throughout, that sources of information to which my readers are referred for the extension of their personal studies, do not mean, except casually and occasionally, the sources from which I have myself derived. The dependence in my own .case has been usually from knowledge at first hand, though this has been checked and expanded in many directions, possibly most of all from sources in MS. or from private texts which it would be inadvisable to specify by citation. My study under the title of *Grades of the Ancient Alliance* can be checked by recourse to four classes of texts, but one of them concerns the ANCIENT AND ACCEPTED SCOTTISH RITE, which I shall have occasion to speak of later, and the particulars are therefore postponed. For the Grade of *Mark Master Mason* and the work of a certain Craftsman therewith connected consult : (*a*) *Le Rameau d'Or d'Eleusis*, by J. F. Marconis ; (*b*) the work of Eckert already cited ; and (*c*) Ragon's codification of Rituals connected, by his hypothesis, with the Degree of Royal Arch. For the *Holy Order of the Royal Arch* itself, the bibliography is considerable, and the first item hereinafter mentioned is of palmary importance and authority ; (*a*) W. J. Hughan : *Origin of the English Rite of Freemasonry*, especially in relation to the Royal Arch Degree, 1864 ; (*b*) F. E. Clark : *Notes on the Origin of the Royal Arch Degree*, 1890 ; (*c*) W. G. Warvelle : *The Book of the Law*, Chicago, 1901 ; (*d*) J. M. Ragon : *Rituel de la Maçonnerie de Royale Arche.*

Appendices

For CRYPTIC MASONRY *per se* the two text-books are those of Albert G. Mackey, published under the title in question, and *The Cryptic Rite*, by J. Ross Robertson, Toronto, 1888. ADONHIRAMITE MASONRY is represented by (*a*) *Recueil précieux de la Maçonnerie Adonhiramite . . . par un Chevalier de tous les Ordres Maçonniques*, 1787 ; *Origine de la Maçonnerie Adonhiramite*, referred about to the same date. These are the works which have been ascribed indifferently to Baron Tschoudy and L. G. de St. Victor, who is probably the real author. Those who consult them will see (*a*) full particulars as to the nature of the buried treasures removed from the first Temple, and (*b*) after what manner it would have been possible to recover them for use in the later Temple built in the days of Esdras.

Book III.—The subject-matter is divisible under three heads corresponding to the three sections. In the first place therefore concerning *Écossais* Masonry, consult : (*a*) Baron Tschoudy : the treatise entitled *Ecossais de St. Andrée d'Écosse*, Paris, 1780 ; (*b*) Nicholas de Bonneville : *La Maçonnerie Écossaise*, 1788 ; (*c*) *La Maçonnerie Écossaise comparée avec les trois professions et le secret des Templiers*, 1788. The cycle of literature which has gathered about the Grade of Rose-Croix is as large as the variations of the Degree itself are numerous, but naturally the works which deal exclusively therewith lie in a smaller compass than the descriptions and references scattered through the great body of Masonic literature. Particular monographs are as follows : (*a*) *Les plus secrets Mystères des Hauts Grades de la Maçonnerie dévoilés, ou la Vrai Rose-Croix*, 1768 ; (*b*) Henry O'Connor : *A Few Words upon the Degree of Grand Prince Rose-Croix*, including its alleged transmission in Ireland from the fourteenth century, 1843 ; (*c*) Goblet D'Alviella : *Du Rituel des R.R. + +, et de sa signification symbolique*, 1890 ; (*d*) R. A. Withers : *Rose-Croix Masonry*, 1900 ; (*e*) Ragon : *Ordre Chapitral —Nouveau Grade de Rose-Croix*.

The Secret Tradition in Freemasonry

Book IV.—I will take in the first place the works dealing with the history, symbolism and system of the ANCIENT AND ACCEPTED SCOTTISH RITE. There are primarily the writings of Ragon, as already specified, and his selection of particular Rituals according to French workings. Other texts are as follows : (*a*) J. E. Marconis : *Le Menteur des Initiés*, 1864 ; (*b*) E. H. Darnty : *Recherches sur le Rite Écossais*, 1879 ; (*c*) *Books of the Ancient and Accepted Scottish Rite*, published by the Supreme Council, 33rd Degree, U.S.A., about 1880 ; (*d*) W. H. Peckham : *The Ancient and Accepted Scottish Rite in the United States of America*, New York, 1884 ; (*e*) C. T. M'Lenachan : *The Book of the Ancient and Accepted Scottish Rite*, Northern Jurisdiction, U.S.A., New York, 1885. The Order of the Temple, as originally constituted and in its several Masonic revivals, has also an extended literature, some of which is exceedingly valuable. The original Order is outside our horizon and I will therefore mention only the work of C. G. Addison, published in 1842 under the title of *Knights Templar*. It is a tolerable account and is ready to the hand of inquirers. Other texts are as follows : (*a*) James Burnes : *A Sketch of the History of the Knights Templars*, 1837—a work dealing more especially with the revival under the Charter of Larmenius ; (*b*) *Knight Templarism Illustrated*, Chicago, 1888 ; (*c*) R. Greeven : *The Templar Movement in Masonry*, Benares, 1899 ; (*d*) *Quelques réflexions sur les origines de la Francmaçonnerie Templière*, Brussels, 1904 ; (*e*) *Ordre des Chevaliers du Temple*, 1840 ; (*f*) Chevalier Guyot : *Manual of the Knights of the Order of the Temple*, 1830 (I have not seen the French original). The question of the revivals is also mentioned by Abbé Gregoire in his *Histoire des Sociétés Secrètes Religieuses*, 1830, and by C. H. Maillard de Chambure in his *Régles et Statutes Secrètes des Templiers*, 1840. The work enlitled *Knight Templarism Illustrated* may also be consulted for the *Knights of the Holy Sepulchre* as well as the connected Degrees.

Appendices

Book V.—I do not suppose that Masonic readers, unless they are drawn very strongly by the claims of the Secret Tradition, are in the least likely to undertake at first hand the study of alchemical texts. I may mention, for their better equipment, that in the very imperfect bibliography of Lenglet du Fresnoy the works extended to nearly 2500 separate tracts. But in a case of this kind it is never quite wise to be certain, and if any one should open the door of this cryptic library he may be counselled to take down from some shelf the *Bibliotheca Chemica Curiosa* of Mangetus, in two folio volumes, date 1702. It contains sixty-seven texts, all notable after their own manner and some of high authority. The mystic side of Alchemy is represented in England by one remarkable book published in 1850, under the title *A suggestive Enquiry into the Hermetic Mystery*. It is not, however, final or satisfactory as a critical study ; indeed, in some respects it is a morass rather than a pathway. There is also *Remarks on Alchemy and the Alchemists*, by an American writer, Mr. E. A. Hitchcock, but to the deep subject he had not brought a consideration which was also deep.

Coming now to the Hermetic or Alchemical side of Masonry, I regard bibliographical references as practically out of the question in respect of Pernety and his brotherhoods, while the works referable to himself have been mentioned already in the text. Baron Tschoudy is represented adequately by *L'Étoile Flamboyante*, which has been printed several times, and I have spoken of it at great length. The question which therefore remains is concerning the two colossal Rites of Mizraïm and Memphis. In respect of the first the authorities, such as they may be held to be, are : (*a*) Veruhas : *Défense de Misraïm et quelques aperçus sur les divers Rites Maçonniques en France*, Paris, 1822 ; (*b*) Marc Bédarride : *L'Ordre Maçonnique de Mizraïm*, practically the adventures of the writer, who was one of the founders ; (*c*) *Statuts Généraux de l'Ordre*,

1844. The authority for Memphis is J. E. Marconis, who had also a hand in its establishment. His chief works are *Le Sanctuaire du Memphis* and *Le Rameau d'Or d'Eleusis*, already mentioned. Dr. J. A. Gottlieb has written a brief and uncritical *History of the Masonic Rite of Memphis*, which was published at New York in 1899. We have seen that the system was reduced and reappeared in this form as the ANTIENT AND PRIMITIVE RITE. There is no account of it that is really worth mentioning, but some of its Public Ceremonies were published about 1885, and a short sketch of its history appeared some three years later.

Book VI.—Cagliostro and his Egyptian Masonry are represented by innumerable descriptive accounts scattered through Masonic literature on the Continent and in England ; by several formal biographies, from that which was issued in Italy under the authority of the Holy Inquisition to the excellent reconsideration of all the evidence published, in 1910, by Mr. W. R. H. Trowbridge under the title : *Cagliostro : The Splendour and Misery of a Master of Magic* ; and finally by a piecemeal but serviceable summary of the Egyptian Rituals, which appeared some years ago, and is now practically entombed in a French periodical entitled *L'Initiation*.

Earlier and later Martinism is another very large subject, and I will mention only : (*a*) Papus : *L'Illuminisme en France.—Martines de Pasqually*, 1895 ; (*b*) Papus : *Martinésisme, Willermosisme et Franc-Maçonnerie*, 1899 ; (*c*) Franz von Baader : *Les Enseignements Secrets de Martinés de Pasqually*, 1900 ; (*d*) Martines de Pasqually : *Traité de la Réintégration des Êtres*. The life of L. C. de Saint-Martin, represented by various memoirs, his autobiographical notes and his letters, does not enter into Masonry save by his connection with the RITE OF ELECT COHENS, and of this enough has been said in the present work.

Book VII.—The literature of Rosicrucianism in its

Appendices

Masonic aspects and connections is practically worthless, and I do not propose to burden this appendix with useless or mischievous references. The general history of the subject is not in much better case. I have intimated that modern American publications are the work of illiterate imposition. *The Rosicrucians : their Rites and Mysteries*, by the late Hargrave Jennings, was exposed in respect of its pretensions, nearly twenty-five years since, by myself. This leads me to remark that I have throughout omitted all reference to my own writings, in part for obvious reasons and for the rest because their bare titles have been specified elsewhere in these volumes. Readers of German may be referred to the old *Collections* of Solomon Semler, and for Masonic aspects to C. G. Von Murr's *True Origins of the Orders of Rosicrucianism and Freemasonry*, 1803. The history of the Fraternity has not been attempted in France.

The intervention of Swedenborg in Masonry has no literature, but the speculation attracted such dreamers as Reghelline and Ragon, who continue to be regarded as oracles by the French school of modern Martinism.

I trust that the scope and intention of this rough list will not be misconstrued. It contains many noticeable and a few excellent works, but the citation of none is intended as a mark of approval or as operating to the exclusion of others. There are several points of view from which most are negligible, except for the collection and collation of facts and their separation, when it can be made, from the fictions in which they are imbedded.

VI

Summary of Head and Tail Pieces

The description of these has been deferred, because in many instances it is necessary to speak of them at greater length than would be possible in a note attached to each. The accounts follow hereafter in the exact order of their appearance.

P. vi.—A circle inscribed with the words : *There are three miracles—God and Man, Mother and Virgin, Three and One.* Within the circle is a Hexagram or Seal of Solomon, inscribed with the letters B.S., signifying *Salvator Benedictus,* Blessed Saviour. It is the descent of the light in Christ, represented by the white inverted triangle. There is a Cross in the midst of the Hexagram rising above a smaller circle inscribed with these words : *The Centre in the Triangle of the Centre.* Within this second circle there is a third containing a point ; this is the familiar symbol of eternity. The angels of the four quarters of manifest creation encompass the whole figure, which represents in brief summary the thesis of this work.

P. viii.—The Sign of the Son of Man in the centre of that sun which is the light of the earth, and beneath these is the symbol of the Sun of Justice, which is the Word of God. The sentence written on the cross signifies : *In this sign shalt thou conquer.* It is the message to the Craft Grades uttered by the High Grades.

P. xix.—The symbol of catholic or universal Freemasonry : a winged heart, representing love and goodwill at their highest. There is a solar light in the centre, and within it is a double square or octangle, the mystic symbol of Christ. Within this is the Eternal Triad. It shews forth the manifestation of God in Love. The message is that the Divine is in the heart of Masonry and it is also the Providence above, represented by the triangle and the All-seeing Eye. Various Masonic emblems are inscribed on the heart.

P. xx.—The Four Living Creatures of Ezekiel,

corresponding to the four parts of heaven and the divisions of the human personality, which are consecrated in Masonry.

P. xxi.—The Seal of Solomon, another form of the Hexagram on p. vi. Both embody the doctrine of Hermetic correspondence, the analogy between the Divine and the human, the seen and unseen. It has many Masonic applications.

P. xxxi.—A *cornucopiæ* or horn of plenty, representing the Masonic good things of the Lord in the Land of the living. It is much more therefore than the conventional sign of refreshment.

P. xxxii.—The genius of Freemasonry, a vested virgin like Isis, crowned with seven stars, and uplifting that globe over the whole surface of which is diffused the beneficence of the Masonic Institution.

P. xxxiii.—The figure of Hermes the Messenger, bearing the Caduceus. He is here as the beautiful feet upon the mountain, bringing glad tidings near. The original is in the Museo Borboniso.

P. xxxv.—An emblematic figure of the Law of Masonry in the act of proclamation *urbi et orbi*.

P. xxxvi.—The emblematic figure of the Master, clothed with the power of Masonry and with the sun of its light behind him, illuminating the work which he performs.

P. 1.—A variant of the symbol at the back of the foretitle. It may be said further concerning it (*a*) that the cross is that of the Supernal Father (down line) and the Son (cross line) above the circle of manifestation ; (*b*) that the cross above the circle is also the sign of Venus reversed, and as such it may be compared with what is said in the text respecting the mystery of the Garden of Venus.

P. 18.—An open book, which is that of the Law, supporting a square and compasses, stands on an unhewn altar with horned angles. There is also the rough delineation of a human face. A few scriptural references to the horns of the Altar of Burnt Offerings will be in the mind of the reader, *e.g.*, Ps. cxviii. 27.

P. 20.—A coffin whereon is a black pentagram, signifying the perfect soul in concealment. Beside the coffin are a spade and mallet. The acacia, type of immortality, blooms at the head. The reference is of course to the passing of the Master-Builder.

P. 24.—The Ark of the Covenant, supported by the Four Living Creatures.

P. 25.—A variant of the Winged Heart on p. xix, with the same meaning.

P. 67.—An imaginary delineation of the Temple of Solomon, illustrating unconsciously its completion, apart from the original plans communicated by Divine Wisdom.

P. 68.—The square and compasses, with the letter G in the centre, signifying God, geometry, etc. Beneath are Masonic tools. The device is familiar in Masonry.

P. 82.—A rose of five petals, having a heart in the centre from which a cross rises. The device is Rosicrucian in its character, and is found among the so-called Secret Symbols of that Fraternity. It is the crucifixion of Divine Love in the life of creation, as if upon an altar, and in this manner it illustrates the *Beneplacitum termino carens* which operated in creation according to Kabalistic doctrine. In more Masonic language it is the Divine goodwill manifested in all things, and reflected in the goodwill which is the counsel in chief of Masonry to all its Brethren.

P. 83.—A variant of the symbol which appears on p. 68.

P. 100.—Another representation of the unhewn altar, with the Book of the Law thereon and Masonic emblems represented upon it. The meaning is that the knowledge and remembrance of the Law is kept alive or open like a book by means of Masonry. The three Lesser Lights stand about the altar.

P. 101.—The Rose-Cross in the centre of a glory

or nimbus. It means here the sacrifice of the whole creation on the altar of the Divine, by which sacrifice creation in fine attains the glorious end of its existence. Masonry is also a rose, and so also is it crucified, that so it may attain in fine.

P. 133.—A variant of the device on p. xxxi, having the same meaning.

P. 134.—Masonry summarised in the form of a monumental tablet, bearing the symbolic jewels allocated to the various offices of the Craft. Symbolically it stands upon the earth and overlooks the world of waters.

P. 136.—The vision of Jacob.

P. 137.—The symbol is allocated to one of the High Grades, but is in analogy with the Legend of the Master-Builder. The candle which burns on the coffin has the same significance as the acacia. In a sense also it signifies that the Adept or Master, being dead, yet speaketh. He speaks under a veil in Craft Masonry; in Christian Masonry he returns with the Word of Life, or such at least is the hypothesis.

P. 139.—This device is in analogy with that on p. xxxvi. Here, however, the light is solely from the letter G, signifying the Divine Light diffused in Masonry.

P. 140.—The Pillars of the Porch of the Temple and the winding stairs beyond.

P. 141.—From one point of view this is the Altar of Incense, and in the form delineated it belongs to the Grade of Prince Adept. There is the vessel of Incense beside an open book and the pentagram is placed upon the surface. The three lesser lights surround the altar, as in a previous diagram. The Altar is sometimes held to represent the tressle-board, when the latter is understood in a symbolical and speculative sense.

P. 170.—The five orders of architecture. Some of the emblematic correspondences are specified in a Craft Lecture, and there are others which have not passed into writing, though they are not external to the horizon of Masonry.

P. 171.—Vessels of consecration for use in Temples and Lodges. In the centre there is a horn containing wheat, on the left is the cup of wine, and on the right hand that of oil.

P. 192.—A commemoration of the just made perfect in their passage from this life. The motto might be: *In memoria eterna erit justus.* The broken pillar is the sign of mortality. The genius of Masonry is reading from the Book of the Law. She uplifts a branch of the acacia as a sign of eternal life. Behind her is Time with his scythe. He is raising one of her abundant tresses. The reference is to 1 Kings i. 42 : There shall not a hair of him fall to earth. . . It is another reference to the immortal nature of man.

P. 193.—Mount Sinai and the surrounding plain.

P. 204.—Another view of Mount Sinai, shewing the convent of St. Catherine.

P. 206.—The perfect arch of symbolical Masonry, when it is understood on the moral side. The words are Justice and Equity. The one is represented by the sword and the other by the balance. But above these there is a triad formed of ten Hebrew Yods, shewing that above the law of human equity and above morality there is the higher and eternal sanction which resides in Divine Grace and Power.

P. 207.—The Temple of human aspiration open to all the quarters and raised upon five steps, representing the elements of our natural personality and the spirit which overshadows these. Above is the inextinguishable flame which ascends from the Sons of Desire.

P. 210.—The double-headed eagle with a crown above. It is really the badge allocated to the 33rd degree, but it has a wider application as the union of the two covenants, and as such is a fitting symbol preceding the consideration of the New Alliance in Freemasonry. In Alchemy it signifies that which is called

Appendices

Rebis, being a mystery of the substance of the wise during its passage through the first process of the Great Work.

P. 211.—An important and rare symbol. The words are : *This do, and thou shalt live.* The joined hands signify union ; they are clasped in front of an anchor, which is that of eternal hope, familiar in Masonry. From the union of the hands there springs flame, and the heavenly dove, symbol of the Holy Spirit, descends thereon. It is a perfect sign of the New Alliance in love. On one side there is a fallen pillar, because heaven and earth may pass away but the word of God shall remain for ever.

P. 227.—A pelican in its piety, the symbol of Christ and that of the 18th Degree.

P. 228.—The Cross of St. Andrew.

P. 240.—The Divine name *Tetragrammaton* is surrounded by an ineffable glory and is placed within an inverted triangle, shewing the descent of the Divine Influences. A key is suspended from the triangle, meaning that the descent of those influences and the law of their communication is the key of all things. In the ANCIENT AND ACCEPTED SCOTTISH RITE it is the device of the 4th Degree, being that of Secret Master. The symbol is described in the historical discourse attached thereto, and the account is curious because of its Christian references at that early stage of the system, but the true explanation is wanting. I have myself withheld something.

P. 241.—In this symbol the cross which on p. 82 is shewn above the heart is now placed within it. It is the taking of the Divine Sacrifice into the human heart, because he who is crucified with Christ shall also reign with Him. This is the message of the Christian Grades in Masonry.

P. 263.—An alternative device of the 18th Degree and especially the form in use by the Supreme Council of Spanish South America. It will be noted that in this case the Rose is above the Cross, which does not improve the symbolism.

P. 264.—The extended symbol of the 18th Degree, shewing, within a glory, the Cross of eternal life above the Pelican, the Hermetic Rose being on one side and the acacia on the other.

P. 266.—The plan of the Third Temple, which, according to Éliphas Lévi, was to have been rebuilt by the original Knights Templar, if their design had not been discovered.   See pp. 300 to 303 of the text.

P. 267.—The Egyptian symbol of the Winged Globe. It is the sign of immortal life—that which passes through all things and is not changed thereby.

P. 274.—An incised slab representing Frère Gerars of the Commandery of Villers le Temple in the district of Liège.   Temp. 1273.

P. 275.—Effigy of Jean de Dreux, referred to the year 1275.   In the eighteenth century it was still preserved in the church of St. Yved de Brame, near Soissons, France.   See *Monuments de la Monarchie Française*, by Montfauçon.

P. 287.—Knight Templar, from a Hollars engraving, date 1656.

P. 288.—Mounted Knight Templar and Standard-bearer from Adrien Schoonebeek's *Histoire des Ordres Militaires*.   Amsterdam, 1699.

P. 307.—A Knight Templar in military clothing. From Helyot.

P. 317.—A Knight Templar in ordinary clothing. See Helyot, *Histoire des Ordres Monastiques, Religieux et Militaires*.   Paris, 1721.

P. 318.—A transparency attributed to the Grade of *Knights of the East*.   The letters L.D.P. have been held to signify *Lilia pedibus destrue*, or Trample the lilies under foot, and so constituted a supposititious motto of the Revolution.

P. 330.—Statue of a Knight Templar in the Hall of the Inner Temple, by H. H. Armitage, date 1875.

Appendices

P. 331.—St. Bernard of Clairvaux, after Fra Angelico.

P. 353.—The seal and arms of the old Order of the Temple.

P. 369.—Masonic Arms connected with the Order of the Temple.

P. 379.—The ancient habit and armour of a Knight Templar in the Sublime Degree of Masonry, from a stipple engraving of 1796. First example of the kind and without Masonic devices.

P. 388.—A Teutonic Cross, attributed to the Grade of *Sovereign Grand Inspector General.* From a Spanish South American source.

P. 398.—St. Helena, mother of Constantine the Great, bearing the true Cross. From the Boisserée Gallery.

P. 399.—A Grand Master of the Order of the Temple. See *La Chevalerie et les Croisades,* a compilation from the writings of Paul Lacroix.

P. 410.—The Councillor Karl von Eckartshausen.

P. 411.—Banner of the Temple as adopted by the Grade of *Kadosh.*

P. 417. Another Banner belonging to the same Grade.

P. 418.—The Glory of the Divine Triad enclosing the Divine name *Tetragrammaton,* and the familiar symbols of Craft Masonry. The letters beneath will be also familiar to all Masons, but the symbol is derived from a High Grade source and there is little doubt that they signify Jacobus Burgunders, *i.e.* Jacques de Molay.

VOLUME THE SECOND

P. iv.—The Ark of Noah, which, according to certain Mysteries, carried the secrets of initiation across the waters of the Flood and thus insured their transmission from the days of Enoch. The rainbow in this sense was the covenant of their perpetuation and the sign of alliance between the two epochs.

The Secret Tradition in Freemasonry

P. v.—The great pentagram of life surrounded by spiritual presences.

P. vii.—The Hermetic Master reading from that which is termed in Rosicrucian literature the Book M., containing the knowledge of things within and without.

P. viii.—The Pillars of Hermes, shewing on the one hand the winged globe encircled by the serpent, which is that of the loss and the trespass, but on the other the Brazen Serpent, which is that of Christ the Deliverer. These Pillars are referred to a High Grade, but they are of universal meaning in Masonry, being symbolic of the two covenants and of the Craft and Christian systems.

P. 2.—The sacred Dionysius, from the painting at Pompeii. According to Baron Tschoudy, the Mysteries of this god were carried over into Emblematic Free-masonry.

P. 3.—The hexagram, or seal of Solomon, encompassed by a solar glory. The two triangles are connected by a horizontal line to indicate their unity in the essence of both.

P. 7.—The conventional figure of a hermit or pre-server of mysteries.

P. 8.—The figure of Hermes wearing the mask of Anubis and encompassed by all his emblems.

P. 9.—A king in the guise of a pontiff, wearing a triple crown, is seated on a throne. At his feet are the sun and moon, with the five planets. He is a symbol of the Great work in its fulfilment. From the *Theatre of Terrestrial Astronomy*.

P. 20.—Hermes and the Great Mother watching over the picture of a grey-headed student consulting the records of the past. His motto might be : *My days among the dead are past*. The inscription says that the dead are the best counsellors.

P. 21.—A hand issuing from a cloud replenishes the oil of a lamp set upon a closed book. It typifies light upon the Mysteries.

P. 38.—The reversed alchemical triad of spirit, soul

426

and body, the soul, by a particular . convention, meaning the highest part. The inscription on the circle says: Visit the depths of the earth ; by rectification thou shalt find the hidden stone. On the circle is placed the heptagram of the planets, with a human face in the centre, signifying the alchemical King, whom we have met with in the symbolic diagram on p. 9. The present emblem represents the Great Work and the working secret, according to the doctrine of Basil Valentine. I am dealing here only with its most obvious elements ; it has been the subject of many commentaries. The figure behind the diagram, and veiled thereby, is the secret essence or root of the metallic nature.

P. 39.—The same face reappears in this emblem, but here the figure is winged and is seen rising from the square altar of material things.

P. 52.—The double patriarchal cross in its application to Alchemy. The sense of the inscription is that all external honour is a barren contest, but the blessed stone containeth all things in itself. The sun reflects upon the moon below, and her face is turned downward, as if to shed light on material things.

P. 53.—The inscription on the circle is that of Basil Valentine's Key ; the planetary symbols are within, and other emblems of transmutation, such as the Green Lion and the double-headed eagle. This diagram is sometimes regarded as connected with the Table of Emerald, attributed to Hermes.

P. 80.—This is the treasure of all the treasures of Alchemy, and is supposed to expound the secret doctrine of Paracelsus. The chest which contains the treasure has proved Pandora's box for many and too many.

P. 81.—This diagram presents the universal key of Raymond Lully in symbolic form. It is said to contain all things which are necessary for the accomplishment of the Great Work and to expound them for those who can see in a clear manner.

The Secret Tradition in Freemasonry

P. 90.—The seal of Hermes inscribed with the word
"chaos" on the circle and the four seasons within. The
square refers to the Salt of the Philosophers and the
triangle is elemental water.

P. 91.—The seal belonging to the Sovereign Primitive
Ancient and True Masonic Order of Memphis in the
United States. Two variants of the design have been
described in the first volume.

P. 97.—The basin or sea of the wise, into which
the glory of the alchemic sun is reflected. It is an
illustration to Roger Bacon's *Mirror of Alchemy*.

P. 98.—The Risen King placing crowns of gold upon
the heads of his servants, who represent the base metals.
The word *Oro* is embroidered on the sleeve of his
vestment. We have met with this King in the symbols
on pp. 38 and 39. *Zallo* is a technical term, the
significance of which is wanting.

P. 108.—The tree of the seven planets.

P. 110.—The symbolic figure of Hermetic Magic.
From a design by Éliphas Lévi.

P. 111.—The hexagram in its magical application.
This is also a design of Éliphas Lévi.

P. 115.—The Great Hermetic Arcanum, according
to Lévi, containing the divine Tetragram, with the
words *Taro* and *Inri*.

P. 120.—The character or sigil of Adepts according
to the work entitled *Chymicus Vannus*. It is the expounded form of the mystic aphorism : *In cruce sub
sphæra venit sapientia vera*, and the long inscription
celebrates the glories of the Cross. He who is acquainted with its mysteries does not fear to die ; he
knows of another refuge, and—as in a glass—he sees
the life to come before him. The black Calvary Cross
changes into the Rose-Cross, and thereafter the White
Cross shines. The way of the Cross is the Way to God.

P. 121.—The key of the Great Work in *Magia*,
according to Éliphas Lévi. It formulates the doctrine
of correspondence between things visible and invisible.

428

At the summit of the circle is the Divine Triad encompassed by seven crowns, symbolising the seven spirits before the Throne of God. Above the belt of the Zodiac are Saturn, Jupiter and Mars, two of them with their signs reversed, that is, directed towards the unseen. Beneath the belt are the four other planets of ancient lore, the sun immersed in the sea, and Mercury presiding over a mountain which I take to be that of initiation. It is a very curious symbol, and some readers may remember concerning that sun which shines at midnight beneath the surface of things.

P. 126.—The Key of Black Magic, according to Éliphas Lévi.

P. 127.—The horned Altar of Burnt Offerings, according to another symbolism.

P. 131.—The Hermetic Cross of Count Cagliostro, with the Four Living Creatures in the angles.

P. 132.—A symbol connected with the Grade of Grand Elect, Perfect and Sublime Mason. A blazing triad is placed within a pentagram. The ill-formed characters have the appearance of a *Shin*, *Lamed* and *Aleph*, followed by a cross.

P. 147.—The occult alphabet of Cagliostro, but it is a question whether this is not an invention of the bibliophile Christian, who once wrote a great romance and called it a history of magic.

P. 148.—A variant of the Rose-Cross, with inscriptions referable to occult thought in America.

P. 182.—St. Martin of Tours, after Martin Schoen.

P. 183.—The apocalyptic Christ, between seven-branched candlesticks, holding the unsealed book, inscribed with the letters *Alpha* and *Omega*.

P. 190.—Lux Crucis.

P. 191.—The Divine Tetragram—*Jod, He, Vau, He*—according to Athanasius Kircher.

P. 197.—The Kabalistic *Macroprosopus* and *Microprosopus* as designed by Éliphas Lévi. It is another illustration of the occult doctrine of correspondences.

The Secret Tradition in Freemasonry

P. 189.—Éliphas Lévi's key to the *Sepher Yetzirah* or Hebrew Book of Formation, regarded as the root-matter of Kabalistic philosophy.

P. 200.—Rosicrucian seal affixed by the Comte de Chazal to the document certifying the reception of Sigismund Bacstrom into the Secret Order.

P. 201.—St. John the Evangelist represented with the head of an eagle, indicating his place among the symbolic Kerubim of Ezekiel.

P. 206.—The Zodiac in its alchemical attributions surrounding the four elements, with the Great Secret in the centre. The Secret is termed Wonder of Nature, and at the angles of the heptagram are the signs of the metals and planets. Salt, Sulphur, Mercury, and other alchemical symbols are within the angles of the star.

P. 207.—The Mystic Rose, according to Robertus de Fluctibus. The inscription says that the Rose gives honey for the bees.

P. 225.—Another form of the Rose-Cross.

P. 228.—The arms of J. V. Andreas, a reputed founder of the Rosicrucian Fraternity. It will be seen that four roses are emblazoned within the angles of a St. Andrew's Cross.

P. 229.—The double-headed eagle, attributed to the Grade of *Sovereign Grand Inspector-General*. We have seen that it has wider applications, and the device signifying the development of order out of chaos belongs to universal Freemasonry.

P. 237.—The crowned Rose-Cross, a badge of the *Societas Rosicruciana in Anglia.*

P. 238.—Light on the path of quest and the hand that guides therein. It belongs in one of its aspects to the Grade of *Knight of the Brazen Serpent*, but it is also a general—that is to say, a catholic—symbol.

P. 267.—The phœnix rising from his ashes, a symbol of Christ and His resurrection, signifying the completed sacrifice.

P. 268.—This is inserted because the cone or fruit of

the pine was an important symbol in the Mysteries of Ceres, as also in those of Bacchus. It has descended thence to the Secret Orders of modern times.

P. 282.—The Brazen Serpent lifted in the wilderness of this world, and therefore the term of quest.

P. 304.—The Woman clothed with the Sun.

P. 330.—The waters of creation, the waters above and below, and the Divine Dove bearing the Eucharist.

P. 331.—The pentagram as a sign of man in the stature of his perfection, encompassed by the Divine Name. It is one of Lévi's symbols and has attributions drawn from Hermetic literature, Kabalism and the Tarot. Reproduced by permission from *The Occult Review*.

P. 339.—The union of the Calvary and the St. Andrew's cross, the crosses of active and passive, of voluntary and involuntary sacrifice.

P. 360.—A votive hand connected with the old Rites of the *Mater Deorum*. The mystic pine-cone is fixed to the top of the thumb, and it connects therefore with the design on p. 268.

P. 361.—The Seven-Branched Candlestick. It has many interpretations in Masonry and the other Mysteries.

P. 437.—Another figure representing the meditative genius of Freemasonry. The book is again that of the Holy Law, and the Law is symbolically understood.

VII

THE FULL PAGE PORTRAITS

WITH the help of references in the text, the portraits which illustrate my work really speak for themselves, but there are a few points of information which may interest the general reader.

I. ELIAS ASHMOLE.—He was born at Lichfield in 1617 and died in London in 1692. Apart from any personal interest, he seems one of the important figures of his period for the subject of Masonry and things connected therewith. So far as there were Hermetic Schools in England at that time, he may be said to stand for these. He had definite Rosicrucian connec-- tions, his spiritual father in Alchemy being William Backhouse, whose records are known to a few in MS. He states that he received from this person the secret of the Great Work on the physical side. Perhaps, by the evidence of Ashmole's life, it may not be advisable to take this statement too literally ; probably it was a secret concerning the reputed First Matter without the process, or a process in the absence thereof. The work was not followed personally by Ashmole.

II. ATHANASIUS KIRCHER.—He was born in 1601 and died in 1680. A member of the Jesuit Society, he was perhaps the palmary example of encyclopædic learning ; all his works are monuments, having regard to their period ; practically all are still of curious interest. *Œdipus Ægyptiacus* is the rarest and most valuable ; it is usually obtained in four folio volumes, and herein is a summary account of Jewish Kabalism which, within its limits, is perhaps the best of its kind and the most readily intelligible. It has been made available recently in the French language. It is more especially by reason of this tract that his portrait has been included here.

III. JEAN MARIE RAGON.—He was born about 1789 at Bruges, and died in Paris, 1866. The portrait is from a private source, and represents an earlier period than that which was prefixed to *Orthodoxie Maçonnique*.

IV. PRINCE CHARLES EDWARD STUART (the Young Pretender).—The portrait is after the engraving by Edelinck.

V. JACQUES DE MOLAY.—He was born at Besançon

in Burgundy about 1240, and was burnt, with other Templars, in front of Nôtre-Dame, 1314. I do not know that his immolation is the greatest blot on the scutcheon of the Church in France, but it has not been expiated in the succeeding centuries and it must be called indelible.

VI. N. C. DES ÉTANGS.—He was born on 7th September, 1766, and died on 6th May, 1846. I have said that in his Masonic activities he was actuated by worthy and even excellent motives, but his attempted reformation of Rites was apart from all illumination and was practically still-born.

VII. ARCHBISHOP FÉNELON.—He was born on 6th August, 1651, and died on New Year's day, 1715. The suggestion of Reghellini and the French Martinist, Dr. Papus, that the Chevalier Ramsay was *soigneusement initié* into Templar Masonry by this prelate, who, by implication, had therefore a hand in preparing the French Revolution, is one of those points which students should keep in memory as a test of value about anything thought or said in the French occult schools. It is for this reason that I refer again to the point and have inserted a portrait of Fénelon, lent me by Mr. Ralph Shirley.

VIII. THE EARL OF KILMARNOCK.—He was forty-two years of age at the time of his picture, and was executed as a Jacobite rebel in 1746.

IX. ÉLIPHAS LÉVI. — He was born in 1810 and died at Paris in 1875. So much has been said regarding him in the present work and in other books of mine that no addition is necessary. The portrait shews the French occultist in the robes of a professional magician.

X. FREDERICK THE GREAT.—He was born on 25th January, 1712, and died on 17th August, 1786. There is no question as to his Masonic initiation, but there is also none as to the falsity of the claims made by several Masonic Rites in respect of his concern therein. There is no object in debating the question here.

XI. ALBERT PIKE.—The great American Mason has become almost a sacred memory for the whole Southern Jurisdiction of the ANCIENT AND ACCEPTED SCOTTISH RITE. The portrait is from an authorised source and represents the later period of his life.

XII. ROBERT FLUDD.—He was born at Berstead, Kent, in 1574 and died in 1637 at London. His Latin works are numerous, and represent, broadly speaking, a modified Kabalism applied to cosmology and the study of things physical. His literary connection with the Rosicrucian Fraternity was practically coincident with the first published accounts concerning it. He was visited by Michael Maier, the German alchemist, and the latter is the one person who can most reasonably be identified with the Fraternity, supposing that it had been incorporated in the early years of the seventeenth century.

XIII. FRIEDRICH LUDWIG ZACHARIAS WERNER.—He was born at Koenigsberg, 11th November, 1768, and died at Vienna, 17th January, 1823. He was author of the long dual dramatic poem entitled *The Sons of the Valley*, which I have mentioned several times in the text. It represents the High Grade theories regarding the origin of Masonry in Palestine, and it exalted those theories by a suggestive mode of presentation. The Sons or Children of the Valley were a mysterious Eastern Brotherhood, the power of whose protection preserved the Templars wheresoever located, until their corruption led to their abandonment. The transit of Molay and his companions from Cyprus to France at the bidding of Philippe le Bel corresponds to the moment when the

Appendices

Order was left to its fate. Werner died a priest of the Catholic Church, and the Masonic elements were removed in consequence from a later edition of his poems.

XIV. A Court de Gebelin. — I have not come across the date of his birth, but he died in 1784. He was an Orientalist of distinction in his day, and is one of the characters who, according to P. Christian, had a part in the questioning of Cagliostro at the Lodge of the Philalethes. This took place, by the report of my witness, at the Masonic Convention of 1785, and appeal is made to an account of De Gebelin in MS. The story is a wilful invention and the record does not exist. Cagliostro was invited to the meetings as the founder of Egyptian Masonry and because of his colossal claims, but the price which the Magus demanded was that the great French Lodge should burn its archives. The Lodge dispensed with his presence.

XV. Comte de St. Germain.—The unenlightened disposition of history says that he was born in Savoy about 1710, and that he consented to the experience of physical death at Schleswig in 1783. We have seen that according to more exotic opinions he is still alive, and it may be added that, either by his own story or by tales which he permitted to circulate, he was a contemporary of Christ in Palestine.

XVI. Marc Bédarride.—I am unacquainted with the date of his birth, but he died in April, 1846. If there were any importance in the Rite of Mizraïm he would be called important for its history. There is none, as I have sought to shew, and it must be added that his memory is on the whole that of an adventurer with little talent and perhaps less principle.

XVII. Professor John Robison.—He was born in 1739 and died in 1805. He is of no interest outside

The Secret Tradition in Freemasonry

The Proofs of a Conspiracy, which is one of the most entertaining books ever written against Masonry. It may be added that it has done no harm, and I almost regret the animus with which some brethren of the Craft have felt it just to speak of his polemic and his memory. The portrait is after Raeburn.

XVIII. JACQUES CAZOTTE.—He was born at Dijon in 1720 and was guillotined on 25th September, 1791. I believe that his daughter accompanied the venerable and illustrious man in his last moments. He is an exceedingly interesting figure in High Grade Masonry and report connects him with Secret Orders behind it. The portrait is from a print in the *Bibliothèque Nationale*.

XIX. COUNT CAGLIOSTRO.—Speculation as to his date of birth is now idle, as his identity with Joseph Balsamo has become a matter of serious debate. He is supposed to have died about 1795 in the castle of St. Angelo, under the wings of the holy Inquisition. This date also is doubtful. Reproduced from *The Occult Review* by permission of Mr. Ralph Shirley.

XX. MARTINES DE PASQUALLY.—I have mentioned the date of his birth, and he died in 1774 at Port au Prince, Island of St. Domingo. The portrait, which is from a French periodical source, is exceedingly bad as a print, and for its genuineness I cannot vouch, but there is nothing else available.

XXI. COMTE D'HAUTERIVE.—I know nothing of his birth or death, but he was a friend of Saint-Martin, a member of the RITE OF ELECT COHENS and a writer on French illuminism.

XXII. J. V. ANDREAS. — He was born on 17th August, 1586, and died 27th June, 1654. He is accredited with the authorship, as we have seen, of the first

Rosicrucian documents, but I think the ascription doubtful. By his own confession he wrote the *Chymical Nuptials of Christian Rosy Cross*. Reproduced from *The Occult Review*.

XXIII. CHRISTIAN ROSY CROSS.—This is generally unknown, and will interest the few who believe in the historic personality : they are very few indeed.

XXIV. EMMANUEL SWEDENBORG.—He was born at Stockholm on 29th January, 1688, and died in London on 29th March, 1772. I have said enough of his alleged connection with Masonry and he has no other interest for the present purpose. From *The Occult Review*.

XXV. LOUIS CLAUDE DE SAINT-MARTIN.—He was born at Amboise in Touraine on 18th January, 1743, and died at Aunay on 13th October, 1803. He is the mystic *par excellence* in France towards the end of the eighteenth century ; the records of his life and a considerable part of his works are of permanent interest and value.

XXVI. ST. THOMAS AQUINAS.—From Ghevet's *Portraits des hommes illustres*.

INDEX

439

Index

441

Index

Index

445

The Secret Tradition in Freemasonry

446

Index

www.ingramcontent.com/pod-product-compliance
Lightning Source LLC
Chambersburg PA
CBHW031950060726
47497CB00016B/1021